U.S. Orientalisms

U.S. Orientalisms

Race, Nation, and Gender in Literature, 1790–1890

Malini Johar Schueller

ANN ARBOR

THE UNIVERSITY OF MICHIGAN PRESS

Copyright © by the University of Michigan 1998
All rights reserved
Published in the United States of America by
The University of Michigan Press
Manufactured in the United States of America
⊗ Printed on acid-free paper

2001   2000   1999   1998   4   3   2   1

A CIP catalog record for this book is available from the British Library.

Library of Congress Cataloging-in-Publication Data

Schueller, Malini Johar, 1957–
    U.S. orientalisms : race, nation, and gender in literature,
1790–1890 / Malini Johar Schueller.
        p.   cm.
    Includes bibliographical references and index.
    ISBN 0-472-10885-9 (alk. paper)
    1. American literature—Oriental influences.   2. American
literature—19th century—History and criticism.   3. Asia—In
literature.   4. Africa, North—In literature.   5. Stereotype
(Psychology) in literature.   6. Nationalism in literature.
7. Imperialism in literature.   8. Race in literature.   9. Sex in
literature.   10. Asia—Foreign public opinion, American.   I. Title.
PS157.S38   1997
810.9'325'09034—dc21
                                                        97-21206
                                                           CIP

For my children, Divik, Maya,
and Neena, and my husband, John

Preface

After the Federal Building in Oklahoma City was torn apart by an explosion on April 19, 1995, but before Timothy McVeigh was arraigned, speculations on possible perpetrators ran rife. Several of the most distinguished Middle East experts went on the air to proclaim the explosion an Arab deed, a clear case of the workings of the crazed Arab mind. These analyses forcefully testified to deep-seated anti-Arab sentiments within the national psyche. More recently, when Democratic fund-raiser John Huang was being investigated for accepting illegal campaign contributions, Reform Party nominee Ross Perot seized the occasion not simply to criticize his Democratic opponent but also to ridicule Huang's ethnicity.[1] Scrutiny of Democratic campaign funds is revealing an ever-increasing array of illegal funds by Asian businessmen, channeled through Asian Americans.[2] At issue in the publicity and interest surrounding these donations is not simply their legality (the acceptance and subsequent return of Canadian contributions by the Dole campaign scarcely received publicity) but an anxiety about the devious Asian infiltrating the body politic. Even though conservative columnist William Safire called the Asian money Clinton's "green peril" and not a yellow peril, the very distinctions call attention to the particular genealogy of Asian xenophobia to which the current scrutiny of campaign funds could be connected.[3] While the accusations surrounding the Oklahoma City incident and those surrounding the investigation of campaign fund-raising evoke very different types of representations— the terrorist and the tycoon—and have current, historically specific origins, the former deriving from the Gulf War and the latter from fears about a recessionary U.S. vulnerability, they are both part of an Orientalist discourse that admits a diversity and multiplicity of often contradictory positionings within an ideal of a whole, inviolate, and strong imperial nationhood, an ideal that these representations at once depend on and facilitate. Ideas about the immoral, cowardly, and bloodthirsty Arab helped define the nation as moral, brave, and peace-loving; images of sneaky, rich but corrupt Asians draw on a complex conjuncture of ideas of the nation as virtuous, legitimately and rightfully powerful, and Anglo.

U.S. Orientalisms suggests that the cultural mappings of such an Orientalist discourse, in its multifarious positionings and discrete historical specificities, begins in the postrevolutionary period of the late 1700s and derives its sociopolitical impetus from different imperial discourses about the Orient that are central to ideas of U.S. nationhood. Without positing a unified or transhistorical trajectory, I emphasize the prevalence of intersecting discourses of the Orient and empire for a century before the 1890s, the decade traditionally viewed as the beginning of the imperialist phase in U.S. history. I argue, therefore, that contemporary discourses on the Orient—discourses treating sneaky infiltrators and fanatical demolitionists—can be better understood as latter-day manifestations of earlier U.S. visions of the Orient, refracted variously through millennial fervor, racial-cultural difference, and ideas of westerly empire.

Specifically, *U.S. Orientalisms* examines the construction of the Orient by selected USAmerican poets, dramatists, essayists, and novelists from the 1790s to the 1890s.[4] I argue that the earliest U.S. literary Orientalism was not simply an abstract and mystical phenomenon but an important indigenous discourse in which questions of nation, empire, race, and gender were intimately connected. An important way in which U.S. nationhood in the nineteenth century defined itself was through imaginative control over various Orients, positioned divergently through different historical and ideological contexts: the moral war against the so-called Barbary States; the missionary fervor to head the Western race to save the Orientals; the imperial-hermeneutic imperative (shared by the British and the French) to decipher the real Orient; the desire to fulfill Columbus's original mission to "find" the Orient; and the conception of nation as the latest westerly empire (a continuation of the medieval *Translatio Imperii*), destined for expansion. I argue that the construction of the Orient in these works followed a complex and internally contradictory trajectory. It enabled the compensatory projection of a protoimperial narrative for the nation based on versions of the dichotomies of USAmerican righteousness, morality, energy, and vibrancy versus Oriental corruption, deviance, lassitude, and passivity, dichotomies which helped mystify internal racial schisms. Yet, the imperial body of the nation constructed in these texts was always a figure in crisis, dependent upon the cathected Orient it sought to control, and fraught with raced and gendered anxieties.

U.S. Orientalisms examines literary constructions of the Orient through three major contexts. The Orientalism generated by the U.S.–North Africa conflict of the late eighteenth century is evident in such works as Royall Tyler's *The Algerine Captive* and Susanna Rowson's *Slaves in Algiers,* in which the idea of the nation embodying freedom and virtue is both contested and evoked through narratives in which the hero or heroine simultaneously participates in and condemns slavery and sensual excess. In the Near Eastern Orientalism of the nineteenth century, fueled by Egyptology and missionary fervor, writers like John DeForest and Maria Susanna Cummins satirize yet proclaim the hermeneutical presumptions of the missionary/archaeologist; in contrast, Edgar Allan Poe, Harriet Prescott Spofford, and Herman Melville critique the idea of New World hermeneutic power by reversing the gaze, destroying the raced and gendered certainties on which the imperial-hermeneutic identity of the hero depends; simultaneously, former slave David F. Dorr reveals the omnivorous appeal of Near Eastern Orientalist discourses by appropriating and rewriting their imperial imperatives. The Indic Orientalism of the nineteenth century, I suggest, was spurred by both scholarly Indology and visions of the westerly movement of empire. Emerson's raced construction of India as a passive and spiritual Other is an anxious attempt to co-opt the idea of unified space to negotiate the idea of a fragmented nation, at the same time as it is an effort to redefine the New World as the new empire. Similarly, Whitman's embodiment of the nation as youth/child embracing the Indic Orient is dependent on yet contoured by a strategic exclusion of presentness and historicity.

I intend my use of the term *Orient* throughout this study to both evoke and delimit Edward Said's usage. For Said, the term *Orientalism* has three applications: those that write about or research the Orient; a style of thought based on ontological and epistemological distinctions between the Orient and the Occident; and, most importantly, a Western style for having authority over the Orient.[5] In all cases, Said sees a syncretic and unchanging Orient. I retain the use of the term *Orient* (and its derivatives *orientalist* and *oriental*) to evoke the issues of power inherent in Said's usage, but I emphasize the deformative power of both particular writers and specific contexts. As my study demonstrates, many writers enunciated challenges to dominant cultural discourses on the Orient, while, as Reina Lewis puts it in her study of women writing the Orient, "dominant ideological formations" partially recouped some of these transgressions.[6] My study also demonstrates how the nineteenth-century cultural imagination was responsive to discrete varieties of specific locations—Algeria, the Near East, and India—all of which might well be othered, but in distinct ways, each site producing an internally complex discourse.[7] My use of such terms as *Near Eastern Orient* or *Indic Orient* emphasizes the specificity of the Oriental configuration.

I also intend my use of the term *Orient* to call attention to the shifting gendered valences inherent in cultural constructions of different Orients. Whereas Said sees Orientalism as a male domain and theorizes desire to be exclusively male, I rely on the work of contemporary feminists who question the unproblematic association of the feminine with the oppressed, lacking its own agency.[8] In addition to examining the work of several women writers in this book, I also foreground the numerous moments when the Orient reverses its gaze, as it were, questioning both the masculinity and the power of the USAmerican subject.

Methodologically, this book is situated at the intersection of postcolonial and feminist analyses. Nineteenth-century U.S. literature has traditionally not been seen through the lens of postcoloniality, because it lacked the dominion over far-flung locations characteristic of, for example, the European empires of Britain and France. Instead, recent critics have suggested a colonized status for early U.S. literature.[9] As my analysis of the investment in Oriental discourses suggests, however, the nineteenth-century literary imagination was acutely sensitive to the imperial possibilities of the New World. Throughout this book, I also pay particular attention to the coextensive investments in racial and gender differences of literary Orientalist works. In revealing the interrelationships of the two categories, this study contributes to the growing body of scholarship by feminists who have long questioned the singular attention to gender.[10] My focus on the blurring of raced and gendered boundaries in these texts at the very moments when a vibrant, whole nationhood is being proclaimed reveals the mutual imbrication of categories of nation, race, and gender stimulated by the Oriental context.

Acknowledgments

In the fall of 1991, I taught a graduate seminar on U.S. Orientalisms. The conversations and debates generated in the seminar were immensely useful to me in thinking about many of the texts I discuss in this book. I wish to thank the students in the seminar—Aeron Haynie, Susan Mickleberry, Betsy Nies, Stephen Powers, and Marianne Waltz—for their energetic participation.

While working on this book, I have received useful suggestions from many colleagues. During the many months I spent conceptualizing this book, conversations with Brian Richardson helped crucially with its organization. I am grateful to the many generous people who read and commented on different portions of the book. My greatest debt is to Russell Reising, who read the book carefully and offered invaluable revision suggestions. Lee Quinby and David Leverenz read and copiously commented on large sections of the book and enabled me to make important revisions. Daniel Cottom, Susan Hegeman, Brandon Kershner, James Paxson, and Stephanie Smith were kind enough to critique parts of the book. Without John Seelye as a reference guide, and without John Van Hook's help, I would not have discovered many of the texts. I also wish to thank Pat Craddock, then Chair of the English Department at the University of Florida, for encouraging me to begin work on this project before I had completed my first book. Marsha Bryant, Elizabeth Langland, and Anne Jones were among my many supportive colleagues. I also wish to thank LeAnn Fields, the editor of the University of Michigan Press, for her assistance in seeing this manuscript through its different stages, and Kristen Lare, the copyediting coordinator, for her careful attention to its preparation.

I worked most intensely on this book in Peoria, Illinois, while I was on sabbatical leave. It would have been impossible to work had I not been allowed to use the library at the University of Illinois–Urbana. I wish to thank Richard Wheeler for securing me faculty borrowing privileges at the library. My friend Donna King used her local library card to get books on interlibrary loan for me while I was in Peoria.

I owe the greatest debt to my husband, John, for supporting me in my work by taking on sometimes unfair burdens of child care, for his constant affection, and for his faith in me. This book would not have been possible without him. My children, Divik, Maya, and Neena, have been irrepressibly delightful; writing would have been no fun without them. The pride that the women in my family have had in me has been sustaining; I particularly want to thank my mother, Usha Johar, my sister, Kavita Nayar, and Beata Schueller.

A part of this book, in a different version, was published earlier as "Harems, Orientalist Subversions, and the Crisis of Nationalism," *Criticism* 37, no. 4 (fall 1995): 601–23.

Contents

Introduction: A Cultural Aesthetics of U.S. Literary Orientalisms

There is, perhaps, no better indicator of the political significance of the Orient in the USAmerican cultural imaginary than the fact that even poems of the revolutionary period linked nationhood with command over the Orient.[1] For instance, in "America, or a Poem on the Settlement of the British Colonies, Addressed to the Friends of Freedom and Their Country," published in 1780, Timothy Dwight assumed the mantle of poet of the nation, narrating its evolution and prophesying its future glory. The poem starts by tracing the beginnings of civilization in Asia and the subsequent barbarities and depravities there and moves on to commemorate Columbus's voyages, which signal a new era as "America's bright realms [arise] to view" and as a haven for the persecuted is created in the New England colonies. Then, in a dream vision, the goddess of freedom, in "robes of pure white," prophesies the glory of the nation as it imperialistically extends its dominion:

> Hail Land of light and joy! thy power shall grow
> Far as the seas, which round thy regions flow;
> Through earth's wide realms thy glory shall extend,
> And savage nations at thy scepter bend.
> Around the frozen shores thy sons shall sail,
> Or stretch their canvas to the ASIAN gale,
> Or, like COLUMBUS, steer their course unknown,
> Beyond the regions of the flaming zone. . . .
> For thee, proud INDIA's spicy isles shall blow

Bright silks be wrought, and sparkling diamonds glow;
Earth's richest realms their treasures shall unfold
And op'ning mountains yield the flaming gold.[2]

America marches triumphantly over savage nations, emerging as leader and bearer of civilization. In recognition of America's glory and power, India pays obeisance to it. What is prefigured in the poem took concrete shape twenty years later, when Dwight became one of the founding members of the American Board of Commissioners for Foreign Missions in 1811. A major agenda of this organization was the conversion of heathens in the Orient.

A century after the publication of Dwight's poem, an equally patriotic John Fiske, an eminent philosopher and historian, delivered a series of lectures titled "American Political Ideas, Viewed from the Standpoint of Evolution." The most popular lecture in the series was called "Manifest Destiny." In this lecture, Fiske reviewed the future of Europe during the Protestant and Catholic struggles in the sixteenth century in light of Columbus's discoveries and argued that Europe could either progress or "fall forever into the barren and monotonous way of living and thinking which [had] always distinguished the half-civilized populations of Asia."[3] The discovery of the Americas, however, ensured that Europe would not be consigned to Asian lethargy. Here opened up an enormous region, and it was clear to Fiske that "the race which here should gain the victory was clearly destined hereafter to take the lead in the world."[4] Fiske proclaimed that "In the United States of America a century hence we shall . . . have a political aggregation immeasurably surpassing in power and dimensions any empire that has as yet existed."[5] In time, continues Fiske, "it will be possible to speak of the UNITED STATES as stretching from pole to pole."[6]

Dwight's postrevolutionary poem and Fiske's lecture, the latter written just before a period of rapid overseas expansion, demonstrate the remarkable persistence with which ideas of empire and the Orient were linked in the cultural imaginary for over a century.[7] In Dwight's poem, the Orient (specifically Asia) is a naturalized trope for the imperial imaginary because it is simply a part of historical progression, a final realization of Columbus's thwarted attempts. In Fiske's lecture, control over the Orient is a supreme signifier of imperial power. And for both Dwight and Fiske, the idea of civilization and empire moving west, culminating in the New World, is a powerful raced one that thrives on distinctions between EuroAmerican uprightness and Oriental degradation.

Incarnated as the goddess of freedom in white robes, America, it is suggested, has a natural right over Asia. Yet the Asia that Dwight was writing about had at that time entered the imperial consciousness of Europe as Britain began to exercise control over India, a fact that Dwight, as a future missionary organizer, would have known well. In envisioning for the United States a cultural, material, and political dominion over India, Dwight was asserting the imperial right of the new nation over the Orient, a right that had hitherto been assumed by Europe but that "naturally" belonged to USAmerica from the time of Columbus. In Fiske's evolutionary scheme, Asia is associated both with barbarism and inertia; it is a pernicious contagion to be avoided or, as Fiske suggests later in his lecture, a passive entity improving through British rule.

Dwight's and Fiske's conception of Asia as part of the imperial imaginary was repeatedly invoked in literary works. For at least a century, from the 1790s to the 1890s, poets, dramatists, essayists, novelists, and short-story writers routinely wrote about different Orients and produced a series of literary works in which the nation was variously embodied as vigorous, active, masculinized, and morally upright Columbia-as-empire, against versions of a decaying, passive, demasculinized, deviant, or spiritual Orient. Yet this imperial body was, to use Judith Butler's terminology, very much a "figure in crisis," dependent on the Oriental qualities it sought to (control and) dissociate itself from.[8] Thus, a naturalized discourse of empire, predicated on oppositions, was interrupted by a violent destabilization of these oppositions, usually revealed in moments when questions of national incoherence surfaced. The Orient served the dual purpose of containing national schisms and constructing an imperial nationhood. The problematic configuration of the imperial body and the mapping of raced and gendered oppositions in USAmerican Oriental works as varied as Royall Tyler's *The Algerine Captive*, John DeForest's *Irene the Missionary*, Emerson's "Fate," and Whitman's "Passage to India" is the focus of this book. These texts testify both to the importance of Orientalism as a needed, compensatory, raced rhetoric in the cultural imaginary and to the interest of the reading public in matters relating to the Orient, and they defy the insularity traditionally ascribed to eighteenth- and nineteenth-century U.S. literature and culture.

I begin this book with an examination of the literature of the "Barbary" Orient generated by the U.S.–North African conflict of the late eighteenth century, including the works of writers Royall Tyler, Susanna Rowson, and Washington Irving. I then move on to the Near Eastern Orientalist literature of the nineteenth century in light of Egyptology and the growth of missionary fervor, including the works of novelists John DeForest and Maria Susanna Cummins, poet Herman Melville, and short-story writers Edgar Allan Poe and Harriet Prescott Spofford. Finally, I consider the Indic Orientalism of the nineteenth century in the context of Indology, British colonialism, and the push for Asian trade in the United States, focusing particularly on Emerson and Whitman.

As the plural term *Orientalisms* in the title of this book suggests, these literary texts created multiple and diverse varieties of imaginary Orients. In different ways, writers maintained a dialogue with or strove to create an indigenous Orientalism premised on the idea of civilization and empire moving west, from Asia, through Europe, to culmination in the New World. The New World thus displaced Britain as empire. The Orient was seen as the new frontier against which the United States—variously represented as Columbia, Libertad, or Atlas, but always powerful and whole—could define itself in terms of virtue and world mission.

This task of imperial self-definition, however, was anxiety-ridden. The rhetoric of empire that permeates these works relies on various raced and gendered distinctions between Oriental despotism, sensuality, idleness, moral flaccidity, effeminacy, and sexual aberrance, on the one hand, and USAmerican democracy, rigorous Anglo-American morality, industry, healthy heteronormativity, and masculinity, on the other. But these oppositions are deployed to repress or allay fears about the wholeness and stability of the nation in the face of diverse ethnic immigration and African American and Native American presences. Similarly, the gendered polemic within these works resists the discourse on empire by questioning both the masculine and the heteronormative gender constructions of the New World.

As noted in the preface, I use the term *Orient* in this study strategically both to invoke Edward Said's polemical definition and to critique it. In his book *Orientalism*, Said describes the Orient as a European invention, "a place of romance, exotic beings, haunting memories and landscapes, remarkable experiences," and also Europe's "deepest and most recurring images of the Other."[9] Thus, Western representations of the Orient, no matter where and when this Orient might be located, include features that are disturbingly similar. Said uses Foucault's notion of discourse as outlined in *The Archaeology of Knowledge* and *Discipline and Punish* to describe Orientalism. Orientalism has functioned as a disciplinary practice "for dealing with the Orient—dealing with it by making statements about it, authorizing views of it, describing it, by teaching it, settling it, ruling over it: in short, Orientalism as a Western style for dominating, restructuring, and having authority over the Orient."[10] Said demonstrates how from the eighteenth century onward, Oriental representation has always been linked to Western colonialism and imperialism. More importantly, Said shows the relation between the Westerner and the Orient/Oriental to be sexual and gendered. The Orient, uniformly associated with sexual promise, sensuality, and unlimited desire, is an "exclusively male province; . . . women are usually the creatures of a male power-fantasy. They express unlimited sensuality, they are more or less stupid, and above all they are willing."[11] The prototype of such images is Flaubert's Kuchuk Hanem. In the Westerner's view, the Orient always invites penetration and insemination.[12]

The impact of Said's *Orientalism* on disciplines as diverse as history, literature, linguistics, and political science cannot be exaggerated. In literary studies, *Orientalism* generated enormous critical activity in the decoding of texts heretofore seen as simply symbolic and existential and revealed them to be texts of high imperialism, complicit with empire. Like many postcolonialists, I too remain indebted to Said's pioneering work. I depart from Said's theoretical formulations, however, in two crucial respects: in pursuing issues of gender from a feminist and non-heterosexual imperative, and in emphasizing the discrete, rather than simply the unchanging, nature of Orientalist discourses within the United States.[13]

In critiquing the persistence of Western characterizations of the Orient as passive, supine, available woman/body, Said obviously draws attention to the power relations inherent in constructions of the Orient. This configuration, however, problematically assumes desire to be a male prerogative alone and situates masculinity as always powerful and separate from that (Woman) which it seeks to control; it also assumes a heterosexist model for gender relations. My study of U.S. Orientalisms challenges all these presumptions. First, the very contribution of women writers such as Susanna Rowson, Maria Susanna Cummins, and Harriet Prescott Spofford—belies the idea of Orientalism as a male domain. These women continually critique the patriarchal impulses of imperialism and explore the consequences of racial blurring, even as their transgressive positionings are partially reclaimed by the dominant imperial impetus of the discourses of Orientalism. Many U.S. Orientalist works also break down the traditional gendered dichotomies of mind and body that Said invokes. In the writings of Indic Orientalists, for instance, the muscular, athletic, imperial

body of the nation depends on an evocation of India as a dematerialized and disembodied spirit or soul; the investment in materiality and
body is USAmerican, while the association with spirit is Oriental. Second, as my analyses demonstrate, the autonomy and wholeness of the
imperial body is highly fragile, dependent on the raced/gendered
Other that it presumes to control. Here, I am guided by Judith Butler's
attempts to resituate femininity out of the paradigm of dominated/oth-
ered and by Homi K. Bhabha's theorizations on the stereotype as an
"ambivalent, contradictory mode of representation," based as much on
anxiety as on assertion, the enunciation of a split subject.[14] Third, many
U.S. Orientalist texts challenge heterosexist presumptions because the
Oriental encounter opens up possibilities of homoerotic gendering that
cannot be freely articulated at home.[15]

My second major departure from Said is from the idea of Orientalism as an unchanging discourse. Most obviously, the construction of the
Orient changes according to different contexts, and Said himself
acknowledges that his focus is largely on the Muslim Near and Middle
East. As my study demonstrates, the parodic U.S. Orientalism of the
Near East, as exemplified in the works of such writers as DeForest and
Cummins in the mid-nineteenth century, is very different from Emerson's reverent Indological Orientalism during the same period. Similarly, the nationalistic fervor generated by the capture and enslavement
of U.S. sailors in Algiers enters the representation of the Orient in the
drama and novels set in Algiers in a different manner than does Egyptomania and missionary activity in the Near Eastern Orientalist literature a generation later.

In departing from Said in these two crucial areas, however, I do
not simply embrace ambivalence and hybridity apolitically and ahistorically, as universally applicable.[16] The major contribution of Said's
Orientalism was to make it impossible to think about Western constructions of the Orient in purely spiritual, philosophical, or symbolic terms
and, by analogy, to make it problematic to deal with any construction
of an Other without thinking about relations of power. To simply
ignore such relations and questions of hegemony is, as Ella Shohat has
suggested, to "sanctify the *fait accompli* of colonial violence."[17] I thus
use the term *Orientalism* throughout this study to call attention to the
historicity of U.S. literary writings about various Orients and their participation in raced discourses of empire in the nineteenth century, not
to suggest an unchanging, seamless, repetitive tradition. The three different Oriental sites explored in this study—Algerian, Egyptological,

and Indic—generate a wide variety of concerns within the omnivorous framework of imperial ideology; examining them together, however, points to the sheer magnitude of U.S. literary Orientalisms for a century prior to the 1890s.

My use of Said's and Foucault's terms in the plural forms *Orientalisms* and *discourses* also indicates my need to open up these terms to the possibility both of different kinds of literary Orientalisms and of different kinds of discourses on the Orient. For example, although Poe and DeForest both critique the idea of mastering the Orient through Egyptology, Poe's stories demonstrate the destructive consequences of this mastery tragically, while DeForest's novel does so comically. Similarly, although many appeals for increasing trade with Asia were made on the grounds of national power, missionary appeals made on similar grounds were far more concerned with representing the wretchedness of Asia than were political diatribes.

Because the idea of discourse has so often been linked with disciplinary practice and repression alone, it is important to clarify Foucault's use of the term *discourse*, its relationship to this book, and the departure of this book from some of Foucault's formulations. In *The Archaeology of Knowledge,* Foucault explains the idea of discursive formation. Any type of statements, irrespective of the conventional fields they belong to or the time period when they were written, form a field of discourse if they refer to the same object.[18] Unlike conventional history, however, which unfolds as an oeuvre of collective statements or philosophy where statements are reconstituted as chains of inference, a discursive formation is linked together by systems of dispersion.[19] My pluralization of *discourse* emphasizes the differences that Foucault himself recognizes within a field of discourse. Throughout his career, Foucault remained aware of the ubiquity of the technologies of power through which laws, cultural values, and sexual practices were generated. His effort in *Discipline and Punish* was to present a "genealogy of the present scientifico-legal complex from which the power to punish derives its bases."[20] In an interview in 1982, Foucault described his role as one of showing people "that they are much freer than they feel, that people accept as truth, as evidence, some themes which have been built up at a certain moment during history, and that this so-called evidence can be criticized and destroyed."[21] Resistance, in other words, can come from the act of strategically historicizing discursive formations, a strategy I use in examining literary discourses on the Orient.

Despite Foucault's own massive studies of the juridical system and of the discourses on sexuality, however, his notoriously complex and often contradictory statements on power, knowledge, and resistance have led to a Foucauldian practice, particularly within U.S. literary studies, that all but denies any significance to specifics of power. In the first volume of his *History of Sexuality*, for instance, Foucault writes, "Where there is power, there is resistance, and yet . . . this resistance is never in a position of exteriority in relation to power. Should it be said that one is always 'inside' power, there is no 'escaping' it . . . ? This would be to misunderstand the strictly relational character of power relationships. Their existence depends on a multiplicity of points of resistance."[22] Foucault comes so close to collapsing notions of power and resistance here that it is no wonder that many Foucault-inspired new historicists, Foucault's denial of the inclusiveness of power notwithstanding, minimize the significance of power relations.[23] Many people, taking the idea of circulation and localization of power to mean a scrutiny of the local power alone, have ended up denying the relevance of such issues as colonialism and imperialism. The result, as Jonathan Arac and Harriet Ritvo have suggested, is that much of this work, "however fine its local analysis, comes to little conclusion except that any significant cultural practice is complicit in the power it might think to be opposing."[24]

My own analyses benefit from Foucault's notion of discursive formations in that I see U.S. literary Orientalist texts as inextricably related to discourses on the Orient. I pay particular attention, however, to the deformative power of both particular writers and contexts. Throughout this study, I note the numerous ways in which writers enunciate resistances to the mechanisms of power that seem inevitable in discourses on the Orient. But I do not suggest that these enunciations were simply complicit with furthering an imperial will or a stereotypical Orient. Instead, I focus on the specific nature of the challenges against the systemic discourses on the Orient.

I use *nation* and *empire* as related terms in this study because of the frequency with which the nation was constructed as an empire in Orientalist works. The close connection between ideas of nation and those of empire has also been noted by theorists of nationalism. Timothy Brennan has pointed out how European nationalism was motivated by European colonial activity: "The 'national idea,' in other words, flourished in the soil of foreign conquest."[25] Both Benedict Anderson and George L. Mosse also situate the beginnings of modern European nationalism in the late eighteenth century, a period coextensive with the beginnings of colonialism.[26] It would be a mistake, however, to think of nationalism and imperialism as identical. Even though the founding fathers often thought of the United States as an empire, the very nature of the connection between nation and empire necessarily changed with different historical and social contexts. *Nation* and *empire* are relational and related terms, one dependent on the other.

Here we come to a crucial difference between U.S. and European Orientalisms. Colonialism, with its ensuing violent contact with non-European others, ensured that for European countries, particularly England and France, the narrative of empire as unquestioned was inherently unstable and needed to be supported by ideas of firm national character. In the United States, however, imperialism, particularly with respect to the Orient, could be constructed much more benevolently, as teleology. Since the "discovery" of the Americas by Columbus was popularly transmitted as the outcome of a vision to reach the Orient, contemporary arguments about seizing Oriental trade or civilizing Orientals through missionary activity were accompanied by visionary statements about completing Columbus's original mission. Tropes of expansion and control over various specific Orients were thus mystified as "natural" through the complex genealogy of the country's intimate associations with the search for the Orient.

In addition, in contrast to the situation in Europe, the idea of nation in the United States, predicated as it was on the internal colonization of Native Americans and African Americans, was rife with instabilities. As Toni Morrison has suggested, values that are touted as prototypically "American" and that often form the focus of white U.S. literature are shaped in response to an Africanist presence that had to be either repressed morally and politically or constructed as an absolute Other (primitive, savage), against which a quintessential (white) national identity could be articulated.[27] Morrison's argument compellingly places slavery (as "blackness") and racial alterity at the center of the construction of national identity.[28] Unlike the idea of nation, however, the idea of a U.S. empire, seen as much more benign than the idea of empire in European Orientalist works, was used to both mystify national instabilities and bolster the idea of a strong, expanding nation. It was thus no accident that the most popular figure for the nation in U.S. Orientalist works was Columbia, the feminization of Columbus. Yet, because of this attempted mystification, U.S. literary Orientalism became the site of a triadic encounter in which the Africanist and Native

American presences returned to haunt and question the cultural and political hegemony of the New World.

Of course, the Orient here is not simply a displaced site of national racial issues. The encounter with the Orient works powerfully to articulate and shape national identity in terms of a youthful nation revitalizing the world with messages of liberty and virtue or in terms of a radical historical shift through which the United States becomes the newest seat of empire to which the Orient needs to turn. Of all the discourses on the Orient—political, economic, scientific—literary Orientalism most significantly challenges, even as it evokes, imperialist constructions of national identity and of the Orient, as well as the racial hierarchies at home. In fields like phrenology and archaeology, Egyptomania and interest in the Near Eastern Orient produced massive phrenological studies supporting Caucasian superiority (such as Morton's *Crania Ægyptica*). Yet Poe, during the same time, engaged in compelling critiques of Western imperial will in such stories as "Ligeia" and "A Tale of the Ragged Mountains." Similarly, such novelists as John DeForest and Maria Susanna Cummins both ridiculed and deployed the pretentious figure of the archaeologist venturing east.

It should also not surprise us that these literary Orientalist works were heavily preoccupied with issues of gender and sexuality. Ideas of empire and nation in the nineteenth century, as in the present, were raced, and racial distinctions often depended on gendered distinctions. For theorists of nationalism, nation and gender are often intimately related. Benedict Anderson's connection between nation and gender is perhaps unwitting. Anderson states, "in the modern world everyone can, should, and will 'have' a nationality, as he or she 'has' a gender."[29] Although Anderson assumes that gender is an unproblematic category, something that everyone has, rather than a category that is constructed, his formulation also points to the hegemonic ways in which nation is gendered. George L. Mosse focuses on this latter aspect in the concept of nation. The beginnings of modern nationalism in the late eighteenth century coincided with the Protestant revivals in Germany and Britain, leading to an alliance between nationalism and respectability, "an alliance that regarded control over sexuality as vital to the concept of respectability."[30] Deviance, aberrance, and excess were unnational, while respectability, normativity, and control were national.[31] Nationalism was increasingly associated with an ideal of asensual heterosexual manliness, and even though female national symbols were invoked, these were essentially static rather than dynamic.[32]

Mosse's analyses are particularly relevant in considering formulations of nation in the United States. The curbing of overt sensuality and of promiscuous behaviors that would encourage it was particularly strong in New England, where immigrant purity was routinely contrasted with European libertine excess. But although Mosse's arguments compellingly demonstrate the alliances between nationalism and sexual codes and between nationalism and heteronormativity, they are based on the assumption of literal, oppositional gender constructions (albeit highly politicized ones), the hierarchies of which are dramatic indications of hegemonic, nationalistic power structures. When national icons, as bearers of national ideology, are invoked in the context of empire, however, gender often does not work literally.

Here, Rey Chow's analysis of the journalistic representations of the use of Lady Liberty in the Tiannanmen Square revolt of 1991 is particularly useful. Chow begins by demonstrating the problems inherent in seeing gender literally and as an unchanging category. A feminist friend asks Chow, "How should we read what is going on in China in terms of gender?" Chow responds: "The problem is not how we should read what is going on in China in terms of gender, but rather: what do the events in China tell us about gender as a category, especially as it relates to the so-called Third World?"[33] By reversing the question, Chow demonstrates the mutability of gender categories in a transnational context. Chow suggests that even though Lady Liberty is ostensibly "female," in the Tiannanmen Square context "woman is not the heterosexual opposite of man, but the symbol of what China is not/does not have."[34]

Chow's arguments are especially relevant in thinking about U.S. nationalism in the context of Orientalism. Symbols of nationhood evolved and changed from early European conceptions of the Americas, to early settlements in the seventeenth century, and through the revolutionary period. Europeans pictured the Americas through the body of the Native American woman, resplendent with fruits, a symbol of fertility.[35] By the seventeenth century, the idea of associating the nation with tropes of exploration and conquest coalesced in the figure of Columbia, the feminization of Columbus. In *Magnalia Christi Americana*, Cotton Mather declared that the New World be called Columbia. It was in the revolutionary period, however, that Columbia as a symbol for the United States gained accepted currency. Philip Freneau referred to the United States as both Columbia and New Albion.[36] Undoubtedly, that the music of "Hail Columbia" was part of Washington's inaugural march made the symbology more popular.[37] Simultaneously, the eagle, the symbol of the Roman Empire, was adopted as the seal of the United States in 1782. The spread eagle, bearing a shield on its breast, an olive branch in one talon, and thirteen arrows indicating readiness for war in the other, was often gendered as male.[38] Yet another revolutionary man- ifestation of nation was Liberty, deriving immediately from the liberty cap carried by Britannia on a spear and the Roman goddess of liberty.[39]

For most Orientalist writers, the idea of nation as Columbia was appealing, no doubt because of the trope of exploration and empire inherent in the invocation of Columbus's ventures and his vision of reaching the Orient. Columbus's original dream was idealized and invoked to naturalize ideas of empire. Although strictly in terms of a sex-gender equation Columbia as an early iconic figure for the nation was female, the Columbia invoked as a justification for expansionism and control in the context of the Orient was gendered differently. Columbia as a figure for nation as empire was not associated with such qualities as fluidity, disorder, and emotion, which have, within theories of gender dichotomies, been traditionally associated with femininity; rather, this Columbia was associated with activity, power, athletic vigor, and (virtuous) desire for expansion and control, qualities tradi- tionally coded as male.

In U.S. Orientalist texts, the nation as empire is often embodied as young, vigorous, powerful, and masculinized. But the portrayal of this figure is also interrupted by anxious moments in which its imperial gen- der construction is destabilized through its encounter with the Oriental other. For example, in *El Fureidis,* Maria Susanna Cummins's hero, Meredith, loses his sense of masculinity and wholeness when confronted with an image of two amorous women. Thus, these Orientalist texts do not simply perpetuate a repressive patriarchy.[40] Many women writers, in fact, used the Orient as a site for questioning and undermining the socially acceptable ideologies of womanhood in the late eighteenth and nineteenth centuries. In *Slaves in Algiers,* for instance, Susanna Rowson constructs the harem as a social space for the bonding of women, out of which emerges a critique of the ideal of woman as republican mother. Opened up at key moments in such texts as Cummins's *El Fureidis* and Rowson's *Slaves in Algiers* are possibilities of queer gendering that undermine the heteronormativity and patriarchy on which imperial dis- course rests. As this study suggests, an unstable gendered discourse often works to contest the ideology of superior USAmerican virtue on which the rhetoric of empire within Orientalism depends.

Chapter 1 of this study describes the numerous discourses on the Orient beginning in the postrevolutionary period. Briefly examining the many commercial, political, and literary contacts with the Orient in the late eighteenth and nineteenth centuries, it emphasizes the raced and imperial nature of these contacts and puts under question the model of New England cultural insularity that has dominated most intellectual histories of the period. Oriental travel writing, in particular, enjoyed a success that belies such claims. The chapter then moves on to examine the complex interrelationship between the technologies of race and the discourses on the Orient, by examining two important types of orientalist discourses: phrenology and missionary statements.

Egyptology in the United States generated anxieties about racial hierarchies as much as it did an enthusiasm about decoding the mysteries of the Orient. One can see such anxiety and enthusiasm in Morton's *Crania Americana* (1839) and *Crania AEgyptica* (1844) and in the ethnographic writings of George S. Gliddon, U.S. consul at Cairo. Both writers study Egyptian writings to support polygenesis. Official reports on missionary activity also form an important part of Orientalist discourses. The American Board of Commissioners for Foreign Missions was formed in 1811. The reports of that board offer a fascinating account of the political and racial concerns of the missionaries and of their need to be seen as agents of a major power. The reaction of missionaries to the Oriental churches of the Near East suggests a less than certain ethnocentrism. The alarm of U.S. missionaries at the laxity of Oriental churches and the daily proximity of Christians and Muslims in the Near East underscores an anxiety about cross-cultural and interracial contact that reflects fear of contamination both from people of color within the country and from imperial contacts abroad.

In Chapter 2, I examine a number of literary Orientalist texts of the late eighteenth century that were written in the wake of the U.S.–North African altercation. The capture and enslavement of U.S. sailors by the Algerians created an outrage that went unappeased until 1805, when William Eaton, U.S. consul at Tripoli, coordinated an attack on Derna and raised the U.S. flag on the city walls. The historical occasion thus provided ready materials for dramatizing oppositions between North African despotism and immorality, on the one hand, and U.S. freedom and virtue, on the other. Royall Tyler's *The Algerine Captive* (1797), David Everett's *Slaves in Barbary* (1797), Susanna Rowson's *Slaves in Algiers* (1794), James Ellison's *The American Captive* (1812), Jonathan Smith's *The Siege of Algiers* (1823), and Peter Markoe's *The Algerine Spy in*

Pennsylvania (1787) all participate in the official narrative of the United States as a virtuous empire spreading the light of freedom in a dissipated Orient, the imperial body being constructed through an exclusion of both slavery and deviant Oriental sexuality. But the raced and gendered anxieties accompanying the construction of strong, imperial nationhood are also evident. Slavery surfaces at the center of national consciousness, splitting the coherence and identity of the nation. And all too often the gendering and respectability of the hero embodying the nation is undermined by a willing participation in sensual excess, as a discourse of sexuality contends with a discourse of empire. For instance, in *The Algerine Captive*, Tyler's narrator is made to literally participate in the purchase of human cargo. Later, inside a Muslim enclave, he delights in the "feminization" of his body through ritual scrubbing and oiling.

Chapter 3 focuses on the Near Eastern Orientalist literature of the nineteenth century in relation to the Orientalist discourses of Egyptology and missionary Protestantism. While Egyptology generated a rush of self-styled archaeologists chauvinistically ready to excavate all of the Near East, missionaries prompted concerns about the mixture of races and cultures there. In literary Orientalist works about the Near East, the border becomes a site of anxiety and transgression. Most works appropriate the hierarchical paradigm of white explorer and explored Oriental, but they do this so self-consciously and critically that what emerges is a parodic Orientalism in contestation with the dominant discourses on the Orient, the latter being recuperated only as points of closure. In John DeForest's *Irene the Missionary* (1879), for instance, the vigorous, USAmerican male archaeologist is constantly critiqued in his quest to excavate all of the Near East. These works also reveal the precariousness of the racial alterity on which the missionary-imperial body is constructed, by introducing moments when this body is transformed through interracial contact. In William Ware's *Zenobia* (1837), for instance, Lucius M. Piso fears for his manly body in the Oriental languor of Palmyra. Maria Susanna Cummins, however, uses racial intermixing to both contain and subvert imperial race and gender hierarchies. Exploiting the new possibilities available to women as a result of missionary work overseas, Cummins, in *El Fureidis* (1860), creates Havilah, a woman pure but not bound by domesticity, pious but overly learned, beautiful but more athletic than her male archaeologist suitor. Through this racially mixed character, Cummins challenges the patriarchy within imperialism while still maintaining the raced imperatives of the latter. Finally, chapter 3 explores the tension between the raced and gendered formations of Near Eastern orientalism by examining the interventions of African American David S. Dorr. In *A Colored Man Round the World* (1858), Dorr negotiates his critique of white Egyptology and his willed identification with patriarchal imperial structures that create a space for his contingently "free" body, to reveal the omnivorous attraction of Orientalist narratives of empire.

Chapter 4 examines three of the most subversive Near Eastern orientalist writers: Edgar Allan Poe, Harriet Prescott Spofford, and Herman Melville. These writers critique imperial-hermeneutic power through a raced and gendered destabilization of the body of the archaeologist/traveler/hermeneute. The comic critique of Orientalist power gives way here to a demonstration of its tragic consequences. Poe critiques both the repressive discourses on the Orient and the suppression of the facts of Western colonialism in the U.S. imaginary. "Ligeia," the most complex of Poe's oriental tales, demonstrates the crisis of identity consequent on the inability of the narrator to support either an imperialist national identity or Southern nationalism. The character Ligeia, suggestive of an Oriental and Africanist presence, undermines through her power the narrator's attempts at coherent raced and gendered self-fashioning. In "Desert Sands" (1863), Spofford critiques the objectification of the Other inherent in the aesthetics of Oriental authentication. By literally equating the artistic triumph of the hero (a triumph won by a mastery over the Oriental landscape) with the death of the woman, Spofford exposes the repressive patriarchal basis of Western imperialism. Writing contemporaneously with Spofford, Melville, in *Clarel*, problematizes the idea of USAmerican hermeneutic power by dramatizing the resistance of the Oriental subject to appropriation and control. Through Clarel, a young theology student journeying the Near East, Melville eroticizes the relationship between the New World and the Orient and demonstrates how the racial-cultural difference of the Orient cannot be contained by a creation of race hierarchies or through phallocentric othering. Instead, *Clarel* questions the oppositions between the New World and the Near East through the circulation of homoerotic desire.

Chapter 5 focuses on popular Indian Orientalist writers, the complex cultural discourses on Indology, the push for Asian markets, theories about the westerly movement of empire from its inception in Asia, and the colonization of India. It then examines Indic Orientalist writings, including works by such poets as William Rounseville Alger and James Russell Lowell, which contrast a youthful USAmerica with a spent and dissipated Orient. The enormously successful Bayard Taylor, often dismissed as sentimental and romantic, exhibits in his travel writings a keen historical awareness and a self-consciousness about constructing the Orient that opens possibilities for a transgressive Indic orientalism.

In chapters 6 and 7, I specifically analyze the Indic Orientalist texts of Emerson and Whitman in the context of the political, economic, and philosophical discourses on India sketched in chapter 5. In chapter 6, through an examination of Emerson's "Indian Superstition," "Plato," *English Traits,* and "Fate," I show how Emerson's raced construction of India as a passive and spiritual Other against an active and material New World is an anxious attempt to recuperate the nation as vibrant and whole. As Emerson became more involved with issues of slavery and race, he increasingly sought to exclude the social-material Asia and its raced bodies (and create a transhistorical Asia, free of divisive racial politics) to facilitate the construction of the nation as a strong, whole, athletic body. Yet race powerfully surfaces in Emerson's essays through his engagement with theories of racial evolution and Anglo-Saxon destiny. And at significant moments in Emerson's construction of the Indic Orient, the normativity and wholeness of the nation is questioned as it becomes evident that the idea of a powerful (male) nationhood depends greatly on a homoerotic nationhood that needs to be suppressed.

Chapter 7 examines several of Whitman's Orientalist poems, including "Salut Au Monde," "Facing West from California's Shores," and "Passage to India," and traces their construction of India as a maternal trope and a raced Other lacking its own agency. I suggest that in these poems, particularly in "Passage to India," the fantasy of cross-continental unification does not simply exist in a spiritual imaginary where power relations are suspended. "Passage to India," for instance, historicizes India but does so strategically, excluding the realities of British colonialism. This excluded history contours the embodiment of the nation as youth/child innocently embracing the world.

My analysis of specific U.S. literary Orientalisms as related to political and commercial issues and to questions of nation, empire, and race stands in contrast to most studies in this area, which have reduced literary interests in various Orients to the allure of a syncretic, European-constructed Orient, conceived as simply philosophical, spiritual, or exotic, or have seen the deployment of certain tropes for the Orient as unrelated to the field of power relations. Arthur Christy's statement about Emerson, "He turned both inward and Eastward," typifies the ahistorical nature of these studies.[41] Christy's book, published in 1932, is admittedly dated, but even Beongcheon Yu's *The Great Circle: American Writers and the Orient* (1983) doggedly refuses to admit issues of power.[42] This lack of a sociopolitical approach to U.S. literary Orientalism until very recently can be explained by two long-standing tenets of U.S. literary studies: the centrality of Puritan New England culture to the nation and the insularity of this culture; and the assumed lack of an imperialist tradition in the United States.

In *Nathaniel Hawthorne and the Romance of the Orient*, Luther S. Luedtke brilliantly shows how the New England of Hawthorne's time was, in fact, far from insular. Drawing on a wide variety of materials, including records of Hawthorne's readings, the logbooks of Hawthorne's father, Nathaniel S. Hathorne, and various maritime histories, Luedtke delineates the active commerce and interaction with the Orient in mid-nineteenth-century New England. Luedtke's findings allow him to examine Hawthorne's writings through a context far more cross-cultural than any available before.[43] Looking specifically at U.S. attitudes toward the Near Eastern Orient in the nineteenth century, Fuad Sha'ban sees USAmerican Orientalism as an expression of the New World belief in its chosen destiny, as the "symbolic kingdom of God," to spread the light in the Muslim world. In the nineteenth century, this missionary goal coalesced with expansionist impulses, leading to "a more physical aspiration to establish that Kingdom in the Holy Land."[44] Both Luedtke and Sha'ban demonstrate the significance of the historical-material Orient to the culture of nineteenth-century USAmerica. My study expands Luedtke's scope to include the relationship of literary texts to imperialist discourses, and it goes beyond Sha'ban's by emphasizing the secular as well as religious impulses of USAmerican Orientalisms.

Until recently, U.S. literary and intellectual history have simply not acknowledged the existence of imperialism as a significant ideology within the United States. Indeed, the most accepted model for literary and cultural studies of the United States was Perry Miller's model of Puritan origins (a model that Amy Kaplan has shown was formulated by the imperial conditions that brought Miller to the Congo on an oil tanker);[45] the second influential model derived from Frederick Jackson Turner's thesis that the vacant frontier was the enabling condition of U.S. democracy.[46] The major challenge to these approaches came from critics who placed intercultural contact and conflict at the center of national culture. Richard Slotkin suggested that the colonists' brutal suppression of Indians made the idea of regeneration through violence the defining metaphor of national identity.[47] In the works of Ronald Takaki and Richard Drinnon, the idea of empire came to the forefront in U.S. cultural studies. In *Iron Cages*, Takaki proposed that the "iron cages" of Protestant repression and racial purity, bureaucratic capitalism, and expansionism were interlinked and together explained nineteenth-century U.S. culture.[48] In *Facing West*, Richard Drinnon suggested a direct link between internal colonization and external empire building, by showing how the characteristics attributed to Native Americans and used as a justification to "subdue" them were also used in wars with the Philippines and, later, Vietnam.[49]

As historians have noted, theories of exceptionalism have all but prevented imperialism from being examined as a significant ideology in U.S. history and culture. Such theories maintain that the United States, unlike Europe, was not interested in overseas possessions and that therefore, except for an aberrant period from 1898–1912, imperialism is irrelevant to a consideration of its history. This view was challenged by two almost contemporaneous works, William Appleman Williams's *The Tragedy of American Diplomacy* (1959) and R. W. Van Alstyne's *The Rising American Empire* (1960). Williams and Alstyne both demonstrated the long history of the United States as an empire much before the end of the nineteenth century. More importantly, Van Alstyne traced the history of the ideology of empire and showed how the United States was continually thought of as an empire by statesmen and policymakers from the time of the revolution. This view was supported by Williams in his later work *Empire as a Way of Life* (1980).[50]

For our purposes, the importance of these studies lies in their demonstration of imperialism as not an aberrant but a central and enabling ideology of U.S. culture. The Revolutionary War severed the economic and military bondage of the colonies to Britain, but it did not break many of their ideological ties, particularly the idea of Anglo-Saxons creating empires and holding sway over people of color.[51] The founding fathers had no difficulty thinking of the nation as an empire: America was quite naturally to be one. Thomas Paine, for instance, had no doubt that the war of independence involved more than the rights of the thirteen colonies. Paine wrote, " 'Tis not the affair of a city, a county, a province, or a kingdom; but of a continent—of at least one eighth part of the habitable globe."[52] As early as 1783, Washington used the term *ris-*

ing empire to describe the United States.[53] By the early nineteenth century, the idea that the United States represented liberty and freedom for
which, paradoxically, it needed more territory and influence was
acceptable to many statesmen. Jefferson, whose most frequently used
word was *liberty*, described the United States as an "empire for liberty."[54] "Trusted with the destinies of this solitary republic of the world,
the only monument of human rights, and the sole depository of the
sacred fire of freedom and self-government," Jefferson wrote, "from
hence it is to be lighted up in other regions of the earth, if other regions
of the earth shall ever become susceptible of its benign influence."[55] Jefferson's formulation mutually implicates the sacred and the secular, the
national and the imperial. Being trusted with guarding the "*sacred* fire of
freedom" (emphasis mine) paradoxically means ensuring its expansion.
Freedom and influence, liberty and empire—such was the paradoxical
language of U.S. empire building. This rhetoric, couched in the familiar
and acceptable language of USAmerican freedom, was different than
the British rhetoric of empire, in which empire building was cast as a
civilizing mission.

It was also clear to the early leaders that spreading freedom did not
simply mean (although it could include) rallying to the cause of revolu-
tions for freedom in other countries. John Quincy Adams wrote to his
father in 1811, "The whole continent of North America appears to be
destined by Divine Providence to be peopled by one nation, speaking
one language, professing one general system of religious and political
principles. . . . For the common happiness of them all, for their peace and
prosperity, I believe it is indispensable that they should be associated in
one federal Union."[56] What Adams had speculated about as the imperial construction of the nation would be circulated in popular parlance as
indisputable through the appellation *America*, a term signifying the
imaginary welding together of two continents.

Only very recently, however, have literary critics recognized the
importance of ideas of empire to U.S. literary studies.[57] David S. Shields
has shown that until the mid–eighteenth century, the poetry of the
United States featured a discourse of empire. After 1750, this myth was
simply shorn of its British imperial frame and applied to the "republican
glory of the rising glory of America."[58] While Shields emphasizes the
centrality of empire to eighteenth-century literature, Wai-Chee Dimock
demonstrates its significance to the mid–nineteenth century. By placing
Melville's writings in the context of antebellum discourses of empire,

Wai-Chee Dimock analyzes Melville's imperial articulation of individualism.[59] The essays collected in *Cultures of United States Imperialism* (cited earlier in this introduction, in n. 45) attest to the growing acceptance of imperialism as an important ideology in the study of U.S. literature.

My study of U.S. literary Orientalisms similarly situates texts in relation to discourses on empire endemic in the country since the Revolutionary War. I suggest that U.S. literary Orientalism was not simply a mystical, ahistorical phenomenon or an imitation of British Orientalism but an indigenous discourse deriving its impetus both from immediate sociopolitical circumstances and from theories of the westerly movement of civilization, culminating in the New World—theories that naturalized the idea of a USAmerican empire. I also show how works of writers seen as central to the mid–nineteenth century, such as Poe, Emerson, and Whitman, need to be read through postcoloniality. The construction of the nation as a strong, though benevolent, empire, continuing in the Orient the original quest of Columbus, served both to distinguish this new empire from those of Europe and to mystify and contain internal racial schisms, conflicts, and violence.

My study of U.S. Orientalist literature in the century prior to the 1890s demonstrates the international interests of USAmerican writers in a period that has largely been seen as insular. These writers sought to appropriate the imperial imperatives of European Orientalist discourses within a Columbiad vision, changing, questioning, or accommodating these imperatives to the exigencies of the New World. An understanding of how literary Orientalism works in the early period of the nation's history is therefore crucial in comprehending both the global dimensions of definitions of nation and the dual nature of early U.S. culture as both postcolonial and colonizing.

This book excludes many texts in which issues of orientalism and imperialism might be significant, because I have focused on the literary Orientalisms arising out of only three specific contexts. The numerous works produced in fear of the yellow peril, for instance, need to be read in the context of the Chinese immigrant cultures of California more than in the context of imperialism, although, no doubt, the two are related. Even within these contexts, my purpose is not to engage in an exhaustive examination of Orientalists works, but to focus on their different discursive possibilities. Similarly, I have not dealt with works relating to the Pacific Islands, because of the very different Western constructions placed on oral versus print cultures; primitivism and Orientalism cannot simply be collapsed as structures. Travel writing about the Orient likewise serves only as a point of departure, because of the different manner in which issues of representation and mimeticism need to be theorized there. Finally, I end this study just before the 1890s, because of the proliferation of new Oriental contexts and because the perceived activity of "real" empire making generates qualitatively different discourses of empire that affect discourses on the Orient.

1

Race(ing) to the Orient

A major component of USAmerican culture in the late eighteenth and nineteenth centuries was a race to the Orient: it was a competition among various business and scholastic interests; it was a race with prominent European powers; it was also an inquiry into racial difference and the origins of races. Merchants competed to earn profits from trade to the Near East and Asia, tourists eagerly rushed to visit the Holy Land and marvel at the pyramids, travel writers churned out numerous books on Near Eastern and Asian travel for an omnivorous readership, and the public at large consumed vast quantities of Oriental goods. The cultural proximity between the United States and the Near East and Asia created by these contacts fostered a climate that generated a rich body of literary Orientalist works. Although this orientomania has been noted by many scholars, what has escaped attention is its ideological dimensions: the preponderance of discourses involved in race(ing) the Orient and with which contact with the Orient was intimately connected.[1] For instance, visions of the westerly movement of empire, culminating in the United States, were invoked in arguing for a greater share of trade with Asia; missionaries, alarmed at the lapsed Christianity of Oriental churches in the Near East and at the mixture of races there, wrote their anxieties into popular travel narratives and tracts; finally, the interest of the nineteenth century in racial classification and phrenology was intensified by debates about the racial origins of the Egyptians. This race(ing) of the Orient was an integral component of the cultural imaginary in which literary Orientalist works participated. After briefly examining the commercial and scholarly links between the

United States and the Orient until the mid–nineteenth century, this chapter will focus on a few of the raced discourses on the Orient. I intend these forays into Oriental reading, writing, and trade not as explanatory histories but as rhetorical interventions, questioning the dominant scholarly paradigm of U.S. cultural and political insularity in the eighteenth and early nineteenth centuries.

Oriental Readings

It is important to realize that reading about the Orient was nothing new to nineteenth-century USAmerica. Even the earliest New England colonists, fascinated perhaps by Columbus's highly mythologized quest to reach the Indies, were widely read in travels to different parts of the Orient. For instance, the elder William Brewster, who came on the *Mayflower*, carried with him a copy of Richard Hakluyt's *Principall Navigations*, a work that covered travel to the Orient and advocated colonization. Among about fifty books that the soldier Miles Standish left at his death were *History of the World* and *Turkish History*.[2] By 1723, Harvard could boast of a large list of Orientala, including Thomas Fuller's *A Pisgah-sight of Palestine*, Aaron Hill's *A Full and Just Account of the Present State of the Ottoman Empire*, and Richard Hakluyt's *History of the West Indies*.[3] The intellectual excitement created by works about the Orient is evident in Cotton Mather's letter to John Winthrop in 1720 in which he particularly mentions, "I have newly received large packetts from *Tranquebar* in the *East-Indies*."[4] Mather's own language was understandably sprinkled with such phrases as "the Arabian proverb" and "a certain proverb in Asia," a feature Thomas Goddard Wright sees as an example of the knowledge of the Orient that all literate colonials of Mather's class had.[5] It seems clear that even in this early period the New England intelligentsia considered knowledge about the Orient important.

Academic institutions in New England also stressed the importance of Oriental knowledge. For example, Harvard College, from its very inception, required the study of such languages as Chaldee and Syriac.[6] Such learning did much to awaken interest in the oriental churches in Syria and Lebanon, leading to the first foray of missionary activity in the region in the early nineteenth century. The same period also witnessed both scholarly and popular interest in the Near East as a result of Napoleon's Egyptian expedition in 1798. Jean-François Champollion's deciphering of hieroglyphic writings with the help of the Rosetta stone in 1822 created intense excitement in both Europe and

USAmerica. By 1831, Champollion's discoveries and the controversies surrounding them were enough for Edward Everett to write a long essay in the *North American Review* defending Champollion's findings over those of Britisher Thomas Young. Such scholarly excitement incited by Egyptology had its popular counterpart as well. The first U.S. display of an ancient Egyptian object (a mummified ibis) took place as early as 1803 in the Peabody Museum in Salem, Massachusetts.[7] P. T. Barnum acquired two mummies, which were displayed at Peale's Museum and Gallery of Fine Arts in New York in 1826. Even Chicago acquired its first mummy in the 1830s. Not to be outdone by British archaeologists and collectors, U.S. adventurers ventured forth into Egypt. In 1832, Colonel Mendes Cohen of Baltimore returned from Egypt with 680 artifacts to establish the first private Egyptian collection in the United States.[8]

By the early nineteenth century, the United States, like Europe, would also feel the effects of what Raymond Schwab has called "the Oriental Renaissance." According to Schwab, the arrival of Sanskrit texts in Europe in the late eighteenth century created an intellectual renaissance greater in impact than the renaissance following the arrival of Greek manuscripts in the fifteenth century.[9] For scholars in the United States, the work of William Jones intensified interest in India and its languages and spurred inquires into the origins of the Caucasian race. In 1795, just a decade after William Jones's journal *Asiatic Researches* had started publication, the Massachusetts Historical Society elected Jones as a corresponding member.[10] U.S. literary interest in India continued with the printing of act 1 of William Jones's translation of the Sanskrit *Shakuntala* in the *Monthly Anthology and Boston Review* in July 1805. A similar flurry of interest accompanied Hindu reformist Rammohan Roy's visit to England in the 1820s. Ralph Waldo Emerson's aunt, Mary Moody Emerson, wrote glowingly about Roy to Emerson and urged him to read Roy's writings. Emerson, skeptical at first, recognized Roy as a major thinker in later years. Already in 1817, the Boston publication *The Christian Disciple* published in its "Religious Intelligence" column an article on Roy titled "A Remarkable Hindoo Reformer"; in March of the following year, another Boston publication, the *North American Review*, published an essay titled "Theology of the Hindoos, as taught by Ram Mohun Roy."[11]

An indication of the importance of the Orient in the cultural imaginary is the speed with which literary orientalism was circulated and domesticated in the postrevolutionary period, with even statesman and politicians dabbling in Oriental tales and letters. Benjamin Franklin wrote a short story titled "An Arabian Tale," which was structured around an argument between Albumazar the magician and Belubel, a spirit.[12] Federalist lawyer Benjamin Silliman used the genre of Oriental letters to attack republicanism. His "Letters of Shahcoolen, a Hindu Philosopher, Residing in Philadelphia; to his Friend El Hassan, an Inhabitant of Delhi" began to appear in Noah Webster's *New York Commercial Advertiser* in October 1801. The letters received such favorable notice that they were collected into a book published by Russell and Cutler in Boston in 1802. A major event in the circulation of Orientalist literature was the publication of *The Arabian Nights* by H. and P. Rice of Philadelphia in 1794; the book sold over forty thousand copies in its first decade. Two decades later, in 1817, Thomas Moore's *Lalla Rookh* sold more copies than any other book published in the United States that year.[13]

For readers in the United States, Oriental literatures were not simply exotic, trivial entertainment but literatures that warranted commentary and critique. Although many of these appraisals were predictable, as was, for example, Silliman's conception of Eastern writing as "florid," "brilliant," and full of "wild similitude and extravagant hyperbole,"[14] others attempted to undertake a serious study of different Oriental writings. Between June and November 1840, for instance, the *Southern Literary Messenger* published three articles on Arabian literature. The first article broadly enunciated the major types of Arabian languages and the regions in which they were spoken; the second was an analysis of the Book of Job, taken to be the oldest Arabic production; the third was a translation of selected Arabic poems and biographical sketches of the poets.[15]

New World Westerly Empire and Trade with the Orient

In addition to the availability and popularity of Orientalist works in the postrevolutionary United States, increasing commercial interests both in the Near East and in Asia also brought the Orient closer to the New World, the commercial often signifying more than simply profit, being invested with raced cultural ideologies. As Luther S. Luedtke suggests, New England was engaged in a flurry of international trade. Salem was a major international port, where products from all parts of the Orient were far from foreign. The area was so cosmopolitan that Luedtke contends, "During an age that thought in terms of universal history it

would have been surprising to discover an educated citizen of Massachusetts whose cultural horizons stopped short of the Orient."[16]

Brisk commerce with the Orient quickly followed independence,
and the United States soon became an important force.[17] Oriental trade
was obviously important, both in itself and as a sign of national power.
Revolutionary statesmen emphasized the need for the United States to
compete with European colonial powers in participating in the opium
trade. Jefferson appointed William Stewart as consul at Smyrna in 1802.
The main object of trade with Smyrna was opium for China, and the
United States cornered the Smyrna market.[18] By the 1830s, after a commercial treaty with Turkey was negotiated, trade with the Tripolitan
states became well established. It is estimated that in 1832 alone, forty-
six U.S. ships landed at Smyrna and fourteen in Constantinople.[19] In
the 1830s the U.S. merchant fleet was second in size only to Britain and
was highly regarded. In fact, the construction and power of U.S. ships
impressed the Turks so much that the sultan hired Henry Eckford, an
eminent New York naval architect, to overhaul the shipyard of the
Turkish navy on the Golden Horn. In what might be the first instance
of U.S. technological dominance, Eckford commanded an operation
comprising fifteen U.S. craftsmen and about six hundred Greeks,
Turks, and Italians.[20]

More than trade with the Near East, trade with Asia was vigorously
sought after, pursued, and accomplished. It was presumed that the
leader in this trade would lead the world; yet, for many, the issue of
commercial dominance over Asia was as much racial and cultural as
economic and political. Philip Freneau, for instance, celebrated the voyage of the *Empress of China*, the first U.S. ship to sail to the Far East,
"Where George forbade to sail before."[21] Journeying to the Far East and
trading with it were signs of New World independence and incipient
power. For many other thinkers, Far Eastern trade exemplified the idea
of civilization coming full circle. It was properly held that empires had
started in the Far East, had moved to Europe, and were heading to the
New World. As early as the 1750s, Englishman Andrew Burnaby commented when he visited the United States, "an idea, strange as it is
visionary, [had] entered into the minds of the generality of mankind, that
empire is travelling westward; and every one is looking forward . . . to
that destined moment when America is to give law to the rest of the
world."[22] A half century later, in 1807, John Adams concurringly wrote,
"There is nothing, in my little reading, more ancient in my memory than
the observation that arts, sciences, and empire had travelled westward;

and in conversation it was always added since I was a child, that their next leap would be over the Atlantic into America."[23] The idea of the newest Western empire exploring and dominating the East therefore had utopian implications beyond those of trade alone. Jefferson had been fascinated with the idea of "the North American road to India" since 1787 and hoped that an overland route to the Columbia River would help divert Oriental trade from Europe to the United States. The Lewis and Clark expedition sent by Jefferson opened such a route in 1804–6.

The idea of the North American road to India was taken up again by Senator Thomas Hart Benton of Missouri, one of the most vigorous proponents of Asian trade in the early nineteenth century. Benton prophesied great prospects for Asiatic trade and the consequent burgeoning of St. Louis as one of the greatest cities of the world. He incessantly pushed for a railroad to the Pacific to enhance Asian trade. More interestingly, he cast his arguments about trade in terms of human race and civilization moving west and the return of republican ideals to Asia.[24] Such arguments were complexly transformed into cultural and gendered embodiments in the works of such literary figures as Emerson and Walt Whitman.

Whatever the ideological reasons for Asian trade may have been, merchants began to agitate for Chinese trade in Salem as early as 1783. By 1790, when the elder Elias Hasket Derby's ship, the *Astrea,* returned to Salem from Canton, it brought a cargo for which duties were paid amounting to an unheard of twenty-seven thousand dollars.[25] The public craze for goods from the Far East ensured that trade was lucrative.[26] However, the biggest moneymaker by the 1830s, as all the major colonial powers realized, was opium.[27] All leading U.S. firms handled the sale of Turkish opium to China, and soon, in direct competition with the British East India Company, they dealt in the more profitable opium from the native states of Western India. Clearly, dominance in trade with the Far East was a signifier of imperial power, and the United States sought for this dominance.

The effects of Asian trade, however, were not simply economic but, as importantly, cultural. The import of Asian goods both created and satisfied the demands of the public. Even as early as the 1650s, Puritan severity notwithstanding, the import of painted Indian calicoes via England was taking place.[28] By the early eighteenth century, silken goods and nankeens were enjoying popularity. Handmade and hand-painted chinaware, porcelain, jade, and chessmen were increasingly becoming signs of class for the well-to-do, a fact that Washington Irving noted in *Salmagundi.* In addition, popular interest in curiosities from the Orient was also rising. The Salem East India Marine Society exhibited its collection of instructive materials from the Orient, including a stone hand from the cave temples of Elephanta in Bombay, a hookah, and figures of Hindu deities, such as Krishna, Rama, and Sita. By the 1870s and 1880s, "odalisques, cloisonne, sandalwood, and other Oriental bric-a-brac" had become part of the atmosphere of New England;[29] cultural proprietorship over the Orient was as much New England's as Europe's.

Travel Writing about the Orient

Although oriental goods and knowledge of Oriental literatures and customs were widely circulated in New England, the race to the Orient was limited to merchants at first and later to merchants and missionaries. Only with the introduction of steam packets in the 1830s did tourists from the United States start to choose Oriental destinations. Once the touristing started, however, Egypt and the Holy Land were the most popular Oriental destinations. U.S. appetite for Oriental travel is evidenced by the fact that by the winter of 1838–39 Egypt had more travelers from the United States than of any other nationality but the British.[30] Tourists were awed at the antiquities and collected many of them, but they never lost sight of their roles as emissaries of a contemporary power. Traveler George English, for instance, floated on a raft in the Nile in 1820 singing "Hail Columbia! happy land!" while John Leydard described the Nile as no bigger than the Connecticut River.[31]

For the people who did not travel to the Orient, there were the accounts of fellow citizens who did. Eager citizens crowded the lecture circuit to hear talks about different Eastern countries. Exotic accounts of a syncretic, monolithic Orient were routinely challenged with more concrete, scholarly talks about specific Orients, even though the raced prerogatives of the former were often retained. In April 1856, for instance, crowds battled harsh weather in New York to hear an arcane discussion about the two distinct classes of people in Syria.[32] Travel writing about the Orient was also plentiful and popular. The journal of the American Oriental Society, in its first volume, lists forty-nine titles under the heading "American Voyages, Travels, and Other Works Relating to the East and Polynesia."[33] Out of these, thirty-four are travel works about Asia, the Near East, and the Middle East, all published between 1823 and 1843.

SCENES IN ASIA,

FOR THE

AMUSEMENT AND INSTRUCTION

OF

Little Tarry=at=Home Travellers.

⋘●◉●⋙

BY THE

REV. ISAAC TAYLOR,

AUTHOR OF "SCENES IN EUROPE."

⋘●◉●⋙

STEREOTYPED BY JAMES CONNER, NEW-YORK.

HARTFORD:
PUBLISHED BY SILAS ANDRUS
::::::::::
1830.

Even missionaries, whose sole purpose was to demonstrate the depravities and degradations of the Orient and thus illustrate the need for Christian conversion, attempted to present their works as entertaining travel writings.[34] For instance, Rev. Isaac Taylor, author of *Scenes in Europe*, published in 1826 a pocket-size book called *Scenes in Asia, for the Amusement and Instruction of Little Tarry-at-Home-Travellers*. The title page carries a picture of a composite Orient that bears little relation to and indeed complicates the rhetorical purpose of missionary salvation (see fig. 1). In the picture, a bearded man with long, flowing robes, leaning over what looks like Chinese pottery, rests under a Japanese-looking umbrella and fans himself with a Japanese ladies' fan. He sits on a Persian rug, an elephant behind him, and a sword visible among his possessions. The book opens with a flippant invitation to the reader to explore the Orient: "A going, a going, we'll set off in style, / The wonders of Asia to see / We'll take our farewell of Old England awhile, / And give a good jump o'er the sea."[35] Once he has captured the readers' attention with this syncretic Orient, however, Taylor proceeds to list the depravities of different Oriental cultures.

Other travel writers focused more on the picturesqueness and exoticism of the "backward" Eastern races, though some, like Bayard Taylor, questioned theories of racial evolution by critiquing European colonization.[36] Many of these travel writers, such as Nathaniel Parker Willis, enjoyed immense popularity. Willis's *Pencillings by the Way*, an account of a cruise on the Eastern Mediterranean in 1833, no doubt fascinated readers with its raptures over Mediterranean sunsets, twilights, and veiled women. Similarly, John Lloyd Stephens attained almost overnight success with his two books of Oriental travel, *Incidents of Travel in Egypt, Arabia Petraea, and the Holy Land* (1837) and *Incidents of Travel in the Russian and Turkish Empires* (1830). Stephens was well received both in the United States and in Europe, his royalties reaching an unheard of twenty-five thousand dollars.[37]

Travel writing continued to enjoy popularity in the mid–nineteenth century, with George William Curtis's *Nile Notes of a Howadji* (1851) and *The Howadji in Syria* (1852). The first is an account of a journey along the Nile, the second a description of travels across Cairo, the Arabian

FIG. 1. Title page of Rev. Isaac Taylor's *Scenes in Asia, for the Amusement and Instruction of Little Tarry-at-Home-Travellers* (1826; reprint, New York: James Conner, 1830).

deserts, Jerusalem, and finally Damascus. Curtis's books demonstrate the persistence with which constructions of the Orient intersected with raced concerns at home. *The Howadji in Syria* begins, for instance, with exotic images of "acacia groves," "costumes whose picturesqueness is poetry," and the harems of the pashas.[38] Yet Curtis suggests that Oriental civilization is all in the past: "The Poets at the cafés tell the old tales. The splendors of the Caliphat flash, a boreal brilliance, over an unreal past. . . . Thus oriental life is an echo and a ghost."[39] Curtis employs binary oppositions that circulate in much of U.S. Orientalist writing, such as past and present, unreal and real, spectral and material. However, it is apparent that even here the imperial rhetoric attempts to displace the anxieties attendant on raced hierarchies in the nation. Curtis writes: "For what more are these orientals than sumptuous savages? As the Indian dwells in primeval forests, whose soil teems with mineral treasure, . . . so lives the Oriental."[40] For Curtis, as for many travel writers, Oriental travel writing was both a foray into another culture and a site where disturbing racial issues at home came to the surface. Even more than the Native American, the African always entered the Oriental landscape questioning the rhetoric of freedom and liberty and drawing attention to the racial discourses that comprised ideas of empire overseas and of colonization within the country.

The most prolific of Oriental travel writers was Bayard Taylor. Taylor recorded his two and a half years of travel in three volumes: *A Journey to Central Africa; or Life and Landscapes from Egypt to the Negro Kingdoms of the White Nile* (1854); *The Lands of the Saracen; or Pictures of Palestine, Asia Minor, Sicily, and Spain* (1855); and *A Visit to India, China, and Japan in the Year 1853* (1855). In addition to plays, poems, and biographies, Taylor continued to write a number of Oriental travel works, including *Japan in Our Day* (1872) and *Travels in Arabia* (1872). He also edited *Central Asia: Travels in Cashmere, Little Tibet, and Central Asia* (1874) for the multivolume collection of the Illustrated Library of Travel, Exploration, and Adventure. Although Taylor had a flair for the dramatic, and although his appearance on the lyceum circuit clad in Arab clothes and holding a scimitar is reported to have made women swoon, many of his works, imbued with a sense of present-day materiality, made no attempt to recuperate a fetishized Orient of the past. The popularity of his works thus attests to the public receptivity of a variety of Orientalist travel writings, not simply the exotic and dematerialized.[41]

Much of Taylor's *A Visit to India, China, and Japan,* for instance, corrects misconceptions about "ignorant" natives created by previous Orientalist writers, recounts the complex diplomatic maneuvers of Commodore Perry, and satirizes the imperial presumptions of his countrymen.[42] Taylor was surely not acceding to stereotypical imperial representation when he wrote of the trip to Loo-Choo, "We landed and marched directly into the interior, without so much as saying, 'by your leave.' We had not proceeded more than half a mile, however, before we were overtaken by a native mandarin of the fifth rank, with several subordinate officers, who had been sent in all haste to follow us and watch our movements. Their faces exhibited considerable surprise and alarm, as they beheld eight armed men, with the cool assurance natural to Americans, taking the direct road to Shui, their capital."[43] As Taylor's perspicuous narrative indicates, Oriental travel writing often contested the raced imperial ideologies of nineteenth-century USAmerica.

The interest in Oriental literatures, the travel to the Orient, the popularity of books on Oriental travel, the push for trade with different Oriental nations, and the demand for goods and crafts from China, India, and the Near East in the two generations following the revolutionary period are all indicative of a cultural intimacy with the Orient and an eagerness to embrace things Oriental that energized and popularized literary Orientalist works. At the same time, however, this orientomania also intersected with theories of racial and cultural primacy that were widely circulated in the nineteenth century and that were part of the complex genealogy of Oriental representation. Two major racialized discourses on the Orient that were evident in the United States in the early and middle part of the nineteenth century were ethnography/phrenology and missionary Christianity. An organization closely connected with the latter, although with interests ostensibly more scholarly, was the American Oriental Society, formed in 1842. A brief examination of the polemics of phrenologists, missionaries, and scholars reveals common raced ideologies and points to the extent to which Oriental representations were implicated in highly charged, raced anxieties.

Egyptology, Phrenology, and Polygenesis

That Egyptology was the site of enormous ethnographical and phrenological activity for scholars in the United States, often to support polygenesis and justify slavery, is one of the little-known facts about U.S. culture in the nineteenth century. The mid–nineteenth century witnessed a heated debate between monogenists, who believed in a single story of creation, and polygenists, who argued for multiple versions of creation. The contentions arose mainly because of the explanation of racial difference through the biblical account of creation. Supporters of monogenesis argued for the unity of human beings delineated in the story of creation in Genesis. Because all people were descendants of Adam and Eve and the three sons of Noah, they argued that all races had the same origin. Polygenists, in contrast, could not accept the idea of the fundamental unity of races and looked to scientific theories to support their beliefs about complete and absolute separation of Caucasian and African races. Of course, the classification of races in the works of Linnaeus, Buffon, and Blumenbach in the late eighteenth century set the stage for later advocates of polygenesis. Although Blumenbach believed in the concept of a single human species, his division of people into five races—Caucasian, Mongolian, American, Ethiopian, and Malay—was hierarchical. Caucasians were presented as the primary race, and all others were degenerations from this type.[44] By the early nineteenth century, particularly in the United States, arguments for polygenesis grew stronger, and even monogenists embraced the idea of different races with different capabilities within a single human species. Constructions of the Oriental civilizations and Oriental peoples could not well be isolated from these theories that permeated the cultural imagination.

Egyptology, in particular, created considerable consternation for both phrenologists and theorists of racial classification, because of the non-Caucasian features of Egyptian monuments like the Sphinx, and because of the existence of people with African negroid features in many of the carvings and parchments of Egyptian antiquity. Dr. Charles Caldwell had already initiated USAmericans into racist phrenology in the early nineteenth century. In the late 1820s he examined skulls dug out of Indian mounds and compared them to the heads of Indians from different tribes. Predictably, he reached the imperial conclusion that only the half-breeds, who had been interbred with the white race, had advanced at all.[45]

Caldwell's highly polemical, raced construction of phrenology was taken up by ethnographers, Egyptologists, and, later, poets like Walt Whitman.[46] One of the scholars most adept at linking phrenology to ethnography was Samuel George Morton. In 1839 he published *Crania Americana; or A Comparative View of the Skulls of Various Aboriginal Nations of North and South America.* The huge volume contains numerous plates of skulls of various Native Americans, but the most interesting part of

Crania Americana is Morton's long introductory essay (running over a hundred pages), titled "An Essay on the Varieties of the Human Species." The major intent of the essay is clearly to prove the superior attributes of Caucasians. Following Blumenbach's fivefold division of the human species, Morton describes the characteristics of each race, prioritizing the physiognomy, intellect, and power of the Caucasians. The Caucasian race, says Morton, "is characterized by a naturally fair skin, susceptible of every tint. . . . This race is distinguished for the facility with which it attains the highest intellectual endowments."[47] He characterizes the Native Americans as "averse to cultivation, and slow in acquiring knowledge; restless, revengeful, and fond of war."[48] He describes the "negro" as "joyous, flexible, and indolent," adding that "the many nations which compose this race present a singular diversity of character, of which the far extreme is the lowest grade of humanity."[49]

Yet, even in this general essay on the types of races, Morton is inordinately interested in racial classification in Egypt. The disproportionate part of the essay devoted to the subject of black races in Egypt reflects the extent to which Egyptology had generated anxieties about the capabilities of different races in the United States. Morton was evidently schooled in Egyptology, for he quotes extensively from John Lloyd Stephens's *Egypt,* Burhardt's *Travels in Nubia,* and Wilkinson's *Ancient Egypt.* In a long note, "On the Supposed Affinity between the Egyptians and Negroes," Morton questions the opinions of writers like C. F. Volney who had classed the ancient Egyptians with the Negroes. Of one such writer, C. F. Volney, Morton writes that he

> looked upon the Sphinx, and hastily inferred from its flat features and bushy hair, that the Egyptians were real Negroes: yet these circumstances have no weight when we recur to the fact, that the Buddhists of Asia . . . represent their principal god with Negro features and hair, and often sculpted in black marble; yet among the three hundred millions who worship Buddha, there is not, perhaps, a solitary Negro nation. . . . There is no absolute proof, moreover, that the Sphinx represented an Egyptian deity: it may have been a shrine of the Negro population of Egypt.[50]

Morton's reaction to such an overdetermined figure as the Sphinx was part of a much larger attempt to undermine the possible challenges that the proliferation of Orientalist knowledge, such as Egyptology, presented to racial hierarchies in the United States. Egyptology had begun to raise the possibility that Euroamerican racial hierarchies were not, in fact, universal. That anxiety about racial-cultural instability is at the root of Morton's concerns about the Sphinx is demonstrated by his linking the Sphinx with the figure of Buddha, another revered Oriental figure presented with negroid features.

Morton attempts to use Egyptological knowledge as a means to validate both polygenesis and the long-standing servitude of black Africans throughout history. For evidence, Morton, a meticulous scientist, is ironically forced to rely both on the writings of Egyptologists and on an idea of shared cultural knowledge, because science alone does not suffice. Thus Morton moves from specific analysis of embalmed Theban bodies to a general hortatory argument about the civilizations of Europe, Asia, and Africa. The vast cemeteries of Thebes, Morton argues, "are crowded with genuine Egyptians, whose remains even now retain almost every feature in perfection. Here are the very people who walked the streets of Thebes, they who built Luxor and the Pyramids; and yet among the thousands . . . I am not aware that a solitary Negro has been discovered."[51] From here, Morton's argument moves on to a frenzied diatribe about African inferiority, in an attempt to allay anxieties about EuroAmerican cultural origins: "It may justly be inquired, if science, art and literature, had their origin with a Negro tribe on the skirts of Africa, how does it happen that the stream of knowledge has never flowed into, but always from that country? For while it has been permanently diffused through Asia and Europe, in Africa itself it cannot be traced beyond the mountains of Nubia. Again, it is now proved almost beyond controversy, that Egypt, and not Nubia, was the mother of the arts."[52]

Morton's phrenological and ethnological inquiries in *Crania Americana* convinced him of the need to conclusively establish the distinction between the cultivated ruling classes in Egypt and the menial blacks. Morton obtained Egyptian skulls from George R. Gliddon, U.S. consul in Cairo, in 1840 and immediately began work on his second major phrenological study, *Crania Ægyptica,* which he published in 1844.[53] In this study Morton had not only the material but also the scholarly assistance of Gliddon, who, in his years of stay at Cairo, had become an experienced Egyptologist. Gliddon's career illustrates the convergence of diplomacy, Egyptology, and scientific racism in the nineteenth century. Gliddon was respected for his knowledge and frequently returned to the United States to give lectures on hieroglyphs. In 1841, Gliddon wrote to Morton, in support of the projected *Crania Ægyptica,* "We, as hieroglyphists, know Egypt better now, than all the Greek authors or the Roman. . . . I urge your pausing, and considering why the ancient Egyptians may not be of Asiatic, and perhaps of Arabic descent. . . . At any rate, they are not, and never were, Africans, still less Negroes."[54]

This correspondence illustrates the extent to which Egyptology was the site of highly charged questions of racial identity in the United States. Although Gliddon's immediate concern was to dissociate Africans from culture, much of Egyptological research also centered on proving the Caucasian origins of the ruling powers of ancient Egypt. Morton's researches in *Crania Ægyptica,* for instance, indisputably linked together in his mind polygenesis and racial and cultural hierarchies prioritizing Caucasians. Morton concluded that

> The valley of the Nile, both in Egypt and in Nubia, was originally peopled by a branch of the Caucasian race. . . . Negroes were numerous in Egypt, but their social position in ancient times was the same that it now is, that of servants and slaves. . . . The physical or organic characters which distinguish the several races of men, are as old as the oldest records of our species.[55]

It is no wonder that Secretary of State John Calhoun read in *Crania Ægyptica* evidence of the historical subordination of races and was impressed with Morton's conclusions.

Gliddon himself, along with Josiah C. Nott, a Southern slavery advocate, published *Types of Mankind; or Ethnological Researches Based upon the Ancient Monuments, Paintings, Sculptures, and Crania of Races and upon Their Natural, Geographical, Philological, and Biblical History* in 1854. The title of the book is itself indicative of the racialization of Egyptological scholarship in the mid–nineteenth century. *Types of Mankind* contains a "Memoir of Samuel George Morton," a tribute in which Morton is celebrated as a pioneer phrenologist and ethnographer of the United States. Nott and Gliddon continued to corroborate Morton's arguments about racial distinctions by scholarly examinations of Egyptian artifacts and writings of different Egyptologists. They argued that the Egyptians had recognized and represented on their monuments many different and distinct races since the fourteenth and fifteenth centuries B.C.[56] Much of their evidence rested on the interpretation of the pictorial representation of blacks in ancient Egypt. They noted how ancient Egyptians had routinely differentiated among different races and how non-white races, particularly African nonwhites, were often depicted as enslaved (see fig. 2).

These questions of raced cultural origins, so important to mid-nineteenth-century culture, and so persistently raised by Egyptology and Indology, affected all aspects of U.S. Orientalism. To add to the cultural and ideological confusions, the mixture of races and religions in the Near East continued to create anxious moments of uncertainty in the literature generated by Egyptology. The works of Morton, Gliddon, and Nott foregrounded these anxieties in a particularly compelling manner and also revealed the extent to which Orientalism was implicated in racial issues at home. Leading African American thinkers, however, used the evidence of there being black Egyptians to demonstrate and lay claims to black Africans being the originators of civilization. Frederick Douglass, for instance, found in Egyptology a means of validating black claims to culture.[57] Other writers also joined in. In 1859 a writer for the *Weekly Anglo-African* in New York derided the arguments of racial classifiers, such as Blumenbach, by using the works of Egyptologists on race. Starting with Champollion's interpretation that the word *Cush* indicated Ethiopia, the writer wryly concluded that because Abyssinia was a mixture of nations and because the Ethiopians had been taken to be the same as Abyssians, the Negroes were a white race.[58] By 1902, Pauline Hopkins had published *Of One Blood*, the story of an African American doctor, Reuel, on an archaeological expedition to Africa; Hopkins attempted to show that "we trace the light of civilization from Ethiopia to Egypt, to Greece, to Rome, and thence diffusing its radiance over the entire world."[59]

U.S. Missionary Activity

While theorists arguing for polygenesis and differences among races embraced Egyptology to buttress their racial theories, proponents of monogenesis turned eastward as missionaries determined to save their degraded brethren, an effort that polygenists like Josiah C. Nott regarded as inherently flawed and thus doomed. In a series of lectures delivered at Louisiana University in 1848, Nott wrote:

> All the historical records of the past tell us of the same moral and physical differences of races which exist at the present day, and we can only judge the future by the past. The numberless attempts by

the Caucasian race, during several thousand years, to bring the Mongol, Malay, Indian and Negro under the same religion, laws, manners, customs, etc., have failed, and must continue to fail. . . . What has been the result of missions to Africa, to China, to India, to the American Indians, & c.?[60]

FIG. 2. Enslaved "Negro" figure from Josiah C. Nott and George R. Gliddon's *Types of Mankind; or Ethnological Researches Based upon the Ancient Monuments, Paintings, Sculptures, and Crania of Races and upon Their Natural, Geographical, Philological, and Biblical History* (Philadelphia: Lippincott, Grambo, and Co., 1854), 249.

Most clergymen who believed in the theocratic version of New England settlements as kingdoms of God did not, however, share Nott's cynicism about proselytizing among different races. Missionary activity was seen as related to nation making and empire making, just as the idea of a U.S. empire was always seen in terms of a mission. Only a single generation after independence, the clergy expanded their reach beyond the New World. In June 1810 the American Board of Commissioners for Foreign Missions was formed at Bradford, Massachusetts. Although spreading "the gospel" was a clearly stated goal of missionaries, political, ideological, and social factors were major components of missionary discourse. Most clergymen saw the development of U.S. missions abroad as important signifiers of national power. Jacob Norton, for instance, used colonial imagery to predict that his countrymen would "go forth into every region of the inhabitable globe, with the everlasting gospel."[61] As our contemporary scholar Charles L. Chaney put it, "budding nationalism was a factor in the close association between missionaries and the Continental Congress during the Revolution."[62] After independence, the mutual implication of imperial and missionary discourses was made abundantly clear through the political semiotics of the show-of-force routines by the navy in support of U.S. missionaries in the Near East. In 1835, Eli Smith, a missionary in Syria, requested official action from the United States, adding that Syrians should be taught "that we are a powerful nation," and claiming that "there is no other way to teach them this but to make them *feel* it."[63]

Missionary activity not only signified national power but also raced itself as distinctly Western. The annual reports of the American Board of Commissioners for Foreign Missions provide fascinating insight into the politics of missionary activity and the construction of the Orient within U.S. missionary discourse. Missionaries viewed all Eastern societies as culturally and morally deprived and in need of uplift from the West. Because of this view, the Christian Oriental churches of the Near East, for instance, were the objects of almost as much solicitude as the "heathens" of India. Let us examine, for a moment, the arguments of Rev. C. H. Wheeler, a missionary in Eastern Turkey, on the benefits of Christianity.

> And shall it be said that godliness, which, in lifting the heathen or nominally Christian nations from the condition of ignorance and degradation, gives them the promise of life. . . . The material advantages which intelligence has over ignorance, industry over idleness, and virtue over vice, are each so many large sums to be placed on the creditor side in striking the balance of advantage which true Christianity has over all false systems.[64]

As Wheeler makes clear, Christian conversion and cultural conversion were perceived as almost identical goals by missionaries. For instance, religious conversion, the ostensible rhetorical concern, is linked with market-driven concerns, such as the advantages of industry over idleness. Even Christian societies in Eastern nations were thus considered objects of conversion, because their morals were considered to be lax.

The 1811 report of the Board of Commissioners reveals the imperial investments of missionary work in the Orient. To solicit more indigenous monies for its activities, the board represents missionary work as a signifier of national might: "Shall the four American missionaries be cast upon the London funds? . . . Would it not indeed be a reproach to our character as a Christian nation . . . should we resign our missionaries to the London Society, under an apprehension that we could not support them?"[65] In November 1811, the three committee members appointed by the board again made the case for missionaries abroad, by invoking national pride in an "Address to the Christian Public": "We are more able to take an active part in evangelizing the heathen, than any other people on the globe. With the exception of Great Britain, indeed, no nation but our own has the inclination, or the ability, to make great exertions in the prosecution of this design."[66] The 1811 report also singles out the East as particularly deplorable and, thus, vital for missionary activity: "The Eastern world, especially Hindoostan, the Malayan Archipelago, and the Birman empire, present the most extensive fields for missionary labors; fields which appear to be fast whitening for the harvest. All those vast regions are full of people *sitting in darkness and in the region and shadow of death.*"[67]

The rapid growth of overseas missionary activity in the early nineteenth century is truly remarkable and belies arguments of historians who view the culture of this period as insular. The formation of the American Board of Commissioners for Foreign Missions in 1811 was quickly followed by clergy journeying to the Orient. On February 6, 1812, five missionaries bound for Asia were ordained at Salem. By 1818 the board was running eleven schools in India alone, instructing an estimated six hundred students. Elated at their success, the board reported, "In these schools, we seem to see a thousand Hindoo hands at work, from year to year, in undermining the fabric of Hindoo idolatry."[68] And although the board had solicited contributions for its missions by appeal to national pride and by urging people to compete with Britain, U.S. missionaries, in racial-cultural solidarity with Britain, found the increasing British dominion over India highly salubrious. The board's 1819 report stated, "By the late war in India, the Mahratta states and territories, on the side of the peninsula or continent adjacent to Bombay, and to a great extent, were subjected to British dominion. This event, as it rendered those countries more easily and safely accessible, gave a new spring to hope and to enterprise."[69] Other U.S. clergymen likewise saw the inhabitants of India as wretched and deplorable and praised any Western influence in the land. Rev. Isaac Taylor wrote with disgust about the "hundred millions of people in India, given up to so false, debasing, and destructive a religion," and he welcomed British efforts to "relieve the perishing inhabitants."[70]

The American Board of Commissioners for Foreign Missions similarly saw the Near East as an area for cultural conversion. Many countries had strict laws forbidding attempts at converting Muslims, but missionaries regarded the Oriental churches as equally fit objects of concern. Because of their close proximity with the Muslims and their shared culture with them, the Christians of the Near East were viewed as only nominally so and were considered even more in need of conversion and purification than their Muslim brethren. Rufus Anderson, the foreign secretary of the board, wrote:

> The continued existence of large bodies of nominal Christians among these Mohammedans, is a remarkable fact. They constitute more than a third part of the population of Constantinople, and are found in all the provinces of the empire. . . . Being so numerous and so widely dispersed, should spiritual life be revived among them a flood of light would illumine the Turkish empire.[71]

Anderson is clearly fascinated by the cross-cultural experiences of Christians in the Near East, at the same time as he considers himself duty-bound to pronounce these culturally interraced Christians as almost devoid of religious life. Rev. C. H. Wheeler expressed the horror with, and attraction to, the cultural mixtures of the Near East more forcefully: "The population of the country [Armenia] is, if possible, even more diversified than the natural scenery, each outcropping stratum of the blended mass of race, language, and religion—which are sometimes thrown together in inexplicable confusion—pointing back to some political upheaving of a past age, or telling of some barbarian avalanche from the East."[72] What seems to fascinate the minister here is the blurring of cultural and racial boundaries, which he then demarcates as outside the bounds of civilization. Racial impurity is associated with "confusion," "upheaving," and impending disaster (an "avalanche"). Much of the U.S. Orientalist literature set in the Near East reflects a similar anxiety about intercultural and interracial contact. Heedful of the need to spread the light in the Near East, the American Board of Commissioners for Foreign Missions established missions in Beirut through a system of schools. Starting with a mere class of six Arab children taught by wives of missionaries in 1824, the schools served three hundred students by 1826 and six hundred by 1827.

The American Oriental Society

The establishment of missionary activity in Oriental countries also facilitated the formation of the American Oriental Society in 1842. This was clearly a scholastic society, the purpose of which was to gain knowledge of Oriental languages and cultures. Yet it was indisputably linked to raced missionary activity. Missionaries served as ethnographers and linguists for the society, and their findings were frequently published by the society. The society's first president, John Pickering, in his opening address to the society on April 7, 1843, began by praising the works of missionaries: "As Americans, deeply interested in the reputation of our country, we cannot but take pride in the reflection, that, at the numerous stations of the American Missionaries in the East . . . we have reason to believe there is a greater number of individuals, who are masters of the languages and literature of their pagan and other converts, than are to be found among the missionaries of any one nation of Europe."[73] He continued, in his address, to stress the symbiotic nature of the relationship between the American Oriental Society and the missionaries, between knowledge and missionary conversion: "While the propagation of Christianity, on the one hand, is opening to us new sources of information in different languages—which are the essential instruments of all knowledge—on the other hand, the progressive acquisition of those languages is constantly placing in our hands new means of disseminating religious instruction."[74]

Missionary outposts in the Near East thus did not exist in isolation either from debates about gender at home or from discourses of empire making at midcentury. Missionary activity was a signifier of national power. In his opening address to the American Oriental Society, Pickering made repeated mention of the exemplary work of American missionaries abroad and compared them with their European counterparts.[75] In the same address, he urged his members to master Oriental languages and cultures in order to complete a "general ethnography of the globe."[76] Knowledge about various Oriental cultures, the establishment of a significant presence in these places, and missionary activity there were all part of the civilizing mission that the United States, as a newly emergent power, wished to claim for its own.

Yet the ambitious scholarly programs of the American Oriental Society could not help but expand the cultural horizons of the United States. The aim of the society was to study "the history, languages, literature, and general characteristics of the various people, both civilized and barbarous, who are usually classed under the somewhat indefinite name of Oriental nations."[77] Diverse scholarly contributions to the journal of the society were made by both missionaries and professional scholars. Essays ranged from discussions of Oriental religions to treatises on Oriental economies and medicine. In May 1844, for instance, at the annual meeting of the society, Edward E. Salisbury, a professor of Arabic and Sanskrit at Yale College, gave a talk titled "Memoir on the History of Buddhism." In the same year, the society's journal published an essay on the history of paper money in China. The variety of interests in different aspects of Oriental cultures continued to be reflected in the journal. In 1848, the journal contained a contribution by Rev. C. V. A. Van Dyck, M.D., a missionary of the American Board of Commissioners for Foreign Missions in Syria; the essay dealt with the condition of the medical profession in Syria.

Thus, by the mid–nineteenth century there was not simply a syncretic Orient as the subject of discourse in the culture at large (although that undeniably was there); there was also knowledge about different countries situated in what had been designated as the Orient. This knowledge had structural resemblances deriving from shared narratives about racial hierarchies and theories about the westerly movement of empire, creating systemic discourses about the Orient, even though the specific racing of this knowledge varied. The effect of these discourses on literary Orientalist texts cannot be measured through their reflection on the literature of the period. Whether the literary texts resisted, reproduced, anticipated, subverted, parodied, or engaged in dialogue with these Orientalist discourses, they were clearly in cultural proximity with these heteroglossic languages (to appropriate Bakhtin's terminology for a moment) in which the Orient was not simply part of an exotic or spiritualized imaginary but, more importantly, part of a political imaginary.

2

Algerian Slavery and the Liberty Vision: Royall Tyler, James Ellison, Susanna Rowson, Washington Irving, Peter Markoe

The first significant group of U.S. Orientalist works had a distinct, indigenous genealogy, deriving their immediate impetus from the diplomatic and military crises between the United States and the so-called Barbary States. These works were polemically structured around raced and gendered distinctions between liberty and slavery, morality and licentiousness—the dualistic rhetoric feeding omnivorously on the discourse as it had been sketched in the cultural imaginary. A brief recapitulation of this narrative helps explain the appeal of the "Barbary" wars to the literary imagination. The Muslim nations of North Africa, as owners of the Mediterranean, had long been receiving passage money from European ships wishing to conduct trade in the region. For most European countries, the idea of paying this money amounted to a ransom demanded by unscrupulous, crafty Muslims, but they continued to make payment, regarding it as a necessary business practice. After the Revolutionary War, however, the United States, being unable to afford the ransom monies, decided to change the practice, and the series of events resulting from the new policy captured the literary imagination.[1]

The drama began in July 1785, when the Algerians captured the *Maria*, a Boston schooner. This capture drew outrage from the public, but negotiations for the release of USAmerican prisoners taken as slaves were protracted. More captives were taken in the following years, and it was only in February 1797 that the Algerians returned them to the United States.[2] Into this bizarre series of events entered Thomas Jefferson. Outraged that the United States should have to pay ransom money for its citizens, Jefferson initiated a series of military and diplomatic maneuvers to defeat the North African nations. The beginning of U.S. victory came with the destruction of a Tripolitan vessel in 1804; in 1805 William Eaton, the U.S. consul at Tripoli, acting like an early Lawrence of Arabia, rescued Hamet Caramanli, the exiled pasha, and rallied the local populace to his cause.[3] With the combined might of indigenous soldiers and U.S. marines, Eaton coordinated an attack against Derna, a city east of Tripoli. The attack ended with the first dramatic show of USAmerican prowess, as the marines raised the U.S. flag on the city walls.[4] Although Hamet Caramanli's cause was abandoned because of the possibility of a treaty with the reigning dey, Eaton became an early national hero, embodying both the manly might and the righteousness of the new nation. A peace treaty with the reigning dey was negotiated shortly after Eaton's attack; however, ransom continued to be paid to the North African states until 1815.

The preceding brief narrative of diplomatic and military events elides the complexly raced imperial impulses and anxieties associated with the altercation. Although the Federalists attacked Jefferson for his botched diplomacy—Thomas Pickering went so far as to call him a "coward and a fool in the conduct of Barbary affairs"[5]—the entire series of events fired the national imagination more than simply in terms of competence or incompetence. What had paradoxically begun as a threat to sovereignty was transformed in the cultural imaginary to a narrative of imperial might. The North African war helped glorify the vision of a powerful, imperial nation. A Senate resolution, for instance, used the iconography of empire to honor Eaton and his marines, who "for the first time spread the American eagle in Africa."[6] Later diplomats would similarly assess the Tripolitan affair in terms of the country's international image. Mordecai M. Noah, the late U.S. consul in Tunis and Tripoli, declared in 1826 that the Barbary conflict was more than a means of abolishing the tribute system; it was "of vital importance to a nation having an infant navy, and desirous of establishing a name and a character among the governments of the earth."[7] As historian Robert J. Allison puts it, "This war proved to Americans their real status as a nation and affirmed that theirs was to be a different kind of nation—different both from the nations of Europe, which were content to pay tribute to the Barbary states, and from the Muslim states, ravaged by their rulers and torn apart by their impoverished and savage people."[8]

Despots and slaves, taken as signifiers of the "Barbary" Orient, generated an imperial narrative based on raced distinctions between Oriental tyranny and USAmerican freedom, a narrative that drew both on the immediate historical moment and on long-standing Western philosophical distinctions between European and Eastern forms of power.[9] Algeria's other signifier of difference was its supposedly aberrant sexual practices. The Algerian male, with his harem of obedient women, represented a moral degeneracy and sensual excess that marked him as unhealthy, deviant, and, ultimately, less than male. In contrast, the USAmerican hero could represent health, vigor, and manly restraint. Most texts of the "Barbary" wars foregrounded this narrative in which the robustness of the New World necessitated its takeover of the degenerate Orient, the imperial body being constructed through an exclusion of both slavery and "deviant" sexuality.

Yet the North African Orient (as despotic) evoked the very anxiety it signified. Thus the oppositional rhetoric of liberty and slavery, for instance, is often constructed by a conscious exclusion of the facts of slavery and racial difference in the New World. Similarly, at pivotal moments in these texts, differences between purity, austerity, and excess are revealed as necessary configurations designed to shore up both a patriarchal structure at home and a strong imperial nationhood abroad.

To see the ideological tensions within the discourse on the North African crisis, we can turn to two important architects of U.S. independence: Thomas Jefferson and Benjamin Franklin. Jefferson saw the problems with the North African states as important enough to warrant including them in his draft of the Declaration of Independence. The pertinent passage, excised from the version approved by the rest of the initiators, reads as follows:

He [King George III] has waged cruel war against human nature itself, violating its most sacred rights of life and liberty in the persons of a distant people who never offended him, captivating and carrying them into slavery in another hemisphere, or to incur miserable death in their transportation thither. This piratical warfare, the opprobrium of INFIDEL powers, is the warfare of the CHRISTIAN king of Great Britain. Determined to keep open a market where MEN should be bought and sold, he has prostituted his negative for sup-

pressing every legislative attempt to prohibit or to restrain this execrable commerce.[10]

Although the passage is meant to be illustrative of King George's
tyranny, most of the invective is directed against the North African perpetrators of slavery. Jefferson dramatizes liberty all the more effectively
in the context of piratical slavery, so that the empire for liberty is simultaneously the empire of virtue. The new nation is literally marked as one
where bodies are not bought and sold: the nation *is* the free body. And
obviously, the distinctions between the United States and Britain work
also as displaced distinctions between Christian and heathen, civil government and despotism, virtue and cruelty.

Yet we cannot help but wonder about the vehemence of tone here
and about Jefferson's inclusion of the passage in his original document.
Jefferson, whose earliest memory was that of being carried on a silk pil-
low by a slave, who publicly opposed slavery even as he privately continued to enjoy his plantation, and who participated in legislation that
awarded revolutionary soldiers three hundred acres and a slave, tried
constantly in his writing to negotiate the tension between liberty and
slavery, the fact that the existence of slavery questioned the very definition of the new nation as the empire for liberty.[11] In *Notes on the State of
Virginia*, when Jefferson represented "those who labor in the earth" (the
majority of USAmericans) as the "chosen people of God," he was simultaneously both excluding the culture of plantations and slavery by presenting the United States as a land of husbandmen and also marginaliz-
ing the backbreaking work of slaves, who were, in fact, laboring in the
earth for no recompense. Similarly, the virulent attack on King George's
acquiescence to the carrying of people "into slavery in another hemisphere, or to incur miserable death in their transportation thither,"
forcefully recalls U.S. slavery and the hardships of middle passage.

The North African Orient at this stage in USAmerican history thus
signified despotism and slavery, which, in turn, both validated imperial
definitions of nation and marked the nation as a free body. While Jefferson masked the parallel between North African and U.S. slavery,
Franklin emphasized it and used it to advance his abolitionist cause.
Parodying the pro-slavery arguments of Mr. James Jackson, representative from Georgia, Franklin presented a speech supposedly delivered by
the divan of Algiers in opposition to *Erika*, a sect petitioning for abolition: "If we cease our cruises against the Christians, how shall we be fur-
nished with the commodities their countries produce, and which are so

necessary for us? . . . And is there not more compassion and more favor due to us as Mussulmen than to these Christian dogs?"[12] The readers were unlikely to miss the parody.

The reading public likewise had a voracious appetite for all literature related to the North African Orient, and writers capitalized on it. The horror of USAmericans being held slaves and undergoing torture and moral degeneration, as much as Eaton's grand march to Tripoli with the "true" pasha, no doubt fascinated people. At least sixteen plays and three novels dealing with the Tripolitan War appeared on the market.[13] Histories similarly fared well. Matthew Carey's *A Short Account of Algiers and Its Several Wars* (1794) saw two editions within its first year of publication.

In the fiction and drama of the Tripolitan War, the Orient functions as a complex site where the construction of the New World as virtuous, respectable, and a free body is predicated on the exclusion of immorality, excess, and slavery, all of which are signifiers of the North African Orient. Yet, interspersed between these attempts at definition of empire are moments when the distinctions between virtuous empire and despotic empire, virtuous body and licentious body begin to blur. The body of the USAmerican embodying the nation becomes associated with a sensual excess that questions the hierarchical raced distinctions between the New World and the Orient. An examination of the moments of national self definition and demarcation, mediated through the body of the hero/heroine, thus reveals the complex ways in which ideas about the Algerian Orient intersected with assumptions about the fledgling nation as free, mighty, and moral.

This chapter traces the different forms taken by the dualistic rhetoric of liberty/slavery and austerity/licentiousness, beginning with Royall Tyler's construction of the nation in the body of the lone USAmerican male captive in *The Algerine Captive* (1797); it then moves on to an examination of James Ellison's *The American Captive* (1812) and Joseph Stevens Jones's *The Usurper* (1841), in which the righteous captive embodying the nation becomes the agent of cataclysmic change, in a manner paralleling Eaton's march. Next, it analyzes Susanna Rowson's *Slaves in Algiers* (1794), examining the complex renegotiation of raced and gendered boundaries that occurs in that work as the discourses of Orientalism and feminism intersect to question traditional USAmerican gender constructions for women. Finally, this chapter examines the challenges to and reinscriptions of the rhetoric of empire through the Oriental narrators, such as Washington Irving's *Salmagundi* (1808) and Peter Markoe's *The Algerine Spy in Pennsylvania* (1787).

Virtuous Captives: Royall Tyler's *The Algerine Captive* and David Everett's *Slaves in Barbary*

In no other text of the Barbary wars is the embodiment of nation as a virtuous body as evident as in Royall Tyler's *The Algerine Captive*. Tyler's novel, written partly as a captivity narrative, traces the fortunes of the narrator, Updike Underhill, as he attempts to find a vocation, first as a schoolteacher in a provincial New England village, then as an apprentice doctor, and finally as a surgeon aboard a slave ship. Captured by the Algerians, Underhill experiences slavery firsthand until he escapes back to his country on a Portuguese frigate. Despite the title, which draws immediate attention to the captivity and the Algerian setting, the structure of the novel makes clear an emphasis on the nature of the new nation and its role in the affairs of the world.

Although the novel is ostensibly divided into New England and Algerian sections—the first dealing with the narrator's struggles to find a vocation in the country, the second with his captivity in Algiers—the ideological trajectory of the two sections validates a discourse of empire. In part 1, the narrator is a bumbling comic hero searching for himself in a new country, while in part 2, despite being a captive, he is a wise reporter acting as the agent of the new empire. The narrator's growth thus reads as an allegory of the nation's dual conception of itself as New World and new empire, a conception pointedly emphasized in the introduction and conclusion of the text. The novel opens with an account of Underhill's ancestors settling in Massachusetts in the seventeenth century and intermittently having trouble with the strictures of Puritanism; it ends with the narrator paying tribute to the United States as "the freest country in the universe" and to the "excellent government which [he] [has] learnt to adore in the schools of despotism." He hopes that the case for a strong country enforcing "a due respect among other nations" has been made.[14]

Of course, Tyler is well aware of the problems of reifying a teleological national narrative. He begins the novel, therefore, by complicating the narrative of "free" origins. Early in the novel, the narrator lists several instances of political and religious prejudice in early New England. One of his ancestors is exiled for staring inordinately long at a married woman while in church. Tyler in fact picked anecdotes like these from historical sources so as to dramatize the not-so-perfect beginnings of the country.[15] But even though the narrative of origins is complicated by the acknowledgment of New England intolerance, Tyler makes clear that his work is fundamentally tied to the ideology of a unique New World virtue defined in clearly gendered terms. Making one of the earliest cases for a national literature, Tyler writes that by reading British literature,

> the heart is corrupted. The farmer's daughter, while she pities the misfortune of some modern heroine, is exposed to the attacks of vice from which her ignorance would have formed the surest shield. If the English novel does not inculcate vice, it at least impresses on the young mind an erroneous idea of the world in which she is to live . . . excites a fondness for false splendor; and renders the homespun habits of her own country disgusting. (28)

In contrast to Britain, which is yoked with vices and luxuries, the New World is associated with simplicity and virtue. It is also clear that this New World identity is conceived of in clearly patriarchal terms. In the preceding quotation, for instance, the author, as father/law, defines native virtue through the disciplining of the bodies of women, which in turn function as emblems of national virtue.

It is significant that such native self-definition takes place in a work purportedly about Oriental despots and brave U.S. slaves, thus making amply clear the convergence of sexualized and raced hierarchies in conceptions of nation and empire. That the hero, Updike Underhill, functions as an emissary of a powerful empire is evident in the anthropological status given to his narrative. Although ostensibly a captive, Underhill's account is organized under chapters with titles such as "Sketch of the History of Algiers," "Description of the City of Algiers," "The Government of the Algerians," "Revenue," "Notices of the Habits, Customs &c. of the Algerians," "Marriages and Funerals," "The Religion of the Algerians: Life of the Prophet Mahomet," "The Sects of Omar and Ali," "The Faith of the Algerians," and "An Algerine Law Suit." The structure of the narrative suggests a complete faith in the accuracy of the cultural-ambassadorial observations of the hero. At no point are these sociological observations questioned. In the chapter titled "Marriages and Funerals," for instance, the narrator writes, "I had rather disappoint the curiosity of my readers by conciseness, than disgust them with untruths. . . . I never was at an Algerine marriage, but obtained some authentic information on the subject" (177). Underhill is presented here not simply as a dilettante observer of Algerine life but as an accurate reporter and, to an extent, a judge. The supposed captivity narrative works more like a travel narrative, maintaining many of the raced privileges of that genre.[16]

Yet, while Tyler uses the occasion of Algerian slavery to circulate culturally accepted oppositions between the Algerian Orient and the United States as the newest westerly empire infused with a radical sense of liberty, he also makes clear that the ideology of empire is a constructed one, superimposed on a new nation that is far from being culturally cohesive. The year of the publication of *The Algerine Captive* was also the year in which the initial debates on the Naturalization, Alien, and Sedition Acts of 1798 had begun.[17] Fears about the varied racial composition of the country were beginning to surface. Tyler's narrator, Updike Underhill, is born into a world haunted by the specter of racial otherness.

> My mother, some months before my birth, dreamed that she was delivered of me, that I was lying in the cradle, that the house was beset by Indians who broke into the next room and took me into the fields with them. Alarmed by their hideous yellings and warhoops, she ran to the window and saw a number of tawny young savages playing at football with my head while several sachems and sagamores were looking on unconcerned. (43)

The racial schisms of the nation are literally played out on the body of the narrator. The birth of the narrator, signifying metaphorically the birth of the new nation, is interrupted by the dream of conflict with "Indians." This displacement of the reality of racial conflict onto a dream suggests Tyler's critique of the suppression of cultural plurality in popular ideologies of nationhood. As a raced nightmare, the dream also reflects the barely controlled anxieties of racial contact, here figured through the white body being torn asunder by native savagery.

The ideology of the virtuous empire was signified by the virtuous body, a connection Tyler makes explicit in his preface. Even a decade before writing *The Algerine Captive*, Tyler had presented in *The Contrast* a picture of the New World male—simple, unpolished, honest, and a lover of liberty. This upright hero, tellingly named Manly, continually pontificates on national virtues and cautions against effeminizing foreign luxuries that can sap the vitals of national character. Orientalist writers used the license of exotic surroundings to titillate their readers with descriptions of sexual aberrancies and excesses of the Orient and opposed them to the respectability and normality of the West.

Here, George L. Mosse's arguments about modern European Protestant nationalism and respectability are particularly helpful. As Mosse suggests, Western nationalism was associated with a curbing of passions and sexuality. The "quiet grandeur of the Laocoon," symbolizing the overcoming of baser instincts, suggested the ideal of nationhood.[18] If Mosse had extended his study to the United States, he might well have found an even stronger alliance between nationalism and respectability. Even before the revolution, the founders of the New England colonies feared lapses in social conduct as much as they feared Native American attacks. In William Bradford's *Of Plymouth Plantation*, for instance, Thomas Morton's Maypole, with its overt celebration of open sexuality, was the ultimate site of the unnational.[19]

In USAmerican Orientalist writing, where raced ideas of nation and empire were important, distinctions between the respectability of the new nation and the deviances of the Orient were pivotal. Edward Said has shown that in the Western imagination there is a persistence of the association of the Orient with deviant sexuality. The Orient suggests "not only fecundity but sexual promise (and threat), untiring sensuality, unlimited desire."[20] Yet, as we examine many U.S. Orientalist works, we see that the dramatic structure of the texts resists clean moral distinctions in the very moments when distinctions between respectability and sexual deviance and excess are being loudly pronounced (the dominant ideology being loudly proclaimed). In such narrative boundary sites, the ideology of the virtuous empire is both deformed and reappropriated.

The instability of the raced and gendered polemic of empire signified through the body of the narrator in *The Algerine Captive* can be clearly seen in the episode of the Moslem college, where Updike Underhill receives a reprieve from slave labor in exchange for listening to some Islamic proselytizing. The chapter begins by maintaining an insistence on New England respectability. The narrator describes the Moslem college as a sensual excess, with "refreshing baths, cooling fountains, luxuriant gardens, ample larders, rich carpets, downy sofas." He continues, "I have often observed that, in all countries except New England, those whose profession it is to decry the luxuries and vanities of this world, somehow or other, contrive to possess the greatest portion of them" (136). Here, the lighthearted mockery of New England austerity hides a more ambivalent cultural positioning. The hero's supposed status as an agent of an empire is already complicated here because he is both the representative of New England denial and, in his stay at the Moslem college, the not-too-unwilling recipient of "luxuries and vanities."

In what follows, the body of the hero undergoes an ambiguous gendering and sexualization. The narrator describes the process of his bodily cleansing in the Moslem college:

> I was carried to a warm bath into which I was immediately plunged. My attendants, as if emulous to cleanse me from all the filth of error, rubbed me so hard with their hands and flesh-brushes I verily thought they would have flayed me. . . . I was then anointed in all parts which had been exposed to the sun with a preparation of a gum called the balm of Mecca. . . . In twenty-four hours, the sun-browned cuticle peeled off and left my face, hands, legs, and neck as fair as a child's of six months old. . . . This balm the Algerine ladies procure at a great expense and use it as a cosmetic to heighten their beauty. (136–37)

Readers immediately note the shift to passive voice ("I was carried to," "I was immediately plunged"), which clearly suggests an authorial desire to maintain a distinction between the narrator's will and the sensual excesses his body is subjected to. All evidence of "manly" labor is stripped as his sunburn is scrubbed off. Yet the very eroticization of the body in this process and the narrator's pleasure with the results of the eroticization suggest a need to transgress notions of respectability mythologized in the narrative of U.S. empire making. There is also a clear fascination with ambiguous gendering, as the narrator graphically describes the literal stripping of his outer (male) skin to reveal the fair (female) skin beneath. The body of the New England male is not quite respectable, not quite male, as he undergoes a feminized ritual of beautification. Yet gender alone is not the issue here. The obsessive concern with skin, particularly the idea of whiteness beneath the layers of color, creates an epistemic fracture in dominant nineteenth-century racial thinking based on racial separation. The male/not-quite-male body is also the white/not-quite-white body.

The concern with the disciplining of the body and its resistance to systems of control occurs repeatedly in *The Algerine Captive*. The narrator is fascinated with scenes of torture and with the details of public executions. Yet nowhere was the body so obviously regulated and used in the service of a system as it was under slavery in the United States. The oppositional rhetoric of liberty and slavery invoked in Algerian Orientalist texts thus could not help but also signify on slavery back home.[21] Tyler's treatment of U.S. slavery reveals the split between colonialists' visions of virtuous empire and the realities of the nation; in its tension between the repudiation of slavery and the reenactment of the master-slave relationship, his text recalls the tortured prose of Thomas Jefferson.

The description of Updike Underhill's passage aboard a slave ship is placed strategically between the narrator's account of his bumbling attempts to find a vocation in the United States and his capture by the Algerians. Tyler includes detailed renditions of the barbarities aboard the slave ship, borrowing many of the details from slave narratives, particularly that of Olaudah Equiano.[22] As surgeon of a slave ship, the narrator is forced to face his involuntary complicity in the barbarous institution: "I exacerbated myself for even the involuntary part I bore in this execrable traffic: I thought of my native land, and blushed" (109). Here, the narrator allegorically voices the tortured conscience of the nation and questions the construction of the New World as the land of liberty. Yet the text also resists these absolute oppositions, thus situating itself within a triangulated relationship to the discourses on empire and the Algerian Orient. What occurs in the hero's encounter with slavery is a series of dramatic contradictions.

Updike Underhill is able to simultaneously be an officer aboard a slave ship and a vociferous opponent of slavery. As the voice of conscience, he convinces the ruthless captain to anchor ashore to give the slaves respite from their cramped quarters on the ship. Once ashore and alone with the slaves, however, the bumbling Updike Underhill clearly embodies empire. Under Underhill's supervision the Africans recover, and like grateful and contented slaves, they make him the object of their everlasting gratitude: "Happy was he who could, by picking up a few berries, gathering the wild fruits of the country, or by doing any menial services, manifest his affection for me" (114). Left alone with an African, the narrator's conversion to a New World Crusoe is complete. Underhill sleeps contentedly at night, "the affectionate negro at [his] feet" (116). The narrative moves to unmask the hierarchical racial contradictions underlying the ideology of virtuous empire and to simultaneously support the hierarchies by maintaining a surreptitious master-slave relationship between white and black.

Precisely because *The Algerine Captive* both resists and mirrors the raced idea of empire based on distinctions between liberty and slavery and between virtue and excess, it is a fascinating cultural document in early Orientalist discourse in the United States. Tyler's representation of the Dey, for instance, is bound up as much with desire and fascination as with the creation of the "Oriental despot." In traditional EuroAmerican symbology, the despot could be representative of nothing short of cruelty, corrupted passion, and horrific power. Yet in Tyler's account, the Dey seems anything but evil. The signifiers of his power—his riches and accoutrements—are invested with desire rather than loathing, paralleling Underhill's own earlier satisfaction with becoming an object of worship by the Africans formerly on the slaveship. The sumptuous Oriental despot, a libidinal projection of the benign slaveowner, thus becomes an intimately needed Other in the cultural imaginary.[23]

> . . . the Dey was seated upon an eminence covered with richest carpeting fringed with gold. A circular canopy of Persian silk was raised over his head from which were suspended curtains of the richest embroidery, drawn into festoons by silk cords and tassels enriched with pearls. . . . His feet were shod with buskins, bound upon his legs with diamond buttons in loops of pearl. Around his waist was a broad sash, glittering with jewels, to which was suspended a broad scimitar, the hilt of which dazzled the eye with brilliants of the first water. (122)

The narrator himself, having been bathed, cleansed, and clothed in accordance with the rest of the prisoners, looks at the Dey as if in a mirror. The glittering jewels and the scimitar, which dazzles the eye with its brilliance, reflect back the opulent (though overtly repressed) sensual longings of the narrator. Recognition is here overlaid with misrecognition, as the narrative signifies the mirror image as more complete than the body of the narrator himself.[24] The Dey also is hardly represented as a fierce figure; he is inclined to "corpulency, with a countenance rather comely than commanding, and an eye which betrays sagacity, rather than inspires awe" (122). The narrator, as viewer, is the victim of the despot in only literal, dramatic terms but is metaphorically the despot— the benign ruler/owner—himself.

Tyler's text effects closure by attempting to normalize gender and sexuality through the embodiment of respectable nationhood. The hero, who, as we have seen, was able to speak from a number of gendered positions while a captive in Algeria, now embodies the traditional heterosexual and patriarchal imperative. He vows, when he is back in New England, to "unite [himself] to some amiable woman" and to "contribute cheerfully to the support of our excellent government" (224). The idea of nation is negotiated at the end again through the idea of the virtuous body, as the narrator wishes for the uniting of "our federal strength to enforce a due *respect* among other nations" (224; emphasis mine).

Because Tyler complicates the dichotomies of liberty and slavery and of morality and licentiousness that are raised in other Algerian Orientalist texts of the period, *The Algerine Captive* provides an interesting starting point for investigating narratives of empire as articulated through the "Barbary" wars. The complexity of Tyler's questioning of the raced cultural oppositions of liberty and slavery is evident if we look briefly, in contrast, at some of the more simply dichotomous and polemical dramatizations of North African slavery. David Everett's play *Slaves in Barbary* (1797), for instance, undermines absolute moral distinctions between enslavers and enslaved to reinstate, all the more vigorously, the racial hierarchies perpetuated by New World slavery.

In *Slaves in Barbary,* the bashaw of Tunis is himself a former slave who now "buys" the sick and elderly to better provide for them. A major portion of the play revolves around the fortunes of two Venetian brothers, Ozro and Amandar, brought as slaves to Tunis but set free by the compassionate bashaw. This dramatic movement from slavery to liberty is emphasized at the end of the play in Hamet's speech: "Generous brothers [Ozro and Amandar] enjoy your fortune, and let your father participate in your happiness. . . . Let it be remembered, there is no luxury so exquisite as the exercise of humanity, and no post so honorable as his, who defends THE RIGHTS OF MAN."[25] Everett's decision to let the Oriental bashaw be the mouthpiece for the rhetoric of liberty both erases moral distinctions between the New World and the Orient and attests to the vigorous reaches of the rhetoric. This erasure, however, mystifies the raced hierarchies of slavery that the play continues to maintain.

Among the enslaved in the play are Kidnap, a sadistic Southern slaveholder, and his slave, Sharp. The play negotiates the raced power structure of slaveholder and enslaved by ousting Kidnap from his status but keeping Sharp within his place. Kidnap, whose dreamworld is even pervaded with longings about torturing his slaves, meets his deserved fate by being sold to the most inhuman captor in Tunis. But Sharp, the African American slave, continues to remain in a curiously enslaved position at the end of the play, being now a slave of the kind bashaw to whom he is tied in bonds of filial obedience. Humble, supplicating, and self-effacing, Sharp is the stereotype of the slave advertised by plantation owners in the antebellum South. Speaking of the bashaw, Sharp says, "Dat a good planter, masser. . . . He good to white man; an be he good to poor negur man too?" (110). For Everett, North African slavery becomes a means of containing racial conflict and maintaining the raced hierarchies of antebellum USAmerica.

Umpiring the Orient: James Ellison's *The American Captive* (1812) and Joseph Stevens Jones's *The Usurper* (1841)

Whereas for Tyler the nation was embodied through the lone captive become reporter, for James Ellison and Joseph Stevens Jones this captive was a potential Eaton with the power to change North African Oriental history. Eaton's exploits invited chauvinistic invocations of nation and empire, and in the literary imagination Eaton became a virile, powerful, manly national hero. Eaton's plan to oust the current pasha of Tripoli and install the more amenable, puppet-like Hamet Caramanli was undertaken on a grand scale. Eaton first found Hamet in Alexandria, signed a peace treaty with him, and forced him to agree to reimburse the United States for all expenditures involved in restoring him to the throne. Then, with an army of four hundred, including Arabs, Eaton marched to Derna, a journey no Westerner had attempted since the Muslim conquest.[26] The abandonment of Eaton's cause by the U.S. administration only caused his stature as cultural hero to rise, particularly in the literary imagination. Federalist poet Robert Treat Paine eulogized Eaton's courage and daring thus: "Eaton all danger braves, / Fierce while the battle raves, / Columbia's standard waves / On Derne's proud wall."[27] The plays inspired by Eaton similarly capitalize on his moment of conquest. All end with the restoration of the rightful leader to the Tripolitan throne by heroic U.S. soldiers (as Eaton had planned) and represent the restoration as a fulfillment of the Columbiad vision.

The dedication to Jonathan Smith's *The Siege Of Algiers* (1823) makes the imperialistic appeal of Eaton's march perfectly clear and demonstrates the cultural significance attached to the status of the nation abroad. His drama, Smith writes, will demonstrate how "the United States of America, a minor maritime power, have, by their late coercive measures, evidently proven how this unjust and arbitrary system of tribute demanded by the Barbary powers might be counteracted" and have "set a glorious example in the face of the Christian world."[28] James Ellison similarly sees *The American Captive* as a work "calculated to awaken the feelings of the American reader" and to bring to recollection "the magnanimous conduct of our brave countrymen, Commodore PREBLE and General EATON."[29] Joseph Stevens Jones's *The Usurper* ends with U.S. sailors scaling the palace walls and hoisting the U.S. flag over Tripoli and with a band playing "Hail Columbia."[30]

While *The Siege of Algiers* is clearly an allegorical drama, Ellison's *The American Captive* and Jones's *The Usurper* are more complex dramatizations of USAmerican will, operating through raced distinctions between the New World and the Algerian Orient.[31] Jones's play, with an identical cast of characters, is in fact a revision of Ellison's, twenty-nine years later, and attests to the continuing fascination of Eaton's march in the cultural imagination. A brief comparison of the two versions provides interesting insights into how discourses on the North African Orient and on empire changed within a generation.

Many of Ellison's characters reify a dichotomous Orientalist polemic. The captive in Ellison's play embodies New World manly austerity and democratic freedom, which is set against Oriental despotism and decadence. The bashaw is clad in "sumptuous Turkish habit," with a "large diamond crescent." He has a "rich canopy of silk over his head, from which are suspended curtains of the richest embroidery." In contrast, Anderson, the U.S. captive (and ultimately the Eaton-like liberator), scoffs at richness of parentage and proudly proclaims his New World, meritocratic heritage: "If to be the son of him who served his country, in the time of peril, be that which you call noble, I am of most noble extraction; but if, from pamper'd lords and vicious princes, alone descend this gift, then I am not" (20).

Yet slavery at home questions the absolute moral distinctions between the New World and the North African Orient. Jack, a U.S. sailor in *The American Captive*, restive under Algerian captivity, proudly vaunts the virtues of his native land to the Oriental overseer El Has. The interchange that follows parodies the facile disavowals of racism made by many Northerners.

> Jack. . . . Aye, I'll carry you to the *Theatre*, cast anchor in the centre of the *pit*, . . . you'd think yourself in paradise! . . . And the country too, it's a charming place, Mr. Overseer; no *slavery* there! all free-born sons!
>
> El Has. No *slavery*, hey? go where Senegal winds its course, and ask the wretched mothers for their husbands and sons! what will be their answer? Doom'd *to slavery, and in thy boasted country too!*
>
> Jack. Ohoa! avast there! I'm a *Yankee*—no slaves with us; why a

black gentleman, in our part of the country, is the very paragon of
fashion. (37)

The very casual fashion in which the discussion of slavery is bandied
around and dismissed by a minor happy-go-lucky character is a searing
indictment of the arguments routinely used to dismiss complete emancipation.[32]

Ellison's forceful interjections of racial conflicts complexly triangu-
late the dichotomous rhetoric of respectability and decadence and question the overt narrative of empire projected in the odes to Columbia
interspersed throughout the play. By the time Jones wrote his version of
Ellison's play twenty-nine years later, the ideology of the New World as
a new empire had acquired more circulation. Although the term *Manifest Destiny* would not be introduced until 1845 (four years after the publication of Jones's play), the clamor to control nonwhite races had
become stronger by the 1830s.[33] For example, Sarah Haight's account of
her European and Oriental travels, *Letters from the Old World* (1840), perpetuates the absolute racial divisions propounded by ethnographers.
Describing a slave market in Cairo, Haight does not overtly exonerate
the practice, but she spares no words in describing the ugliness of the
African slaves: "I have never yet seen such a hideous misrepresentation
of the human form divine, as these children of Ham presented. The various degrees of form and feature, from the passably comely to the hor-
ridly ugly and disgusting, almost induced me to believe the theory
which holds that there is a connected chain of animals."[34] Jones similarly allayed the racial instabilities in his revision of Ellison's play. The
most revealing ideological revisions are the complete lack of references
to slavery at home; slavery is contained within the Orient.

Instead Jones adds staple images of the eroticized Orient that associate the Orient with sensuality, languor, and ease, a narrative within
which slavery can be embodied and defused. The play opens with an
image of Oriental plenty. In a "splendid garden" in Tripoli, Oriental
slaves gather flowers and sing contentedly, "Slaves we are but merry,
merry be" (150). Jones's revisions are strongly implicated in the raced
discourses of the period and the changed circumstances of the North
African Orient. The mid-nineteenth-century happy slave, for instance,
was a stock antebellum figure. Also, by the time Jones wrote his revision, European colonization of North Africa had begun with the French
conquest of Algiers in 1830. Both Jones's increased use of stock images
to present the Algerian Orient as a decadent area requiring control and

his rewriting of the Eaton march at this historical moment suggest a stronger need to participate in the rhetoric of empire just as the rhetoric of unified nationhood was being challenged from within.

Feminism, the Orient, and Empire:
Susanna Rowson's *Slaves in Algiers* (1794)

While most male Orientalist writers articulated the raced rhetoric of empire through the righteousness and masculinity of a hero embodying the nation, Susanna Rowson recast the rhetoric in terms of the liberty/slavery of women. Rowson's *Slaves in Algiers* is particularly fascinating in its attempt to negotiate an emancipatory feminist discourse through the possibilities of the Algerian Orient while simultaneously striving to keep the discourse hierarchically raced. Unlike in the works of Tyler and Ellison, the Columbiad vision of the nation as a new empire spreading its message is interrupted in Rowson's text not so much through raced images of slavery but through questions about the limited freedom of women in the New World.[35]

The plot of *Slaves in Algiers* is a series of captures and escapes, revolving around two USAmerican women, Rebecca and Olivia, who embody the virtues of the nation. Rebecca, an older mother figure, is held for ransom money by Ben Hassan, a crafty Jew. Olivia, horrifically, has been captured by the Algerian dey, to be part of his harem. The drama unfolds with Olivia instructing Algerian women about their demeaning roles in the harem and with the plotting of a revolt that finally results in the freedom of all slaves. A familiar racial conflict erupts with the infatuation of the racially mixed Fetnah for Frederic, a USAmerican, but the threat of miscegenation is contained through a plot twist, when Fetnah resolves to remain in Algiers to care for her aging father.

The preceding sketch of plot twists does not capture the complex cultural discourses of nation, empire, gender, and womanliness that circulate in Rowson's text. Like most writers who made literary use of the Algerian altercation, Rowson made sure that popular notions about national ideology were present in her work.[36] Thus, *Slaves in Algiers* bears the subtitle *A Struggle for Freedom*. The United States is celebrated there as a moral meritocracy, "the land where virtue in either sex is the only mark of superiority."[37] The nation, embodied as "Columbia," where one can claim "liberty as [a] birth-right," is the region of "Peace and Liberty" (10, 41). As one of the captives planning a revolt reassures his anxious mother, "An't I an American, and I am sure you have often told me, in a right cause, the American did not fear anything" (50). The play ends with a fervent prayer to the future reaches of empire: "May Freedom spread her benign influence thro' every nation, till the bright Eagle, united with the dove and olive-branch, waves high, the acknowledged standard of the world" (72).

Yet the rhetoric of empire is not the only privileged one. As Rowson makes clear in the epilogue, which is designed to be spoken by the author herself, a major aspect of her drama is a reconceptualization of the roles of women.

> Well, Ladies tell me—how d'ye like my play?
> "The creature has some sense," methinks you say;
> "She says that we should have supreme dominion,
> "And in good truth, we're all of her opinion.
> "Women were born for universal sway,
>
> "Men to adore, be silent, and obey."
>
> True, Ladies—bounteous nature made us fair
> To strew sweet roses round the bed of care
> . . . To raise the fall'n—to pity and forgive,
> This is our noblest, best prerogative.
> By these, pursuing nature's gentle plan,
> We hold in silken chains—the lordly tyrant man. (73)

In this flippant ditty, Rowson manages at once to support the culturally acceptable image of women as ministering angels and to associate women with "sense" or reason, which was traditionally viewed as a male possession. Through her lighthearted tone, Rowson also manages to critique the USAmerican patriarchal culture, in which women are relegated to silence and obedience. The British political satirist William Cobbett was in fact so incensed with the feminist intent of the play that he published a vicious attack on Rowson in 1795.

The feminist concerns of *Slaves in Algiers* should not surprise us. Rowson, author of the best-selling book *Charlotte Temple*, had long been concerned about the roles of middle-class women. In her own life Rowson had broken away from the traditional position of a middle-class woman. She had earned her own living as a governess after her father's deportation to England. After her marriage to William Rowson, a Lon-

don hardware merchant who went bankrupt, she again supported herself and her family, this time by joining a Philadelphia theater company.[38] After 1797, for the last twenty-five years of her life, she devoted
herself to the cause of female education and headed her own Young
Ladies' Academy, where she motivated women, in part, by requiring
them to read her own *Sketches of Female Biography*, a series of vignettes
about famous women in history.[39] Many of her novels, however, were
Richardsonian sentimental tales of seduction, betrayal, lost virtue (a
euphemism for virginity), and suicide. Yet, as Cathy N. Davidson suggests, the sentimental novel as it was adapted by a few writers in the
United States transcended some of the limitations of the genre. Davidson notes that although the sentimental novel appealed to moral critics
because of the connection between "virtuous maidenhood and holy
matrimony," some works "could be dedicated (literally) to the preser-
vation of 'female virtue' yet still exhibit a definite tension between the
public morality apologetically espoused in the preface and the actions
portrayed in the plot."[40]

Many of Rowson's works exhibit a similar tension. Although the
plot of *Charlotte Temple*, for instance, might be said to punish vice—
Charlotte, the fallen woman, dies of grief after having given birth to an
illegitimate child—the preface is directed toward the need of women to
acquire a good education to better fend for themselves. Similarly,
although many of Rowson's novels turned sentiment on itself and
demonstrated that marriages could be unhappy, Rowson used the
didactic plot of the sentimental novel to be accepted by the critics of the
day.[41] Until late in life, she continued to aver that she had never "pro-
mulgated a sentence that could militate against the best interests of religion, virtue, and morality."[42]

The tensions and ambivalences in Rowson's work reflect the conflicting discourses on conceptions of womanhood in the late eighteenth
and early nineteenth centuries. In a sense, the revolutionary period
placed a high premium on the influence of women on national character. Women were regarded as the guardians of culture, and many
thinkers saw crucial links between manners and polity. James Tilton,
the president of the Delaware Society of Cincinnati, observed, for
instance, that while men had more powers in executing laws, "the
women in every free country [had] an absolute control of manners: and
it is confessed, that in a republic, manners are of equal importance with
the laws."[43] But while women were permitted some social equality,
political equality for women was disparaged. The printing of Mary

Wollstonecraft's *A Vindication of the Rights of Women* in the United States
in 1792 was an instantaneous success, leading to a second U.S. edition in
1794, but the work also provoked a series of attacks. Benjamin Silliman,
for instance, excoriated Wollestonecraft's rejection of the inherent "sensibility, timidity and tenderness of women," maintaining that "she
wished to strip them of every thing feminine, and to assimilate them, as
fast as possible, to the masculine character."[44]

Given the simultaneous introduction of the "women's question"
and the pious moralizing against the rights of women, restraints on the
representation of women in literature were inevitable. However, in
Slaves in Algiers Rowson found that she could dispense with many of
these restraints because of the Oriental setting and the major roles
played by women of mixed racial/cultural origins. The result was a sur-
prisingly bold representation of the moral, ideological, social, and sexual being of women.

An interesting subversion of the tainted-virtue fallen-woman type
in *Slaves in Algiers* is the representation of Fetnah, the most racially and
culturally ambiguous woman in the play. Fetnah is British and Jewish
by birth but Algerian and Moslem by rearing (her father having moved
to Algiers and converted to Islam) and Christian by conviction. She is a
white, Christian woman—though with a difference—with whom European and USAmerican women readers could identify. In dramatic
terms, Fetnah is a tragic victim, a fallen woman, because due to her
father's unscrupulous selling of her, she is one of the dey's mistresses.

The fallen woman could never be considered respectable in the
United States, because she had violated a fundamental ethical standard
of eighteenth-century morality that equated chastity with goodness.
Mary Wollstonecraft had eloquently commented on this morality:
"With respect to reputation, the attention is confined to a single virtue—
chastity. If the honor of a woman, as it is absurdly called, be safe, she
may neglect every social duty."[45] Rowson, however, refuses to treat Fetnah as a fallen woman; indeed, her "honor" is hardly made issue of
here. Fetnah discusses her sexual relationship with the dey with a can-
dor and flippancy unthinkable for a female character in a sentimental
novel. When asked by another woman from the dey's harem whether
she might indeed love the dey, she responds,

> No—he is old and ugly, then he wears such tremendous whiskers;
> and when he makes love, he looks so grave and stately, that I
> declare, if it was not for fear of his huge seymetar, I shou'd burst
> out a laughing in his face. (6)

Dorothy Weil sees Fetnah as "Mrs. Rowson's version of a Shake-spearean comic heroine, the girl who shows her spirited, active side."[46] I suggest that by rewriting the current discourses of sexuality in which women's bodies are measured according to a pure/impure dichotomy, Fetnah scripts for herself a gendered space far beyond that of the Shake-spearean heroine. Fetnah talks freely about her sexual experiences with the dey because she is represented as having an agency; her body and sexuality are accessible to her own signification, rather than being deter-mined by the strictures of patriarchal ideology.[47] Yet Fetnah is not pre-sented as the immoral whore, the obverse of the pious woman. Indeed, she is given all the desires and longings deemed acceptable for the woman in the sentimental novel. Fetnah, like the heroine of the senti-mental novel, longs for some man to "fall in love with [her], break open the garden gates, and carry [her] off" (31), and she is indeed rewarded with such a person.

Rowson's subversion of the conventions of the sentimental novel, even if parodic, are to a large extent made possible because she uses the Oriental setting to break free of conventions at home. Women's sexual-ity, for example, was a taboo subject in the United States, in large part because of a clerical shift that contributed to the desexualized represen-tation of women there. Ministers in the seventeenth century had focused on Eve and the sinful, transgressive nature of women. But by the late eighteenth and early nineteenth centuries, ministers were regarding women as guardians "against the encroachments of impudence and licentiousness."[48] Women's sexuality (when acknowledged) had only been regarded as sinful, and it was the middle of the nineteenth century before moral reform groups advocated instructing women in physiol-ogy so that they could understand their own sexual natures.[49]

Rowson's use of the Algerian Orient as an enabling sexual space for women is especially interesting given the prevalent Western association of harems with enclosure. Harems were associated with a sexuality that was for the pleasure of the male alone.[50] In Jonathan Smith's *The Siege of Algiers,* for instance, the two Georgian and Circassian "virgins" brought to the harem choose the respectable way out of their sexual bondage by choosing the ultimate means of separation from the body—suicide. As Circassiana says in her dying speech, ". . . thus did we to the last pre-serve our youthful pledges, and that virgin innocence which is the pride and ornament of our sex."[51] Smith uses the harem to reinforce the morality of the sentimental novel.

In contrast, Rowson represents the harem as a social space where women can form bonds free of the society of men. In the harem, Selima and Fetnah discuss the institution of sexual monarchy, and Zoriana and Olivia form bonds so strong that they are willing to make sacrifices for each other. Indeed, their uncommonly close friendship is repeatedly stressed in the play. The love of both Zoriana and Olivia for the same man, whom they are both willing to give up for each other, is really a displaced love of the women for each other. The eroticized bonding of the women deforms the gender constructions of the sentimental tradition and of the imperial body, which is contoured on the exclusion of "deviance." More importantly, by linking the embodiment of New World virtue with an Oriental counterpart, Rowson undermines the raced divisions inherent in the rhetoric of empire, much as the unmanning of Tyler's hero in *The Algerian Captive,* Updike Underhill, upsets the idea of the heteronormative, manly hero embodying the nation as an empire.

In making the harem a space for female interaction, Rowson was no doubt drawing on the perceived association of harems with imprisonment to question the limited freedom available to women in the land of liberty. Having Algerian women envy the total freedom of women in the United States draws attention to the very real limits on that freedom. Fetnah, for instance, says wistfully, "Oh! it must be a dear delightful country, where women do just what they please" (32). She idolizes "Columbia" as the "land where virtue in either sex is the only mark of superiority," and she chides Selima, the Algerian native, for not being a "woman of spirit" (9, 39). Rowson, of course, knew that women could not do what they pleased. Her own prefaces to her novels, assuring moralists that she was not writing anything that could be construed as licentious, attest to the limitations on women's voices and to the cultural need to construct a socially acceptable woman as pure/desexualized body.

Slaves in Algiers allowed Rowson to construct women's bodies differently and to question the ideologies of womanhood in the late eighteenth century. Yet the discourse on feminism (the free and strong woman's body) signifies on the idea of nation as liberty (the nation of free bodies) and nation as Columbia (the powerful, imperial nation) and depends on an exclusion and control of raced (Oriental) bodies, thus making women's liberty a hierarchical, racial-cultural issue. The woman most content with her status in the harem of the dey is Selima, a native Algerian happy with the customs of her country. Fetnah, British born and Algerian reared, has always had "a natural antipathy to [Moorish] manners" (8). But it is Rebecca, a slave from the United States, who initiates the desire for freedom in Fetnah. As Fetnah puts it, "it was she, who nourished in my mind the love of liberty, and taught me, woman was never formed to be the abject slave of man" (9). Fetnah, the culturally mixed character, learns her lessons so well that she declares, "I am sure the woman must be blind and stupid, who would not prefer a young, handsome, good humored Christian, to an old, ugly, ill natured Turk" (40).

My point here is not to fault Rowson for succumbing to the raced hierarchies of imperialism, for to do so would be to envision an absolute, unified, oppositional subjectivity, one that denies, at the very minimum, Rowson's split position as woman and imperial subject. A more important issue is how Rowson manages to use the dichotomous discourse to articulate feminist concerns. Rowson enriches the discourse on the Algerian Orient by embodying the nation as woman and by introducing the discourse of feminism as a critique of the nation. Her work also opens up the question of the complex relationship of white women to nationhood and empire, issues raised more forcefully in novels of missionary Orientalism written a generation later, in which the need for empire is made by appeal to persistent stereotypes, such as the Oriental woman's "natural" inclination to passivity and slavery. Rowson's Columbiad vision is thus one of womanly virtue and initiative triumphing over the Orient, as opposed to the manly, militaristic visions of Ellison, Jones, and Smith. Within the discourses of Orientalism, Rowson's text is a significant departure. *Slaves in Algiers* questions both Said's views about Orientalism being a male discourse and Sara Mills's argument about women writers formulating a complete break with the imperialist presumptions of their male counterparts.[52] Instead, it suggests that women's compromised status as imperial agents produced narratives that resulted at once in common discourses for women and an anxious racial differentiation among them.

Algeri an Narrators in the New World: Washington Irving's *Salmagundi* (1808) and Peter Markoe's *The Algerine Spy in Pennsylvania* (1787)

Unlike the Algerian Orientalist texts discussed thus far, Washington Irving's *Salmagundi*[53] and Peter Markoe's *The Algerine Spy in Pennsylvania* upset the hierarchical distinctions between USAmerica and the Orient by using a comic mode in which a naive Oriental observer, visiting the New World, inadvertently ridicules the political and social structures he sees. Liberty, for instance, gets recast as self-indulgent and reckless anarchy, both for the public at large and for women in particular, who are coded as frivolous and giddy. Yet this exaggerated transgression of the hierarchy reinstitutes, all the more firmly, the raced and gendered distinctions on which the rhetoric of empire relies. In contrast to Rowson's *Slaves in Algiers*, Irving's and Markoe's texts negotiate imperial hierarchies by maintaining gendered hierarchies at home.

The nine Mustapha letters of *Salmagundi* and the letters of Mehemet in *The Algerine Spy* are presented in the form of the well-established genre of Oriental letters, the indigenizing of which demonstrates the popularity of Orientalist discourses in the country.[54] The observations of a naive/wise Oriental traveling in the West had served effectively as a means of social satire in both France and England. Montesquieu's *Les Lettres Persanes* (1721), popularized by the Oriental Renaissance in France,[55] soon produced its British counterparts in George Lyttleson's *Letters from a Persian in England to His Friend at Ispahan* (1735) and Horace Walpole's *Letters from Xo-Ho* (1757). The trend culminated in the immensely successful *Citizen of the World; or Letters from a Chinese Philosopher* (1760) by Oliver Goldsmith. These works derived their humor from the exaggerated contrast between the Oriental observer and the society he reported on.

Both Irving and Markoe use the Oriental narrator as a means of lighthearted social satire. But if flippant satire was all that was at stake, a European observer coming to the New World would have served the purpose just as well. For Irving, however, the Orient was more than a passing interest. Of Oliver Goldsmith, one of his favorite writers, Irving wrote, he "always [had] a great notion of expeditions to the East, and wonders to be seen and effected in the Oriental countries."[56] Irving suggests that for the Westerner the Orient is never simply a place of travel and inquiry but an arena for action where the agency of the Westerner "effect[s]" change. Irving's views indicate, without questioning it, a certain assurance about the availability of the Orient as a new frontier in the cultural imaginary. The use of an Oriental observer similarly signifies a certain comic subversion of Oriental hierarchies at the same time that it assumes a rhetorical certainty about being able to speak for the Orient.

Irving's decision to choose an Algerian narrator instead of a simply generic oriental narrator also suggests a desire to create an indigenous version of the genre of Oriental letters. The character of Mustapha, the narrator in the Oriental letters of *Salmagundi*, was in fact based on a

Tripolitan prisoner. In August 1804 a Tripolitan vessel was captured by U.S. officers. In the ensuing struggle, seven Tripolitan sailors were captured, and they were brought to New York in February 1805. These sailors were the subjects of newspaper headlines in New York and the objects of great curiosity. Prominent among these sailors was one Mustapha, the captain of a ketch.[57]

The bulk of *Salmagundi* is comprised of polite essays in the Addisonian tradition, written by three fictitious bachelor narrators—Will Wizard, Anthony Evergreen, and Launcelot Langstaff. Interestingly, in the leisured world of the three narrators, the possession of Oriental artifacts signifies luxury and power. Will Wizard's status depends, in part, on the fact that he has traveled to Canton, is accustomed to perusing Chinese manuscripts, and wears a waistcoat of China silk.[58]

In Peter Markoe's *The Algerine Spy,* the rhetoric of nation as empire is more overt. A political conversion narrative, *The Algerine Spy* comprises letters ostensibly authored by an Algerian who comes to the United States in disguise to spy for his country. Experiencing firsthand the fruits of liberty, he is won over by the new country, which he decides to make home. The ruse of a spy allows Markoe to present extended political and historical deliberations about the power of the New World. Mehemet, the spy, muses: "A new nation has started up in America, which, if actuated by ambition (and what power has long resisted its impulse) may invade, harass and subjugate several of the Spanish provinces. The enthusiasm of the invaders, the debility of the invaded, the poverty of the states and the wealth of the provinces, will render the conquest of Peru and Mexico by no means difficult."[59] But these ruminations about a U.S. continental empire are set in the context of Mehemet's musings about the nature of empires, rhetorical interventions that both continue the trajectory of *Translatio Imperii* and qualitatively distinguish the United States from the rapacious empires of the past. Mehemet decides that national character distinguishes the United States from Rome: "Incapable of industry, and confined within very narrow limits, the Romans could not exist without distressing their neighbors" (27). The result of this unbounded ambition of the Romans, the narrator points out, was the destruction of the populace and civilization of Carthage. Yet the rapaciousness of Rome also serves as a warning about the unforseen consequences of imperialistic expansion.

The major dramatic function served by the Oriental narrators and their incredulity with the country they are visiting lies in the raced and gendered contrasts they note between U.S. political liberty and Algerian despotism, between the restrictions of the harem and the freedoms enjoyed by women in the New World. As we have seen with Tyler and Rowson, harems and harem-like spaces could be used to question sexual and gender subject positions at home. Markoe and Irving, however, use stereotypical ideas about imprisonment in the harem and about subdued Oriental women to idealize an absolute freedom for women in the United States, one that denies the restrictions in voting, property laws, and legal redress and the numerous other strictures that women in nineteenth-century USAmerica were subject to. Indeed, by representing USAmerican women as frivolous, giddy creatures, outside the sphere of Enlightenment rationality and thus outside the sphere of nation and empire, Markoe and Irving can, within that circumscribed space, represent women's sphere as free.

Many of the exaggerated and caricatured representations of the overly free women resemble the depictions of corrupting and evil women sketched by people against the "women's question." For instance, Benjamin Silliman, author of books of travel and a tutor at Yale, castigated Mary Wollstonecraft's influence in the United States: "This female philosopher indignantly rejects the idea of a sex in the soul, pronouncing the sensibility, timidity and tenderness of women, to be merely artificial refinements of character, introduced and fostered by men."[60] Wollstonecraft's new philosophy, Silliman declares, has

> induced them [women], in many instances, to expose their persons in such a manner, as to excite passion, but to extinguish respect. . . . the most beautiful actresses exhibit their persons, in robes of lawn, so transparent, and yet, so adhesive, as to discover every latent proportion and beauty. In the robes of the other sex also, they expose their delicate limbs and vainly emulate the firm step, and manly port, which nature has denied them.[61]

Irving's and Markoe's descriptions of women in the United States, though in the comic vein, are strikingly similar to those of Silliman. Oriental servitude and passivity dramatize, by contrast, the unseemly freedom of USAmerican women.

Using the rhetoric of freedom and slavery, Mustapha, the Oriental observer of *Salmagundi*, constantly compares the active, empowered woman of the United States with her passive, voiceless Algerian counterpart. He is shocked at the free bodies of women who, "instead of being carefully shut up in harems and seraglios, are abandoned to the

direction of their own reason, and suffered to run about in perfect freedom" (412); he comments that "Eastern females," in contrast, "shrink in
blushing timidity even from the glance of a lover" (414). Mustapha
notes that women in the United States are "slang-whangers" no less
than the men, whereas the East values the woman's body without
agency: "Thou knowest how valuable are these silent companions—
what a price is given for them in the East, and what entertaining wives
they make" (53). Markoe's narrator, Mehemet, is similarly aghast at the
unguarded conversation of the women he encounters: "They spoke of
their absent friends without reserve, and sometimes with acrimony. . . .
I heard with astonishment more than three female voices at a time" (33).
Mehemet sums up the difference between these U.S. women and Algerian women as exemplified by his wife: "[she] is more intent to hear, than
eager to speak; who satisfied with my love, aims not at the admiration
of others; with whom silence is wisdom and reserve is virtue" (35).

Both works also clearly demonstrate the significance of gender to
conceptions of nationhood. The representations of frivolity are intended
to wake women to the tasks of being chaste and virtuous embodiments
of nation so that they can be guardians of the morality of the country.
Salmagundi begins and ends with concerns about the manners of women
to whom the essays are directed. The narrators of *Salmagundi* express
their hope that when enough numbers are published, the volume may
be "sufficiently portable to be carried in old ladies' pockets and young
ladies' work-bags" (4). *Salmagundi* is advertised, in other words, like an
etiquette manual. The bachelor writers also reassure their readers that
they will watch over "the guardian rules of female delicacy and decorum" (6–7). In the last essay, titled "To the Ladies," Anthony Evergreen
praises the simple, retiring, shy woman "whose blush is the soft suffusion of delicate sensibility," in contrast to those who acquire "artificial
polish . . . by perpetually mingling in the *beau monde*" (462). Markoe's
Algerian spy similarly concludes that the introduction of European
goods and luxuries will inevitably corrupt the simplicity of the
USAmerican woman by introducing her to immoral fashions.

The observations of the Oriental narrators in Irving's and Markoe's
texts establish the freedoms and the necessary virtues of women, who,
in turn, embody New World virtue. In contrast to Algerian despotism,
the United States is embodied as the land of complete liberty, even if
that liberty leads to regrettable excesses, as in the case of women. Irving,
whose Federalist sympathies made him cynical of republicanism, used
Mustapha to satirize what he saw as a political system about to go

amok. Mustapha's incredulity calls into question the unnecessary expense of parades that mark festive days; his genuine astonishment at politicians approaching commoners before elections and ignoring them thereafter exposes the hypocrisy engendered by the system of popular vote.

But although Irving interrupts the discourse of empire by satirizing the excesses and shortcomings of the democratic system, he also makes it clear that these very excesses characterize the United States as vibrant and changing, unlike the static despotism of the Orient. Mustapha derides the voting process and contrasts it to rule under a bashaw.

> ... the only solid satisfaction the multitude have reaped is, that they
> have got a new governor, or bashaw, whom they will praise, idol-
> ize, and exalt for a while, and afterward ... they will abuse, calum-
> niate, and trample him under foot. .... rejoice that, though the boast-
> ing political chatterers of this logocracy cast upon thy countrymen
> the ignominious epithet of slaves, thou livest in a country where the
> people ... have nothing to do but to submit to the will of a bashaw
> of only three tails. (321)

Even though the preceding description ostensibly critiques the "multitude," this multitude is active, lively, empowered, and embodied as a nation/empire, whereas the Algerians are cast as passive and submissive. Like Irving, Markoe also celebrates the limitless freedoms of the United States. His Oriental narrator in *The Algerine Spy*, Mehemet, notes the facility with which censures of the government are accepted in the United States: "Were an Algerine supposed to have imagined only in a dream what a Pennsylvanian speaks, prints, publishes, maintains and glories in, he would suffer the severest of tortures" (97). The free USAmerican body is constructed through an exclusion of, and complete distinction from, the enslaved bodies of Algerians.

Irving and Markoe similarly use the mode of comic exaggeration to travesty the most stereotypical images of the Orient, those of the despot and his harem, while simultaneously reifying raced distinctions between liberty and enslavement. Irving's narrator, Mustapha, talks of his obese wife, who unlike the thin women he sees, had to be carried home in a wheelbarrow; Mehemet, Markoe's narrator, mourns the loss of his wife, who elopes with their gardener in his absence. Still, the major function of the Oriental observer is to validate the new nation as muscular and strong (a potential empire) and free (an abode of civic virtue).

While both Irving's and Markoe's narrators are, to an extent, stereo-types of syncretic Oriental men, there is no question that their specifi-cally Algerian cast was particularly important to their reception with the reading public. For instance, in *Salmagundi* Irving uses Mustapha's status as captured Algerian to point out the importance of giving such events as Eaton's march iconic national significance. Mustapha pities the system of popular decision making that is destined to make Eaton sink into obscurity: "They talked away the best part of a whole winter before they could determine not to expend a few dollars in purchasing a sword to bestow on an illustrious warrior; . . . on that very hero who frightened all our poor old women and young children at Derne." (203). Markoe's *The Algerine Spy* ends as a veritable political conversion narra-tive. Mehemet, who has been declared a traitor in Algiers, gratefully receives the blessings of U.S. citizenship. Cast off from his bondage to the despot, Mehemet declares,

> And thou Pennsylvania, who has promised to succour and protect the unhappy, that fly to thee for refuge, open thy arms to receive Mehemet the Algerine, who, formerly a mahometan, and thy foe, has renounced his enmity, his country and his religion, and hopes, protected by thy laws, to enjoy, in the evening of his days, the united blessings of FREEDOM and CHRISTIANITY. (129)

Through the voice of the regenerate spy, the text consolidates the idea of the nation as a sanctuary for the oppressed and the view of it as a pow-erful beacon that compels outsiders to recognize its power.

The Tripolitan wars spawned the first set of U.S. Orientalist works in which the New World, embodied as Columbia/Libertad, could be imaginatively seen as an empire conquering the East not simply through its might, like its European counterparts, but through its virtue. Cast as the robust, righteous male or the pure, noble woman, this image represented the rightful imperial power of the United States over a dis-sipated Orient. But the raced and gendered dichotomies and the exclu-sions on which the narrative of empire rests are radically undermined when the ideological anxieties of the nation are brought to the surface. The racial schisms, conflicts, and disruptions foregrounded in these moments reveal that the idea of the morally upright, free imperial body roaming the Orient was a necessary construct for a newly emergent nationhood.

It is also clear that questions of nationhood and empire are worked out through questions of gender, normality, and respectability. The North African Orient, with its harems, seraglios, and despots, provided an interesting site, often an imaginary of evil, where USAmerican virtue and liberty were obviously evident. This vision of virtue depended on notions of the virtue of USAmerican women and of the respectability of USAmerican men, characteristics that made possible the power of the empire. And although, as we have seen, virtue and respectability were often shown to be compromised, the rhetoric of moral nationhood was maintained through numerous paeans to Columbia, particularly in the closure of the texts. Through discourses of imperial nationhood in these texts, that is, attempt to contain the disruptive moments occasioned by discourses on gender.

The imaginative space occupied by the North African states was influenced by, but in no way simply mimetic of, the historical events of the U.S. altercation. In fact, in 1797, when eighty-two survivors of Algerian captivity arrived in Philadelphia, they were greeted by a crowd of spectators and wined and dined just for one day. Some small effort was made to collect contributions for them, but on the next day their case was forgotten by the newspapers.[62] What the enslavement signified was more important. The symbolic threat to sovereignty generated numerous attempts at embodying the nation as a virtuous, manly empire that the North African nations would soon recognize as a formidable power. In the geographical imaginary, the North African Orient was to become one of the frontiers of the U.S. empire and would be commemorated (along with Mexico) in a line in the nineteenth-century "Marine's Hymn," "From the halls of Montezuma to the shores of Tripoli."[63]

3

Missionary Colonialism, Egyptology, Racial Borderlands, and the Satiric Impulse: M. M. Ballou, William Ware, John DeForest, Maria Susanna Cummins, David F. Dorr

The Orientalist writing of the late eighteenth and early nineteenth century was occasioned by the immediate diplomatic crises of the Algerian altercation. It reflected the nationalistic fervor and revolutionary zeal of a newly formed nation and the indignation of writers at the enslavement of fellow citizens by the Algerians. The nation, embodied as virtue and liberty, was seen as a regenerative, moral power, needed to awaken and enlighten a torpid Algerian culture. Yet the critique of slavery that framed the embodiment of the nation ensured that nationhood and slavery, free and unfree bodies, were interlinked. Christian slavery in Algiers, no matter how deplorable, mirrored back African slavery and the racial schisms of the nation.

By the mid–nineteenth century, racial attitudes both within the country and in colonial Europe had hardened considerably. Native American dispossession was legalized through the Indian Removal Act of 1830, while fears of black emancipation prompted many people to zealously pursue raced ethnographic research. Samuel George Morton's *Crania Americana* (1839) and *Crania Ægyptica* (1844) were lauded by Southern apologists for separating the "Negro" race from other races. Josiah C. Nott and George R. Gliddon's *Types of Mankind* (1854) further established the irreducible cultural and moral differences among races.

" 'Unity of races,' " they wrote, "seems to be an idea introduced in comparatively modern times, and never to have been conceived by any primitive nation, such as Egypt."[1] In his introduction to *Types of Mankind*, Nott wrote, "In the broad field and long duration of Negro life, not a single civilization, spontaneous or borrowed, has existed, to adorn its gloomy past."[2]

It was particularly fortuitous for writers that in this highly charged political climate, the Orient that became most familiar to the public at large was the Near East, which, with its mixture of cultures and races, questioned the idea of racial and cultural purity. In the literary imagination, the border became a central trope in Near Eastern Orientalist writing. Racial-cultural hybridity questioned the phallocentric ideology of empire embodied in the figure of the venturing archaeologist/savior abroad. Near Eastern Orientalist writers capitalized on the possibilities of this topos, satirizing both archaeological and missionary imperialism, and critiquing their raced epistemologies. If the adventurer in the Orient was admirable, he was also ludicrous; if he was sincere, he was also misguided. The same terms applied to missionary women. The critique of empire, however, was carefully nuanced as comic deflation within a larger structure of imperial dichotomies that the writers felt compelled to retain in some form; the dichotomies—explorer-explored, austere/sensual, industrious/lazy—are acknowledged, yet trivialized by being recuperated only as forms of closure. Thus, in Near Eastern orientalist works, the dominant ideology, intervening as final contestation, appears as a discourse alongside with, but not subverting, the excesses of satire.

The satiric bent of Near Eastern Orientalist writing in the nineteenth century was made possible, in part, because of the increased familiarity with the Near East on the part of both writers and the reading public. Unlike writers of the "Barbary" Orient, the writers of the mid–nineteenth century labored amid much greater awareness and popular interest in the Near East, fueled by Egyptology, the lure of the Holy Land, and an insatiable appetite for travel. Edward Robinson, a leading biblical scholar from the United States, who revolutionized the study of Palestinian archaeology, arrived in the Levant in 1838. His *Biblical Researches in Palestine, Mount Sinai, and Arabia*, published in 1841, was hailed as surpassing all previous contributions to Palestinian geography.[3] Travel to Egypt and the Holy Land was also increasing, and tourists from the United States were reveling in their roles as the new beacons of civilization and empire. One can only imagine the glee of tourist Edward Joy Morris in 1838 as he tore off the Union Jack from the Great Pyramid and substituted the Stars and Stripes.[4] By 1839, there were reportedly more travelers in Egypt from the United States than from any other nation other than Britain; by the outbreak of the Civil War, these travelers numbered nearly five hundred. It is no wonder that by 1867, when the first of the United States package tours started, its fixed itinerary included Egypt and the Holy Land. Mark Twain documented this extravaganza, "the first organized pleasure party ever assembled for a transatlantic voyage," in *The Innocents Abroad*.[5]

The popularity of Near Eastern travel was enhanced by and coterminous with a reading public avidly interested in histories, romances, and tales about the region. By the mid–nineteenth century the obsession with the Near Eastern Orient had found popular and lavish support. Showman P. T. Barnum's three-story mansion called Iranistan, complete with minarets and onion domes, was finished in 1848 in Bridgeport.[6] It is no wonder, then, that travel books about the Near Eastern Orient fared exceedingly well. John Lloyd Stephens's *Incidents of Travel in Egypt, Arabia, Petraea, and the Holy Land* (1837) was enthusiastically reviewed, most notably by Edgar Allan Poe in the *New York Review*, and sold twenty-one thousand copies in two years.[7] Similarly, the first edition (twenty-five hundred copies) of George William Curtis's *Nile Notes of a Howadji* (1851) was exhausted in six months.[8]

The lore of Egyptology also created interests that were popular both to the scholar and to the public at large. Napoleon's Egyptian expedition was relatively short and culminated within three years, when the British and the Turks drove French forces out of Egypt in 1801, but the lasting effect of the invasion was the cultural legacy of Egyptology. Jean-François Champollion's decipherment of Egyptian ideograms was nothing short of remarkable and revealed to the Western world the existence of a language and culture that far predated their own. All these discoveries created intense excitement and consternation about racial origins in the United States. As I mentioned earlier, attempts to disprove any linkage between Africans and Egyptians (who were not viewed as Africans) were furiously undertaken by such Egyptologists as George S. Gliddon, U.S. consul at Cairo. Just as importantly, Egyptology also legitimized the role of the West as cultural authority for and about the Orient. It is no wonder then that the public at large, feeling it could vicariously participate in the hermeneutic power of Egyptology, was fascinated with archaeology and archaeological artifacts. Influential journals, such as the *North American Review*, published several articles on Egyptology, and Egyptian museum exhibits continued to draw crowds.

The Near East was also a particularly interesting area for writers, scholars, and the public because it was comprised of racial and cultural borderlands, where the cultures of ancient Christian churches and Islam mingled, and where distinctions between "enlightened" and "heathen" were extremely unclear. In fact, the supposed paganism of the ancient Christian churches, contaminated as they were from centuries of contact with Islam, led the clergy in the United States to demand and establish missions in the area. Following the disestablishment of Protestant churches in the early nineteenth century, the clergy sought to gain power by popularizing theology and marketing their churches as wares to attract followers. The ensuing millennial fervor in the mid–nineteenth century, as Ann Douglass has shown, was the result of an alliance between ministers and middle-class leisured women for whom involvement in the church provided a means, albeit highly compromised, of gaining social power.[9] Churchwomen gained access to power by exploiting, lauding, and commercializing their feminine identity as society defined it.[10]

Douglass is probably right in critiquing the role of religion in perpetuating the cult of sentimentalism and Victorian womanhood. However, the social visibility in what was perceived to be a just cause also allowed women to transgress the defined sphere of domesticity. Thus, when churches turned to women as potential missionaries in the Orient, they met with great success. As missionaries, women could maintain their socially prescribed roles yet be independent, and they could wield some power over the presumably downtrodden and degraded Oriental women they had to uplift. White missionary women could embody the nation as empire by distinguishing themselves from the raced bodies of Oriental women. The emancipation of USAmerican missionary women was thus symbiotically dependent on the childishness, dependency, and ignorance of Eastern women. Rev. Ross C. Houghton prefaced his account of the social conditions of Oriental women, for instance, by praising the efforts of "those Christian ladies of America whose sympathies and efforts are enlisted in the work of elevating Oriental women through the power of Christian education."[11]

The anxious need of ministers to expand their bases and the attraction of the missionary role as an outlet from domesticity were important factors in the creation and expansion of missions in the Near East. The first United States missionaries went to the Near East in 1820, and within five years the mission saw its first converts. By 1825 missionaries had two firm stations, one in Malta and the other in Beirut. The triumph of missionary activity was the opening of the Syrian Protestant College in Beirut in 1866, now known as the American University of Beirut.[12] And missionary advancement signified the colonialism of the Columbiad vision. A writer for the *American Theological Review* wrote: "The migratory and colonizing character of the Anglo-Saxon peculiarly adapt them for the work of missionaries. This trait belongs to the inhabitants of Great Britain, as well as to Americans."[13]

Although many major missionary societies in New England were male-dominated, women also created their own missionary organizations. Women's missionary societies were formed as early as 1800, eleven years before the formation of the American Board of Commissioners for Foreign Missions.[14] Educated women in particular saw avenues for power in missionary work. It is little wonder, then, that a disproportionate number of graduates from Mount Holyoke College ventured out as wives of missionaries in the early 1800s. The Society for Promoting Female Education in the East was formed in 1834 by women from different denominations; by the 1860s the first unmarried women missionaries ventured East.

Eastern missionary activities were, in turn, related to knowledge about the Orient. Rev. Rufus Anderson's report to the American Oriental Society makes clear the connection between missionary outposts and scholarly knowledge about the Orient: "While . . . the Gospel is the only effective instrumentality for awakening the lethargic heathen mind, and giving it a healthful excitement and direction, it has also shown, that the best use of this instrumentality involves more or less attention, on the part of the missionaries, to nearly all the departments of knowledge contemplated by the American Oriental Society."[15] It is not far-fetched to speculate that if the task of heathen conversion demanded scholarly knowledge about the Orient, the production of this knowledge was also affected by its potential use as a conversion apparatus.

Literary Orientalist writers who focused on the Near East in the mid–nineteenth century capitalized both on the popular interests in Egyptology and on the attraction of missionary activity in the racial-cultural borderlands. Novels of missionary conversion were therefore written to particularly appeal to women readers, because writers knew that many women were active in forming societies for missionary work overseas and that women also constituted a significant part of the reading public. Writers thus produced missionary-colonial novels in which

Western men boldly ventured forth as archaeologists, confident that, like Champollion, they could unearth lost civilizations and languages, scripting to the ignorant natives their own cultures. Western women were most often the conveyers of the gospel, converting Near Eastern women and steadying Western men in their purpose. In these novels, Near Eastern women were frivolous, indolent, and suppressed, while missionary women were independent and intelligent. Rescuing harem women was the task of both the Western man and the Western woman, although ultimately the man was the preserver of moral order. The missionary woman, having experienced some freedom and conversion success, signified her assent to return to the sphere of domesticity by marrying the strong man, a note on which the missionary-colonial novels ended, as did the domestic novels.[16]

But while writers nominally invoked formulaic missionary-conversion plots, they caricatured the ideological presumptions of characters embodying imperial nationhood, such as the archaeologist and the civilizing missionary. And if the missionary-imperial body was constructed through racial alterity, these texts revealed the precariousness of such a construction by introducing moments when this body was transformed through interracial contact. Missionary-colonial novels thus used imperial plots but also critiqued cultural imperialism through satire, and racial difference through the inclusion of racial hybridity. Self-consciousness about the raced and gendered distinctions of missionary and archaeological imperialism was thus an important feature of many of these writings. Beginning with the writings of Henry Brent, Maturin Murray Ballou, John DeForest, Maria Susanna Cummins, William Ware, and David F. Dorr, Near Eastern Orientalist writing finds its most self-conscious expression and critique of the archaeological imperial body in the tales of Edgar Allan Poe and Harriet Prescott Spofford and in Herman Melville's *Clarel*.

The stock features of the Near Eastern Orient were well established in the popular imagination by the mid–nineteenth century. A special *Knickerbocker* article of 1853 devoted to describing the scenes evoked by the word *Orientalism* in the American mind reveals that orientalism meant a combination of luxury, indolence, strange history, and unreality.

> We frame to ourselves a deep azure sky, and a languid alluring atmosphere; associate the luxurious ease with coffee-rooms and flower-gardens of the seraglio of Constantinople; with the tapering

> minarets and gold-crescents of Cairo; with the fountains within and
> the kiosks without Damascus—settings of silver in circlets of gold.
> We see grave and revered turbans sitting cross-legged on Persian
> carpets in baths and harems. . . . we then bespread over all a sort of
> Arabian Night Spell.[17]

Although the description includes such predictable features as flower
gardens, fountains, and Persian baths, one cannot help but note the self-
conscious manner in which these features are presented. The description insists on the act of construction in the creation of the Oriental
scene: "We frame to ourselves . . . ; associate the luxurious ease. . . . we
then bespread over all." As we see in the novels of Ballou, DeForest,
Cummins, and Ware, the sensual Near Eastern Orient was presented as
a deliberately constructed space despite, or perhaps in anxious reaction
to, a space belied by the increasing scholarly, missionary, and travel
activity in the area.

The critical self-consciousness of Near Eastern Orientalist writing,
and the implication of this writing in raced anxieties, can be seen even in
seemingly simple racy adventure stories, such as Henry Brent's "The
Mysterious Pyramid." Brent prefaces his tale with three paragraphs
dealing with the intersection of history and fiction. The narrative begins
with a lighthearted attempt to argue a historical status for *The Arabian
Nights:* " 'Truth is stranger than fiction,' for who could have invented the
Arabian Nights' Tales, those veritable narratives of conjugal confidence
and credulity?"[18] The statement at once mocks both those who confuse
the tales in *The Arabian Nights* with the historical Orient and the improb-
ability of the tales themselves. To further confuse the issue of historicity,
Brent continues, "Alladin's lantern was a true story, as every body who
has travelled in Eastern lands can testify."[19] Even the story proper is
interrupted by remarks that remind us of the sheer unbelievability of
popular accounts of the Near East. After narrating the account of the
death of the stone mason Tekel-Bene, Brent writes: "If the worthy Tekel-
Bene was not embalmed in the memory of his surviving widow and
children, he was certainly embalmed in the swaddling clothes of the
tomb, as any unbelieving skeptic can prove, by stepping down to Barnum's museum."[20]

Brent's story, with its plotline of hidden treasures and intrigue, parodies the adventures and theories of popular archaeologists. Yet even in
this tale, the raced anxieties of the nation come to the surface. The desert
winds are described as winds from "the lone lands of Africa"; the king

whose pyramid is being raided sends out an edict issued to all the "slaves" in the land. By using the term *Africa* instead of *Egypt,* Brent not only makes a semiotic point—after all Egypt was and is part of Africa, as Brent must have known—but also emphasizes that the ideological discourses about Egyptology and about "Africa" in the nineteenth century were widely disparate and deliberately kept separate. While Egypt evoked culture (albeit a lost one), Africa evoked a definite sense of primitivism. The use of the word *Africa* in the tale thus evokes the repressed Other even as the humanity of this Other is denied. In contrast to Egypt, which is peopled, Africa is spatially conceptualized as "lone lands" absent of the very people whose enslaving was an integral part of U.S. national consciousness.

Maturin Murray Ballou's *The Turkish Slave* (1850), a historical romance and a novel of missionary conversion, demonstrates the extent to which Near Eastern Orientalism was both a self-conscious discourse and a site for negotiating the raced hierarchies of the mid–nineteenth century. Ballou presents *The Turkish Slave* as a historical novel bearing some resemblance to events in the late seventeenth century. Yet, as the beginning of the novel makes clear, Ballou clearly positions his work as part of the popular discourse on the Orient. The description of the East in the epigraph to the novel is strikingly similar to the descriptions in the *Knickerbocker* essay on orientalism previously mentioned. Ballou's ode to Constantinople runs thus:

> Fair city of the dreamy East, proud daughter of the sea
> With thy thousand mosques and minarets . . .
> . . . .
> The gilded caique, the opium ship, the Turkish boatman's song!
> . . . .
> From very childhood we have dreamed of romance and of thee![21]

The Orient, as the beginning of the novel suggests, is a scripted site and part of the cultural imaginary: "Constantinople! what a crowd of oriental images throng before the mind's eye at the very mention of this capital of the indolent East" (11). Yet this sensual and gendered syncretic Orient is also specifically the Near East, for which the most important tropes are the border and hybridity. The city includes "the quiet Armenian, the crafty, trading Jew, the haughty Mussulman, with a sprinkling of Arabs from the desert, and slaves from the far East" (11). *The Turkish Slave* begins with this split picture of the Near Eastern Orient, at once defined and fixed but also mobile and racially permeable, reflecting both the process of hegemonic othering and the fascination of writers with the racial-contact zone.

The love plot allows Ballou to naturalize and interrogate the politics of racial transgression and miscegenation, while the courtly setting allows him the familiar device of using the harem as a metonym for a syncretic Orient. Harems were in fact immensely popular with the reading public in the United States. The trend for harem intrigue had been set in England by James Morier's *Adventures of Hajji Baba of Ispahan* (1824), and writers in the United States were quick to follow with works about confined Oriental women (who, it is implied, had to be saved by USAmericans). James Boulden's *An American among the Orientals* (1855), for instance, is subtitled *Including an audience with the Sultan, and a visit to the interior of a Turkish harem*. Ballou's own novella is subtitled *The Mahometan and His Harem*. Even missionaries were not immune from conjuring up stereotypical images of Eastern women to popularize their works. When Rev. Henry Harris Jessup, after seventeen years as a missionary in Syria, published his account of the American mission and anthropological details about Syrian life, he titled his book *The Women of the Arabs*. By the turn of the century, the trend of enticing readers with the word *harem* was pervasive. William M. Delaney titled his assorted collection of songs *In My Harem Songster* (1913) even though it contained only one song about a harem—Irving Berlin's "In My Harem"; similarly, Aloysius Coll's *The Harem and Other Poems* (1905) has one poem about a harem.

Like many of his fellow writers, Ballou capitalizes on the hunger of readers for details about the harem. In *The Turkish Slave,* the harem, a figure for the syncretic Orient because it is popularly coded as mysterious, inaccessible, and sensual, is embodied as woman or eroticized space, awaiting the entry of the male. In the harem of Sultan Mahomet,

> the lovely inmates were listlessly chatting to each other after the midday meal, sipping cool and variously colored sherbets, and playing with the roses and dainty flowers that bloomed in profusion all about the luxuriant and fairy-like apartment. Thoughtless happiness beamed from the faces there in their careless indolence. (48)

What is most interesting in the preceding description from *The Turkish Slave* are the gaps and silences. There is a deliberate erasure of all particularized details of the women. Without any distinctness and agency, they exist as imaginary bodies within the fantasy of the viewer. The harem and Eastern women both serve as metonyms for the Orient, which is figured as passive and nonrational. The Eastern woman, as Ballou puts it, lives "a life of the most listless and luxuriant inactivity. . . . She has but one steadily engrossing object, and that is love" (48). "Unlike her sex in any other part of the world," writes Ballou, "nature seems to have made the women of the East, though noted for their sentiment of character, yet mere toys; Beautiful, indolent, childlike creatures" (16). The gendered mind/body dichotomies of Western metaphysics (signifying male and female) are here mapped onto an Orientalist discourse that differentiates Western and Eastern women.

The discourse of missionary conversion intersects with and interrupts the construction of the passive Oriental woman. In *The Turkish Slave*, Esmah, the daughter of the sultan, rises above the object-like status of her harem sisters and acquires her own agency because she has received instruction in Christianity, letters, and self-esteem from the Greek slave Alick, the embodiment of missionary imperialism. As in most missionary-colonial works, the relationship between the Westerner and the Eastern woman is that of teacher and recipient. Under Alick's tutelage, Esmah rises from body to mind. Alick "instil[s] into [her] heart self-respect and a love of virtue. He [teaches] her the true dignity of her sex, and how woman was esteemed and cherished in other countries" (17). As a result of Alick's tutelage, Esmah acquires a "rare cultivation of mind and refinement of taste" (16).

But this formulaic narrative of harem indolence and the conversion of the degraded Eastern woman is questioned and interrupted by a racial discourse that is at odds with the missionary narrative and that reflects, instead, the racial tensions of the United States at midcentury. Alick, the Greek tutor of Esmah and the embodiment of superior Western culture, is strangely a slave. Western rationality, intellect, and love of freedom (a displaced configuration of the nation) are curiously the property of the unfree body of the slave. Of course, in terms of events of the historical romance, Alick's status is by no means an anomaly. However, in light of the hierarchical theories of race in circulation in the United States, Alick's slave status complicates raced power relations. Although a slave, Alick teaches his Muslim enslavers and is treated humanely by them.[22] Yet Alick's status as teacher only confirms the power of Christianity; because he is a Christian, he can instruct while even a slave.

The title of the novella also provocatively foregrounds slavery, as did many of the works inspired by the "Barbary" wars. Alick, we are told, remembers the Christian instruction he had received from a priest of Negropont, (Ballou uses Negropont instead of *Euboea*, the alternative name for the Grecian island) a place whose name has obvious similarity to the word *Negro*. Much of the plot revolves around Alick's carefully calculated attempts to escape. Just as nineteenth-century slave narratives recounted the significance of doublespeak to successfully outwit white masters, Ballou repeatedly alludes to Alick's mastery of the tongue, through which he keeps the sultan unaware of any plans for escape. And just as in the Southern United States at the time of Ballou's writing, miscegenation (here figured as that between Turk and Greek) is punishable by death. Through ambivalent racially inflected signifiers, Alick's body occupies the dual position of tutor and slave, thus questioning the hierarchies of Near Eastern Orientalist discourses.

Negotiation of racial-cultural hybridity through the conversion narrative, visible in Ballou's work, can be seen much more forcefully in William Ware's *Letters of Lucius M. Piso* in which fascination with the polyglot culture of Palmyra is anxiously tempered through the plot structure of the "fall" of Palmyra. The rational, logical Lucius M. Piso, the masculinized embodiment of the New World as a westerly empire, fears a demasculization in the raced and gendered hybridity that Palmyra represents. *Letters* also reveals the extent to which current interests in Egyptology and the Near East had begun to generate anxieties about racial-cultural primacy, which, in turn, needed to be quelled by an affirmation of the United States as the New Rome.

Zenobia herself was very much a figure of fascination in the nineteenth century. The burgeoning women's movements in Europe and the United States created an interest in strong female figures, of which Zenobia was one of the most significant. Compilations of important women in history included biographies of Zenobia. Zenobia's status was also anomalous because her reign denied the perceived degradation of Eastern women throughout history. Yet Zenobia was recuperated in the U.S. cultural imaginary as the Eastern monarch who had created an exemplary civilization by introducing Roman traditions and thereby uplifting the East. Anna Jameson, in her *Lives of Celebrated Female Sovereigns*, wrote of Zenobia:

> The classical studies of Zenobia seem to have inspired her with some contempt for her Arab ancestry. She was fond of deriving her

origin from the Macedonian kings of Egypt, and of reckoning
Cleopatra among her progenitors. . . . She paid great attention to the
education of her three sons, habited them in the Roman purple, and
brought them up in the Roman fashion.[23]

Similarly, William Gibbon, a chronicler of the Roman Empire and Western hegemony, was fascinated by Zenobia. He wrote, "Zenobia is perhaps the only female whose superior genius broke through the servile
indolence imposed on her sex by the climate and manners of Asia."[24] In
The Blithedale Romance, Nathaniel Hawthorne appropriately gave the
name *Zenobia* to the heroine in command of a utopian, self-managed
community.

The craze about Egyptology in the nineteenth century also contributed to an interest in this Eastern queen. Zenobia considered herself
a descendant of Cleopatra, and in Ware's novel she is appropriately presented as an Egyptologist. Her dinnerware is "most elaborately carved,
and covered with designs illustrative of points of the Egyptian annals."
Moreover, writes Ware, "[t]he walls and ceiling of the room, and the
carpets represen[t], in the colors of the most eminent Greek and Persian
artists, scenes of the life and reign of the great Queen of Egypt of whom
Zenobia reckon[s] herself descendant."[25] But for Ware, the fascination
for the Near East was countered and tempered by the recognition that
the United States—projected into the narrative as the New Rome—commanded the culture and civilization of the contemporary world. The
novel is presented in the form of letters written by a Roman noble,
Lucius M. Piso, who travels from Rome to Palmyra to effect the escape
of his brother Calpurnius from the king of Persia. The ruse of letter writing enables Lucius to describe his wonder at the excesses of Palmyra
and compare them with the austerity of Rome; the novel ends with the
final defeat of Zenobia, who is led, chained, into Rome. Ware makes the
cultural-ideological premises of his novel clear from the beginning.
Writing from Palmyra, Lucius sees everything "different from what the
West presents," so much so that he feels in the "power of a dream" (1:1).
The dream motif, signifying the Orient and a break from the material
world, creates in Lucius the desire to be back in Rome once again.

Rome and Palmyra are set up as gendered binary oppositions in the
novel. While Rome embodies the order, unity, and masculinity of the
New World, Palmyra embodies variety, excess, and femininity. "The
love of the beautiful, the magnificent and the luxurious," which "not
unfrequently declines into . . . effeminacy," characterizes Palmyra (1:31).

Zenobia's palace is dangerously located at the border between wild, mountainous regions, on the one hand, and level and cultivated places, on the other; it is constructed according to the forms of Persian architecture. The empire itself lies between the Romans and the barbarous Sapor of Persia and is home to a hybrid populace. In Palmyra, Ethiopians, Indians, Persians, Syrians, and Egyptians commingle; its city squares are open to pontificators as various as skeptical philosophers, Jewish rabbis, and Christian preachers. And unlike the logical, rational government of Rome, Palmyra is governed by a queen who is the object of the intense adulation and love of her citizens.

Clearly, the attention Ware gives to the mixture of races in Palmyra reflects the preponderance of scientific and cultural theories of race in the mid–nineteenth century. As the United States increased its pace of contact with the East and as the country absorbed an increasingly diverse immigrant population, fears of both racial degeneration and social unrest were rampant. The idea of a society like Palmyra, where different races and cultures intermingled harmoniously, must have been disturbing to Ware. Ware attempts to contain this disruption by using an idealized androgyny to defuse volatile racial issues. He figures Zenobia, who metonymically stands for Palmyra, as a fusion of "feminine loveliness" and "masculine power" (vol 1:119).

But while Ware presents Palmyra as an embodiment of androgynous cultural harmony, he also identifies it with a languor and excess that are in contrast to the energy and discipline of Rome. In fact, Piso, like Tyler's Updike Underhill (discussed in chap. 2), fears for his own masculinity in a culture so temperate and a government so free of the authority of law. Piso writes: "I began to tremble for myself as a Roman. I must depart while I am yet safe" (1:62). As we have seen, nineteenth-century journalists and essayists had repeatedly represented the United States as the latest westerly empire, the logical culmination of the concept of *Translatio Imperii*. In Ware's version, it is figured metaphorically as the New Rome. And even though, as the Roman noble Piso acknowledges, Roman slavery is a blight, Rome must triumph in the end. Ware ends his novel with Zenobia's body being brought in chains into Rome, bearing with her tokens of the numerous cultures of Palmyra. Ware undoubtedly used the overdetermined figure of Zenobia to express his conviction about the righteousness of the United States as the New Rome. Just as Walt Whitman would celebrate diverse cultures offering themselves to the United States in "The Broadway Pageant," Ware recuperates Zenobia's entry into Rome as part of a natural, evolutionary, historical progression. This depiction of the movement of culture from East to West must have pleased readers and reviewers, because when the second edition of Ware's book was released, Ware changed the epistolary title and renamed his novel *Zenobia; or the Fall of Palmyra*. At any rate, the book was immensely popular with readers. From its initial serialization in *Knickerbocker*, the book went through a second edition only a year later, and by 1850 it had gone through eight editions.

Although historical romances like Ballou's and Ware's relied on the idea of cultural conversion, missionary-colonial novels, capitalizing on the growth of U.S. overseas missions, could be structured around the idea of conversion even more forcefully. Yet in these missionary works, resistance to the idea of mission and to racial-cultural purity is present almost from the beginning. Two novels that use satire to complicate the narrative of the New World missionary/archaeologist overseas are John DeForest's *Irene the Missionary* and Maria Susanna Cummins's *El Fureidis*.

The trope of Christian conversion, as Ballou's and Ware's texts illustrate, was popular with the reading public, no doubt due to the fervor with which churches were seeking to augment attendance and to the increasing confidence with which politicians, ministers, and businessmen alike were constructing the Near East as an area in need of revitalization from the New World. The right to empire and the gospel had been linked together in the late seventeenth century by Puritan divines. This imperial religiosity was further fueled by the postrevolutionary Columbiad vision and by discourses on the New World westerly empire. Thus the mid-nineteenth-century evangelical impulse sought, quite naturally, to extend this empire to the Near East. Rev. Leonard Woods of Andover, who had preached at the ordination of the first five missionaries in 1812, declared it impossible "that any man who considers the Christian religion a blessing should not desire its universal diffusion." "Think of the difference," he said, "between the inhabitants of New England, and the people in those countries where pagan influence prevails."[26] Questions of culture, imperialism, and religion were indubitably interlinked in the missionary enterprise.

Similarly, the archaeological imperative to unearth and decode the culture of the Near East assumed an agency embodied in the adventurer that was for the most part, denied the natives. In the novels of DeForest and Cummins, a complex and ambivalent discourse of empire begins to develop, one that questions, yet relies on, the embodiment of the New World as Columbus, as explorer; the raced, imperial body of the hermeneute is contoured by, yet constructed against, the resistant Otherness of the Near East. In John DeForest's *Irene the Missionary* and Maria Susanna Cummins's *El Fureidis,* the bodies of missionary women and male archaeologists are linked in the raced rhetoric of empire in which Eastern women in particular are the most needy recipients of culture; yet the very status given to USAmerican women undermines the phallocentric basis of the imperial rhetoric. And in both works, moments of racial-cultural hybridity question absolute raced dichotomies and the power and wholeness of the missionary/archaeologist hero embodying the nation.

John DeForest's novel *Irene the Missionary* actually incorporated some of his travel experiences. Unlike many of his peers, DeForest had traveled to the Near East. In 1846, at the age of twenty, he went to Syria, where his brother Henry was a missionary and the head of a girls' school in Beirut. DeForest spent almost two years in Syria and undertook the two most popular tourist activities: amateur archaeology and a visit to Jerusalem. A decade later, in 1856, he published *Oriental Acquaintance; or Letters from Syria,* his account of Near Eastern travel, and even later, in 1879, he published the missionary novel *Irene the Missionary.* In the intervening years he wrote prolifically on a diverse range of subjects, his writings include novels of the civil war.

For DeForest, more than for any writer discussed so far, the Near Eastern Orient becomes the site where characters confront, as if in a mirror, the absurdity of the national missionary impulse. *Oriental Acquaintance* begins by invoking a mixture of a Columbian sense of wonder and a familiar sense of the Near Eastern Orient: "Before my western eyes were spread out, in oriental strangeness, the shabby wharves, the fragile minarets. . . ."[27] The dyadic relationship between the New World and the Near Eastern Orient is that between the discoverer and the object awaiting to be, yet always already, scripted. As the narrator's eyes move over the scene, they encounter the familiar display of Oriental lassitude; the active and energetic hero, the embodiment of New World industry, impatiently notes the leisurely pace at which the slothful Orientals work. But soon this formulaic narrative, which bears few signifiers of presentness, is rudely interrupted by the presence of the African.

> But what most struck me, was a negro, who, dressed handsomely in the Turkish style, lounged quietly on a bench near the door, and occupied himself with smoking a meditative pipe. . . . Coming from a country where individuals of this color bear all the marks of a

depressed and despised people, I saw in this man the first of a species. No sneaking, no grinning, no small impertinences. . . . No Turk in the room had more calmness, gravity and intelligence in his air. . . . I saw at once that he had been treated like a man all his life, and that not the least suspicion had ever entered his brain that he was not a man. He gave me new ideas of the possibilities of the African race.[28]

Most nineteenth-century writers who traveled overseas could not help but note their amazement at the relative lack of prejudice there toward Africans. African American writers, especially, narrated their experiences in Europe to further the cause of abolition. In her travels to Russia, free black Nancy Prince, in *A Narrative of the Life and Travels of Mrs. Nancy Prince,* noted the difference in treatment accorded her in Russia not only as compared to African Americans in the South but also as compared to the prejudice free African Americans still faced in the North. But such racial considerations were not part of popular Near Eastern orientalism. In DeForest's narrative, the figure of the African interrupts and undermines the binaries of New World explorer/Near East explored and the idea of mission by asking the reader to reappraise familiar theories about the Western movement of civilization itself. Even though the preceding description of an encounter with an African is implicated in the stereotypes of the sneaking, grinning "sambo" and the calm, grave Turk, its very questioning of racial categories that were so entrenched in the nineteenth century undermines the hierarchical basis on which the discourse of Orientalism rested. And instead of reinforcing the embodiment of the nation as a phallic, Western/westering male, the introduction of the African brings in the real in such a manner as to cause a split in the Western subject.

The narrative of the Near Eastern Orient generated by this split subject is necessarily self-conscious. In *Oriental Acquaintance,* DeForest gives us, in effect, two narrating subject positions—one in which the subject interactively records its encounter with a changing Near Eastern Orient and one in which the subject authoritatively reproduces the syncretic Orient of the popular imagination. Before traveling to the Orient, the narrator writes:

The fat Turk in the geography, and the wealth of the Arabian Nights, formed the warp and woof of my Eastern expectations. I fancied that each oriental possessed an independent fortune, and smoked interminable pipes, seated on luxurious cushions. . . . I was extremely shocked, therefore, to find the greater part of the population at work. . . . The Turkish women confounded my inquisitive eyes with their vexatious veils and swaddlings. . . . They seemed to be absurdly contented with their ghostly way of life; not a soul of them ever solicited me to carry her off from the harem of a tyrannical husband or father.[29]

Instead of confirming the authority of the venturing New World hero by subjecting the innermost recesses of the harem (often a metonym for the Orient) to his gaze, DeForest denies his narrator the power of sight. Instead, the male hero embodying the nation becomes the object of the gaze of the Other, thus upsetting the gendered dichotomies of activity and passivity that have traditionally characterized Orientalist discourse. And while missionary colonialism had coded the harem as a prison, reflective of Oriental tyranny and despotism, DeForest's narrative complicates the easy dichotomies of captive and free bodies.

Irene the Missionary is based on DeForest's stay at the American mission and on his travels in Syria. DeForest uses the novel as a means of examining and satirizing the national will to rule and the imperialist impulse, in which Egyptology is figured as a discovery of the West. The novel revolves around the experiences of two New Englanders, Huberstein DeVries, the amateur archaeologist, and Irene Grant, the missionary, as they travel to Syria. Both learn the manners of the natives and win their trust. The romantic subplot involves Irene's love for DeVries; his casual flirtation with a Syrian woman, Saada; and DeVries's final realization of Irene's "purer" virtues. The novel ends with the couple leaving for New England. As this brief outline suggests, the novel negotiates the interplay of free bodies (representing the free nation) with the gendered limitations on bodies by recuperating dichotomous roles of women. The missionary situation offers gender possibilities far more varied than those prescribed by the cult of true womanhood; these possibilities are, in turn, further complicated by the fact that missionary women are positioned as teachers of native women.

The novel begins with the New England heroine, Irene Grant, the embodiment of the New World missionary calling, traveling aboard a ship bound for Syria, ready to start a life of religious work. Irene (the missionary woman) and the women of the harem are presented as vehi-

cles of ideology through which, paradoxically, both Eastern passivity
and the racist and imperialist assumptions at the heart of missionary
nationhood are revealed. DeForest writes:

> So long as they had their pipes and coffee, and their idle communi-
> cations concerning harem matters, they appeared to care for naught
> beside. From childhood they had been accustomed to see a hun-
> dred types of race and costume. From childhood they had been
> drilled to believe that women should confine themselves to purely
> womanish affairs.
>
> Not so with our young lady from a land where man and woman
> alike are as free as perhaps it is best for them to be. Every one of
> these picturesque fellow-beings was to her an object of curious and
> almost audacious interest. They were entertaining and absurdly
> queer . . . They were foreigners; no matter if they were under their
> native skies, they were foreigners; she alone, the American citizen,
> was a native and possessor everywhere. What were these singular
> creatures bent upon, and did they even know where they were
> going? . . . She had . . . the Anglo-Saxon feeling that only the Anglo-
> Saxon knows fully what he is about, and that the other denizens of
> earth are grown children who need Anglo-Saxons to direct their
> ways.[30]

I cite this passage at length because it demonstrates the extent to which
the construction of an imperial, missionary nationhood was highly self-
conscious within Near Eastern Orientalist discourse. DeForest deliberately sets up familiar raced dichotomies between the free imperial body
and the unfree Orientalist bodies, but he follows these immediately with
a critique so certain and scathing that there is little doubt about his position. The Eastern women first appear as indolent, unthinking creatures,
without agency, content to let the world drift by, satisfied in their ser-
vility to their masters. But even within this stereotypical representation,
DeForest rescripts the idea of Eastern tranquility and docility. The
description curiously suggests that unlike the American heroine, Irene
Grant, the supposedly cloistered harem women have had a far-flung
range of cultural experiences. They have seen a "hundred types of race
and costume."

In contrast, Irene embodies the imperial subject, appropriating all
agency for herself and reducing Eastern women to the passive objects
of her gaze. DeForest unambiguously links internal colonization with

imperialism, which assumes that the non-Western world is a frontier to be conquered either territorially or economically by the New World. Both within and outside the United States, DeForest suggests, the inherent right of the New World imperial body to be a "possessor everywhere" is largely unquestioned. Further, DeForest links the discourse of imperial Manifest Destiny to theories of racial evolution, such as those by Samuel George Morton and George Gliddon, which prioritized Caucasians. These theories, as we know, were debated with great intensity in the mid–nineteenth century, and few Westerners actually believed that the nonwhite races were capable of intellectual achievement. The same set of arguments were also used in the United States to bolster colonization, as well as segregation and lynch laws. DeForest foregrounds the absurd cultural chauvinism of these theories by satirizing Irene's "Anglo-Saxon feeling that only the Anglo-Saxon knows fully what he is about."

DeForest's critique of the racial basis of missionary activity links together the discourses of colonization and evangelical Christianity, the connections between which had been mystified in discussions of overseas missionary activity, though clearly similar discourses had shaped the conversion of various "heathens" in the country. In making the embodiment of the missionary cause the heroine of his novel, DeForest is not only historically sensitive to the growing numbers of missionary women overseas but also recognizes that Eurocentric imperial ideology, with its dehumanization of Eastern women in particular, is not a male prerogative alone. African American women had long recognized the complicity of white women in the subjugation of slave women, particularly after emancipation. Not too long after the publication of *Irene the Missionary*, Anna Julia Cooper and Pauline Hopkins questioned the motives of white feminists and also insistently pointed to the connections between internal and external colonization. The idea of "civilizing" supposedly less advanced peoples, was, to Cooper, embedded in the racial hierarchies of the United States. She angrily asked, "Whence [came] the scorn of so-called weak or unwarlike races and individuals, and the very comfortable assurance that it is their manifest destiny to be wiped out as vermin before this advancing civilization?"[31]

The Near Eastern Orient was a particularly interesting site for mediating the complex interrelationships between racial hierarchies and the ideology of Manifest Destiny, because of the mixture of races and cultures it offered, and because of Egyptology, which spurred both interest in and anxiety about the origins of Western civilization. Such apprehensions were particularly painful for people who envisioned the United States as the new westerly empire and for pro-slavery spokespersons. DeForest makes the anxiety of white USAmericans about racially mixed origins painfully clear by holding up for ridicule the vulgar racial investigations of his missionary-imperial heroine, Irene. Early in her stay at the mission in Beirut, Irene is startled to meet an aristocratic Syrian woman with gray eyes, golden brown hair, and an imposing headdress. Fascinated by the mixture of exotic and white attributes that this woman exhibits, Irene asks to be allowed to see her headdress.

> The lady of the House of Keneasy smiled, and gracefully bowed her gilded and tasselled head. "What a lovely white neck!" whispered Irene, as she studied the network of golden circlets. "This is the blood of the Crusaders." (69)

DeForest uses Irene's naïveté, curiosity, and lack of self-consciousness to reproduce the dynamics of power and desire in the USAmerican contact with the Near East. The Near East figures in the U.S. imaginary as the nearly white, yet Eastern, culture, the investigation and upliftment of which is the mission and destiny of the New World. Yet, as Irene's encounter with the lady of the house of Keneasy suggests, the contact with the raced Other is also a desire for the Other. We also cannot help but think how the dramatic situation of Irene and the Syrian woman replicates the relationship between white and black in the postbellum United States, where the technologies of race reduced the bodies of blacks to their color alone. I do not mean to suggest that DeForest's Orientalism is simply a displacement of black-white relations onto a different arena. Rather, we can say that the very existence of complex racial dilemmas in the United States reproduced in the imaginative literature of the country a far greater concern with racial dynamics within Orientalism than existed in the literature of their European counterparts. In *Irene the Missionary*, for instance, the author distinguishes among different racial types of Syrian women and accordingly assigns them their social-moral functions. Mitra, whose color is "very much that of a handsome brunette from Louisiana or Cuba" (p. 72), is not cast as the sensual Eastern woman, but the dark-eyed Saada, is cast as the vehicle of illicit sexuality.

While Irene embodies the racial paternalism of the missionary impulse, New Englander Huberstein DeVries, the vigorous male for whom the Near East is a new frontier, embodies an expanding, imperial nation, a latter-day Columbia. Energetic, tireless, and supremely self-confident, DeVries embodies the enterprise and industry of the nation, qualities that many industrialists were actively advertising as attributes the Orient could readily use. As an archaeologist, DeVries undertakes to excavate ruins, interpret lost cultures, and write the history of the Near East for its natives. "The whole of Asia Minor ought to be excavated," he declares, "but I must attend to the Philistines first" (35). From his site, the young archaeologist, now in command of a crew of lazy Orientals, writes that he has

> a horde of loafers shovelling. . . . It is an everlasting adventure to rouse out fourscore modern Philistines every morning, and keep them grubbing all day after their ancestors with some decent imita-tion of industry. The laziness and shirking bad faith of the rapscal-lions would be insupportable, if one did not remember that they are the underfed survivors of countless centuries of devastation. (213)

Unlike DeVries, whose appetite for archaeological knowledge is insa-tiable, the natives have little interest in the excavation other than the livelihood it provides. Indeed, DeVries, the hermeneute, interprets the racial origins of the natives for them: "They don't know that they are sprung from the Cherethites and the Pelethites" (214).

Despite exaggerating DeVries's claims to discovery, however, the narrative does not problematize the hero's belief in his right to "dis-cover" Syrian culture and lead the natives of Syria. Thus, through the embodiment of DeVries as a restless, exploring nation, a narrative of empire begins to emerge. And this narrative structure becomes more visible as the novel proceeds, culminating in a recuperation of U.S. might and patriarchal power as both natives and women are refigured as helpless and dependent. As a woman, Irene is often objectified in relation to Huberstein DeVries. On learning of DeVries's fascination with Saada, for instance, Irene becomes the submissive woman fetishized by the cult of true womanhood. Irene wants to become an artifact to please DeVries. But her own status as missionary, particularly in the wake of the findings of Egyptology, is, for Irene, a validation of the westerly course of empire, culminating in the United States. As Rev-erend Payson and Irene discuss the ancient culture of the Near East, Irene exclaims: "Yes, they gave letters to our ancestors. . . . And here we are giving letters to them. How the world turns round!" (160).

The presence of a traditional narrative of Oriental upliftment in DeForest's text, despite the author's contempt for ideologies of westerly empire, should not surprise us. DeForest was, after all, writing at a time when the United States was projecting itself as a cohesive, new westerly empire and a beacon of civilization. That such hegemonic values hardly described the social tensions of the postbellum era or the anxieties about the racial origins of EuroAmericans generated by Egyptology is beside the point. These ideologies were professed precisely because they mystified realities. The U.S. Centennial Exposition in Philadelphia in 1876, the first of the large-scale ritualistic affirmations of national might, fused together empire, culture, and race. The layout of exhibits was racially structured, with the United States in the center, the white nations around it, and the darkest nations at the periphery. This exposition was enthusiastically attended by a fifth of the country's population.[32] In DeForest's novel, raced hierarchies between white USAmerican and Syrian are negotiated by reaffirming the gender binaries of Western metaphysics, where woman as body is denigrated. No matter how absurdly pompous Irene appears to be, she is still pure and noble (without sexuality), a woman to be emulated, while Saada, for instance, is objectified as a sexual body, a "brimming vase of Oriental beauty" (288).

The patriarchal and imperial relationship between the youthful, flamboyant archaeologist and the Syrian woman Saada becomes a means through which DeForest mediates technologies of race and ideologies of empire building. When the mission and its beneficiaries are in danger because of war, the hero suggests a solution for Saada: "I would like to send that one home to my mother. . . . My mother would make a perfect plaything of a Syrian Protestant with such eyes" (260–61). The very ease and frivolity with which DeVries assumes ownership of Saada echoes the imperial assumptions of the Egyptologist. And, in light of the heated racial politics of the Reconstruction, we cannot help but also think how the casual assumption of Saada's body as a commodity to be circulated works as a displaced narrative of white anxiety striving to reinstitute the legalized proprietal relations between whites and blacks.

The creation of Saada as an artifact also works dramatically to recuperate imperialism as a male prerogative. DeVries's intention of taking Saada as a plaything to his mother induces in the heroine, Irene Grant, a desire to become an artifact to please DeVries: "She became humbly anxious to please him, and pondered how she could do it. . . . she was not, like Saada, a Syrian and a curiosity; she was only a poor American minister's daughter, and not suitable for a pet and plaything" (261). Coming close to the end of the narrative, such a disclosure denies Irene the relative independence she possesses at the beginning and refigures her as the pious, pure, submissive, and domesticated woman who, within the nineteenth-century ideology of true womanhood, wielded very little power or, as within traditional male discourse, constituted woman as art object.[33] As noted earlier, in comparison to the circumscribed roles prescribed for women at home, missionary women had a relative degree of freedom, albeit one gained at the expense of the women of color they had to "liberate." DeForest ends his narrative, however, by having DeVries save the mission and its native dependents from a local insurrection. He becomes the embodiment of law and the rightful savior of the local populace. In the process, he wins the hand of Irene, who renounces her missionary task and sails back with DeVries to New England.

If DeForest's recuperation of the imperial plot seems an anachronism in light of his critique of missionary activity, it is so only if we view Near Eastern Orientalism as an uncomplicated discourse. Although DeForest uses a rather standard plot as a basic structuring device, he locates the conflicts and tensions inherent in the construction of the New World imperial body as coherent and uncorrupted. DeVries, who embodies the supposedly free frontier spirit and basic goodness of the nation, for instance, assumes as his right the possession of the Oriental woman as a commodity. Similarly, Irene maintains the fiction of enlightened USAmerican womanhood only by constructing the Oriental woman as a simple Other, imprisoned and without agency. Like DeForest, Maria Susanna Cummins, in *El Fureidis* (1860), also uses the figures of the male archaeologist and the missionary woman to provide a basic structure for the raced imperial narrative of the new frontier. In *El Fureidis*, however, the racial-cultural hybridity of the Near East powerfully intervenes into the dynamics of imperialism by making the Oriental subject resistant to definition and by providing gender possibilities that question the phallocentric basis of imperialism.

Cummins's very authoring of a Near Eastern Orientalist novel suggests the importance of the region in the cultural imaginary and the possibilities offered by the racial-cultural borderlands there. Cummins was, after all, the author of one of the most popular romances of her time, *The Lamplighter* (1854), which sold forty thousand copies in eight weeks and led to Hawthorne's well-known outburst against the "'d—d' mob of scribbling women." Hawthorne asked, "What is the mystery of these

innumerable editions of the 'Lamplighter,' and other books neither better nor worse?"[34] The popularity of *The Lamplighter* probably lay in its
use of what Nina Baym has described as the staple plot of nineteenth-
century women's writing—the story of a poor woman's struggle, her
good fortune in finding a benefactor, and her final marriage.[35] The
orphaned heroine of *The Lamplighter*, who is befriended by Trueman
Flint, is a model of female dependency and purity and is rewarded for
her virtues by marriage to a childhood sweetheart.

    In *El Fureidis*, Cummins intersects the woman's plot with the Ori-
entalist plot and radically reconfigures both. Just as Rowson used racial
ambiguity to reconstruct gender roles in *Slaves in Algiers*, Cummins uses
cultural and racial mixtures to rewrite the gender roles of the conventional courting plot. The liberation of the heroine from the shackles of
the conventional plot is carried out through the ambiguous Near Eastern racial configuration of the heroine, which permits the transgression
of normative gender roles. Yet the anxieties inherent in destabilizing the
racial dichotomies on which the imperial body is constructed come to
the surface when the very same heroine is positioned as the savior of the
degraded Eastern woman, much in the manner of Rowson's *Slaves in
Algiers*.

    Cummins begins the novel by situating it within a discursive terrain
of the imaginary Orient. The scholarly guides of *El Fureidis*, as Cummins
tells us in the introductory chapter, are travel writers and historians like
Edward Robinson, Jacob Burkhardt, and Sir Richard Burton. Through
the male archaeologist, Meredith, Cummins critiques the unreal and
imaginary Orient of the popular imagination. Nearing the Syrian shore,
Meredith enters a dreamworld of "promise, of beauty, of ancient records,
and of sacred lore."[36] Popular Orientalism is a projection of the Westerner's fantasies of sensuality and a site removed from the sphere of
work, a space that Meredith pleasurably creates for himself as he travels
to Syria: "Now feasting his eager eye upon the harmonious picture, then
lifting it with equal wonder and delight to the deep-blue canopy of sky
above . . . and all the while breathing in an atmosphere whose purity and
fragrance are nowhere else inhaled, the Eastern-bound traveller
acknowledges all his longings satisfied, all his day-dreams realized" (2).
But Meredith's fantasy scene also signifies on the wondrous descriptions
of the New World popularized through Columbus's letters and promotional tracts. By mapping the New World imaginary onto the Near East
and exaggerating its effects, the text critiques (even as it evokes) the construction of the Near East as the new frontier.

Just as Cummins ridicules the excesses of Oriental lore, she also undermines the raced hierarchies of imperialism and the stature of the imperial body by representing Meredith, the archaeologist, as overwhelmed by the language and culture of the Near Eastern Orient. The Near Eastern Orient cannot simply be scripted as an Other, the alterity, barbarity, and excess of which can confirm the coherence of the Western body. In Damascus, in the house of a Muslim trader, Meredith finds himself lost within a bewildering variety of forms and figures that undermine the heteronormative gender identity on which the stance of imperial power depends.

> As his eye ranged up and down the lofty walls, he felt himself lost amid mazes of coloring, and bewildered by architectural forms. Arches with fluted pillars . . . on which inscriptions from the Koran were engraved in graceful Arabic characters, light galleries and colonnades festooned with passion-flower . . . all these elements of beauty assailed his senses at a glance, and, reflected in innumerable little mirrors inserted in the wainscoting, were repeated in endless perspective. In vain did the imagination attempt to trace the pattern of flowers and scrolls. . . .
>
> Was it the rippling of a new fountain, just starting into play, which now chimed in with the other sounds. . . . Was it a picture, such as the artist never painted before, or was it a living ideal, which had come to perfect the scene? . . .
>
> Opposite to him, however, mirrored in glass, or possibly in fancy, were two figures, whose loveliness, grace, and picturesque attire harmonized so perfectly with their fairy-like surroundings, that they seemed an indispensable part of the whole. . . . Now they paced slowly around the railed gallery which ran around the court, and then paused to pluck a passionflower or smell a rose, then idled on. Meredith watched them breathlessly for a moment, then they were gone. (288–89)

Instead of scopophilically constructing the scene as the object of his gaze, Cummins's hero is confronted with "innumerable little mirrors" that challenge both his powers of interpretation and his sense of self. Like Royall Tyler's Updike Underhill, whose authority was undermined by his ambivalent racial and gender construction within the walls of the Moslem college, Meredith's imperial, patriarchal position is severely challenged here. Meredith's mental wanderings take place in the proximity of the harem, a space marked not simply as repressive and as a metonym for the Orient but also as a space of women's sexuality. Western writers, in fact, were both disturbed with and fascinated by the idea of "women [in the harem] being freely and continuously together, and the degradation and licentiousness, and corruption that must inevitably ensue."[37] Meredith, in his dream vision, is similarly thrown into confusion by the intimacy of Havilah and Maysunnah. Cultural and gendered otherness intersect to undermine the coherence of the imperial body. Meredith's embodiment of maleness and power is challenged as he is "lost," "bewildered," and "assailed" not only by the "Arabic characters" and Koranic inscriptions that interrupt his cognitive mapping of the Orient but by the women, whose intimacy threatens his sense of heterosexual wholeness. And instead of the Orient mirroring his desire and becoming the narcissistic projection of his needs, Meredith finds mirrored his own inability to create order in a culture whose otherness he has come to interpret.

In representing the epistemological crisis of Western logic and of patriarchal authority in the context of voyaging the Near Eastern Orient, Cummins participates in an important critique of the technologies of imperial knowledge, a knowledge that had been appropriated by the popular imagination in the wake of Egyptology. For some women writers, the idea of the Westerner attempting to construct the Orient as a species of knowledge was quite appealing. Elizabeth Stuart Phelps, in *The Story of Avis,* used the Sphinx, an admittedly overdetermined figure, to demonstrate the resistance of the Orient to the calculations and the control of the West. Avis, the artist whose creativity is stifled under the burden of marriage and child rearing, turns repeatedly to her painting of the Sphinx in an attempt to solve its enigma. Like the male archaeologist of the missionary novels, Avis tries feverishly to interpret the Sphinx: "Against a deep sky, palpitant with the purple soul of Egypt, the riddle of the ages rose with a certain majesty. . . ."[38] Finally, overcome by want of time, money, and fresh inspiration, Avis strikes the Sphinx dumb by painting an Arab child "looking at the sphinx with his finger on his lips, swearing her to silence."[39] Although there are obvious class differences between the leisured and moneyed archaeologist and the impoverished artist laboring in her home, the confidence in being able to interpret the Orient is similar in both. Indeed, Phelps exposes the presumptions of her heroine by having the heroine see the Sphinx in a vision where it stands for all womanhood: "The riddle of ages whispered to her. The mystery of woman-hood stood before her, and said

"Speak for me."[40] White womanhood is invited to speak for all women through a figure that is ambiguous in terms of both race and gender and that is thus an apt symbol of the fear of African womanhood and the alterity of the Near Eastern Oriental woman. Phelps, by dramatizing Avis's repeated frustrations in giving voice to the Sphinx, critiques the idea that the Orient needs to be spoken for.

In *El Fureidis* too, the embodiment of the hero as explorer and interpreter of the Orient is complicated and thwarted by cultural-racial borderlands and hybrid constructions. The ruins of Syria, we are told, have passed through Roman, Christian, and Saracenic dynasties, each of which have left their impress on the culture and resist easy interpretation. Yet the text continues the Columbiad vision, appropriating the Near East as the new frontier. Meredith, a self-exiled aristocrat from England, comes to El Fureidis, a veritable "colony" described in terms that echo New England patriarch William Bradford. El Fureidis is "a beacon set upon a hill," an example to the rest of the country and a means of uplifting the natives. This nineteenth-century, Near Eastern beacon on a hill is a paradigm of the new imperial frontier. Father Lapierre, the spiritual head of El Fureidis, explains:

> Already men's eyes are turned upon us. Western Europe and enterprising America are emulating each other in their beneficent labors in this direction. Science is sounding our harbors, calculating the height of our mountains, surveying our wildernesses, and taking the measure of our streams; and religion lends her aid and sanction to the work, for a faithful band of Christian missionaries are in the van of the reforming army. (272)

The transfer of the rhetoric of colonial New England onto the Near East constructs the latter as a nineteenth-century frontier. And as with the early New England colonizers, racial alterity and anxiety is a fundamental condition of this frontier. Meredith is guided into El Fureidis by the Arab youth Abdoul, of whom he is inordinately suspicious and distrustful. Once at El Fureidis, Meredith falls into a delirium in which the sight of Abdoul "never fail[s] to agitate or disturb" (30).

Cummins's version of the new frontier, however, undermines and questions the patriarchal construction of the westerly vision. Here, the hero's body is subject to the voyeuristic gaze of the Orientals. Lying passive in bed due to an illness, Meredith is the object of curiosity for native children, who "[take] possession of the outer room of the dwelling, and by their juvenile pranks and licensed stares excit[e] the Englishman almost to frenzy" (30). Once recovered from his illness, Meredith sets his sights on Havilah, the daughter of USAmerican businessman M. Trefoil, but is rebuffed. Unlike DeForest's novel, where the self-aggrandizing archaeologist is rewarded from the beginning with the affections of Irene Grant, in *El Fureidis* the racial borderlands of the Near East are used to reconfigure the heroine, undermine the phallocentric and imperial stature of the exploring hero embodying the New World, and rewrite the conventional love plot.

Havilah is differently gendered because of her dual acculturation as Western and Oriental. Her mixture is first described through the traditional oppositions between Western intellect and Eastern passion: "Born beneath an Indian sun, but with the fresh life of the West glowing in her veins, Havilah was at once the imaginative, impassioned child of the Orient, and the active, intelligent representative of a race . . . diverse to the Asiatic type" (62). However, Cummins soon makes clear that Havilah's cultural engendering represents a critique of the construction of woman's sphere in mid-nineteenth-century USAmerica and of the association of intellect with the West alone. Havilah's reading, for instance, is not that "with which a Western belle is wont to beguile an idle hour" but Greek and Syriac manuscripts, French scientific works, and Arabic lore (63).

It is not surprising, therefore, that Havilah becomes Meredith's cultural mentor, deciphering old Saracenic inscriptions and explicating differences among types of ancient architectures. Within the ideology of true womanhood, such a role as Havilah's would have been inconceivable. Although women in the mid–nineteenth century were avid readers and were criticized for this habit, what clergymen found reprehensible was the idea of women's pleasure. Clergymen wrote sternly about the loss of domestic values when idle women spent their time lounging on chairs, engrossed in licentious romances. But even though they were readers, women were seen as passive consumers of novels, rather than as active agents interpreting and transforming what they read. In *El Fureidis*, however, Havilah's mixed cultural embodiment enables Cummins to project Havilah as an active reader. In a dramatic moment that might well be a revision of Hawthorne's *Scarlet Letter*, where Roger Chillingworth is engaged in the process of "reading" the guilty minister, Dimmesdale, Cummins uses the trope of interpretation to describe Havilah's "reading" and rejection of Meredith: "[Havilah] was reading and comprehending him as no mortal had ever done before. . . . she had probed the depths of his unsatisfied soul, and had beheld the void within" (97). In an inversion of the conventional women's plot, Havilah rejects Meredith's suit until he attains (moral) virtue and is rewarded.

Cummins uses cultural hybridity as a means both of questioning the West's ability to create a disciplinary knowledge of the Orient and of subverting the phallocentric and raced bases of U.S. cultural imperialism. Cummins also demystifies the most prevalent symbol of Western imperial desire—the harem—and thereby questions the dichotomies on which the imperial body within Near Eastern Orientalist discourse is constructed. In addition to using the harem, suggestively, as a sexual space that breaks normative heterosexual constructions of gender, Cummins also uses the harem as maternal space. While Havilah and Meredith are returning from Damascus to El Fureidis, they stop at the Bedouin encampment of Abdoul's family. The harem and the Bedouin encampment as a whole become sites through which complex racial questions are mediated and racial hierarchies questioned. Cummins takes us to the interior of the Bedouin structure, where the harem is represented primarily as a gendered, nurturing, domestic social space for women.[41] It is at once "the storehouse, kitchen, bedroom, and nursery of the household" (334). Havilah rests in the harem while the women there engage in the household tasks of cooking and cleaning. Fatigued after the day's journey, Havilah is soothed into sleep "as by a lullaby, for the last sound she heard was the voice of the old woman, who, seating herself on the carpet, swayed her bent form backward and forward, and in monotonous tones invoked the peace of Allah upon her beautiful charge" (337).

This instance of breaking the silence of the Oriental woman is particularly important because it occurs in the harem and through an old woman who is very much part of the harem. In the context of mid-nineteenth-century USAmerica, this productive re-creation of the harem cannot help but recall the peculiar position of black women within the ideologies of womanhood and the sphere of the home. Just as the harem was fantasized as a sexual space (distanced from, yet inviting, the Westerner), the black woman was viewed as a figure of illicit sexuality (who had invited institutionalized rape).[42] As black nanny, however, the black woman was a safe, if unattractive, figure. Cummins's re-creation of the nanny as the Oriental woman (and vice versa) questions forcefully the rigidity of racial gendering and upsets the polarities of Near Eastern orientalism.

Close to the end of the novel, Cummins recuperates the imperial missionary impulse through subplots in which Havilah (who is part USAmerican) saves the physically and morally imprisoned body of the Syrian woman Maysunnah from near death through the power of Christian conversion, while Meredith exposes the treachery and vileness of Havilah's childhood friend Abdoul. Through appeal to Maysunnah's Moslem father, who agrees to his daughter's conversion, Havilah rescues the Eastern woman. Maysunnah is figured as an object of pity; she is "beseeching, pathetic [in her] appeal . . . , encumbered and oppressed by the richness and weight of her costume," "diminutive, feeble, and pale," and "long imprisoned from the light," in the darkness of the harem (290). Such pitiable representations must have held appeal to popular audiences regardless of whether or not any traveler had actually encountered a pitiable woman from a harem. Missionary reverend Henry Harris Jessup, for instance, titled his book on Arab life *The Women of the Arabs*. He delighted, among other things, in depicting the physical abuse of Moslem women and describing in detail torturous happenings he could not possibly have seen.[43] Cummins's use of the figure of the abused Moslem woman, coming so close toward the end of the novel, suggests an analogous need to accede to popular representations.

Similarly, the hero is also shown to acquire imperial status. Meredith, who gains moral stature as the novel progresses by saving El Fureidis from destruction by flooding, feels toward the Arabs and all the "errant children of the earth, paupers in all that is wealth and joy to the civilized man," an appropriate colonial paternalism. The novel ends with the marriage of Havilah and Meredith and with the couple's forgiveness of Abdoul, who forgets his illegitimate desires toward Havilah. The male explorer, transformed by the piety of the mission, unites with the pure (even if somewhat Eastern) missionary, and the specter of racial otherness is rendered harmless.

Near Eastern Orientalist discourses offered popular writers rhetorical and ideological structures through which they could negotiate the vexed imperial narrative of the new frontier. Egyptology, signifying anxieties about racial-cultural origins, when mapped onto the racial borderlands of the Near East, generated a counterorientalist discourse contained only by the recuperation of the patriarchal, imperial narrative as closure in DeForest's, Cummins's, Ware's, and Ballou's works. For African American writers, however, precisely Egyptology's racial-cultural challenge to Eurocentric epistemologies needed to be foregrounded. Eager to join the fray of voices debating the racial origins of Egyptians, African American writers debated with and critiqued the exclusivist ethnological arguments of Morton, Nott, and Gliddon. The negotiation of African American writers with the borderlands of the Near East and with the narratives of frontier and empire, however, was far from simple. If Near Eastern Orientalism as a discourse of power legitimated an imperial subjectivity, could an African American writer in antebellum USAmerica, even though that writer was highly critical of white Egyptology, afford to abrogate the privileges accorded such a narrating subject? David F. Dorr's *A Colored Man Round the World* (1858) and Frederick Douglass's ruminations about Egyptology insistently provoke such a question, thus illustrating the omnivorous attraction of Orientalist narratives of empire.

One of the few African Americans to have traveled around the world in the mid–nineteenth century, David F. Dorr published his travel narrative in 1858. Dorr's account includes his travels in numerous European countries—including England, France, and Germany—and in Egypt, Turkey, and Syria. The structure of the narrative, however, makes clear that the findings of Egyptology are of central significance to the account. In the African American cultural imaginary, Egyptology signified the civilization and power of black Africans. Dorr's preface is an exuberant celebration of Egyptology as a racial-cultural signifier. Dorr opens his book thus:

> The Author of this book, though a quadroon, is pleased to announce himself the "Colored man around the world." Not because he may look at a colored man's position as an honorable one at this age of the world, he is too smart for that, but because he has the satisfaction of looking with his own eyes and reason at the ruins of the Author's ancestors of which he is the posterity. If the ruins of the Author's ancestors were not a living language of their scientific majesty, this book could receive no such appellation with pride. Luxor, Carnack, the Memnonian and the Pyramids make us exclaim, "What monuments of pride can surpass these?"[44]

Because of his lineage, with its antecedents in the race that built the Pyramids, Dorr suggests that he can proudly advertise his book as that written by "a colored man." Even though being a quadroon is a signifier of severely limited agency, once the racial signifier is let loose from the quantifications of the antebellum South, it can operate differently. Egyptology has resignified what being "colored" means. Yet Dorr is painfully aware of the ironies attendant on celebrating blackness. He is only free to write because he is now in Ohio instead of Louisiana, where he "was legally a slave, and would be to-day, like [his] mother."[45] Indeed, the limits to his freedom are made painfully obvious in the dedication that Dorr places immediately before the preface, "To My *Slave* Mother" (emphasis mine); the narrator is apparently unaware of his mother's whereabouts. The book ends with a polemic against polygenesis, with the author citing Dickens, "The European, Ethiopean, Mongolian, and American, are but different varieties of one species."[46] Clearly, for Dorr, as for Morton and Gliddon, Egyptology was intimately connected with the racial discourses of the mid–nineteenth century.

But as we have seen with such writers as DeForest, Cummins, and Ware, the discourses of missionary/hermeneutic Near Eastern Orientalism also generated patriarchal, imperial narratives that were recuperated to maintain the hierarchies of observer/observed, order/chaos, activity/passivity, and morality/licentiousness. Dorr, too, needed the epistemic possibilities of Near Eastern Orientalist discourse, a discourse he could enter into not as a novelist, as could white USAmericans, but through the only form permitted an African American—the nonfictional and testimonial.[47] Yet Dorr retained within his travel narrative many of the tropes of popular Near Eastern Orientalism; in particular, the narrator is especially attracted to the role of knowing, empowered hermeneute elsewhere accorded the USAmerican embodying the nation. The "colored man," whose ownership of his own body was highly contingent in the United States, and who would not be recognized as a citizen, even de jure, for another decade, could claim a freedom and masculinity by embodying the nation when abroad. As an "American" round the world, Dorr fancies himself an empowered hero with constant access to the maidservants that wait on him. The Orient is backward and slothful, but it is also a mystery to be unveiled by the USAmerican male. Thus the title of the chapter on Istanbul (Constantinople) comically reads, "The Dogs Provoke Me, And The Women Are Veiled." Dorr's Turkish women—unreal, inactive, fragile, diminutive, and mystifying, yet inviting—seem to be a metonym for a supine Orient against which the author defines his masculinity. Dorr writes: "I would have given five pds to lift her veil; I know she was pretty, her voice was so fluty, and her hands so delicate, and her feet so small, and her dress so gauzy; she was like an eel. I do not believe she had any bones in her."[48] The Orient as woman is delicate, easily shattered, and without agency. And like the exploring New World hero, Dorr is fascinated with the ultimate signifier of the impenetrable East: the harem, with its women "as pure as silvan nymphs," taking "their baths in all attitudes of pleasure"[49]

Exploiting the patriarchal imperatives of Orientalist discourse answered the needs of Dorr as an African American to affirm his self-hood in a culture that denied him legitimacy both as a subject of a nation and as a male subject.[50] Because slavery was perpetuated by the condition of the mother (the child of a slave mother and free black was a slave), patriarchy was effectively denied the African American male. Claiming manhood was thus crucial in questioning the hierarchies of the slave system. Thus, when Douglass joined the debates about Egyptology and race, arguing vociferously against the conclusions reached by Morton in *Crania Americana* and by such ethnologists as Nott, Gliddon, and Agassiz, he prefaced them by repeated statements about the manhood of African Americans, statements in which the very insistent reiterations and contextual usage of the term *manhood* suggest that it operates more as a gendered signifier than as a signifier for a general humanity. Douglass writes: "The first general claim which may here be set up, respects the manhood of the Negro. This is an elementary claim, simple enough, but not without question. It is fiercely opposed."[51] African American manhood, Douglass suggests, is evidenced by the African American's dominion and control over nature: "You may see him yoke the oxen, harness the horse, and hold the plow. . . . The horse bears him on his back—admits his mastery and dominion. . . . All these know that the Negro is a MAN."[52] These gendered arguments form the preamble to Douglass's later critiques of raced Egyptology and to his conclusion that "a strong affinity and a direct relationship may be claimed by the Negro race, to *that grandest of all nations of antiquity, the builders of the pyramids.*"[53] African American manhood is further validated by the findings of Egyptology.

Dorr's frequent representations of veiled Oriental women, effeminate, sagacious sultans, and wily local Arabs in a text subversive of white racial hierarchies evokes the anxious investment in masculinity and power for African American men. It demonstrates the omnivorous appeal of patriarchal Orientalist discourses even while it simultaneously evokes the contingency of this maleness for a subject whose access to his own body is tenuous at best. Thus, the representation of slavery in the discourse of the Near Eastern Orient disrupts, but is contained within the seamless discourse. Informed by a guide that the Turkish woman who is the object of his gaze is for sale, the narrator jocularly writes, "I told him to go and buy her for me and asked him who owned her, he said, her mother, but I could not buy her because I was no Mohammedan."[54] The unfree body of the Turkish woman, signifying on the unfree slave bodies of the antebellum United States, is assimilated within the hierarchies of orientalism that empower the observer. Similarly, Frank Parish, the free USAmerican of "ginger-bread color," towers over the weak, effeminate, dwarf-like sultan of Stamboul, much in the manner that Maria Susanna Cummins's Meredith, the hero of El Fureidis, towers over his Arab adversary, Abdoul.[55]

As raced discourses, missionary conversion and Egyptology provided popular writers with structures against and within which the tensions and contradictions of the imperial narrative of the new frontier could be articulated. With many of the writers, satire became the means by which the ideological contradictions in the construction of the archaeologist/missionary imperial body of the nation could be unraveled and exposed. The male hermeneute, on a journey to master the Orient, could often be bewildered by the object of his study; the subject of conversion could often resist hierarchical racial definition; and the narrative could state as its purpose the resignification of both blackness and slavery. Meanwhile the recuperation of the patriarchal, imperial narrative at the end of DeForest's, Cummins's, Ware's, and Ballou's works, and as a safe structure within Dorr's narrative suggests both the constraints of the oppositional ideologies of these writers, and of the subversive possibilities of the satiric mode within the context of Orientalism. It remained for Poe, Spofford, and Melville to script the appropriation of the Near East as the new frontier as tragic by undermining the very morality and certainty of the familiar New World imperial tropes of discovery and control.

4

Subversive Orientalisms:
Edgar Allan Poe, Harriet Prescott Spofford,
and Herman Melville

The Near Eastern Orientalist writers discussed in the previous chapter produced texts that were highly conflicted because of their simultaneous critique of missionary and Egyptological power and their investment in theories of the westerly movement of empire and the raced hierarchies of Orientalism. Poe, Spofford, and Melville position themselves more critically against the discourses of Near Eastern Orientalism. The comic and satiric critique of Orientalist power gives way, here, to a demonstration of the tragic consequences of mastery and control. Like the missionary-colonial novelists, Poe, Spofford, and Melville critique the appropriation of the Near Eastern Orient and the naïveté with which USAmericans believe they can, as an ostensibly noncolonizing power, righteously interpret and bring civilization and moral order to the Near East. The tragic Orientalists evoke the idea of the Near East as new frontier through its critique. Resisting ideologies of the westerly movement of empire and New World imperialism, these texts replace the imperialism as closure in the works of missionary-colonial novelists with chaos and nonclosure. In the texts of Poe, Spofford, and Melville, the Near Eastern Orient resists being Othered and causes an epistemological crisis for the adventuring hero from the New World. This chapter examines the critique of imperial-hermeneutic power through a raced and gendered destabilization of the body of the hero in several works, focusing particularly on Poe's "Ligeia," Spofford's "Desert Sands," and Melville's *Clarel*.

The tales of Edgar Allan Poe are among the earliest in Near Eastern Orientalist literature. Of the texts discussed in the previous chapter, only William Ware's *Letters of Lucius M. Piso* (*Zenobia*) was published before Poe wrote the majority of his tales. Yet Poe's tales were also influenced by the vogue for Egyptology and the interest in missionary and quasi-missionary travel to the Near East, just as were the writings of Cummins, DeForest, Murray, and Ware. Like many of his contemporaries, Poe had a deep interest in the Near East. He was fascinated with the discoveries of Jean-François Champollion and with Alexander von Humboldt, the geographer and explorer greatly interested in hieroglyphics, to whom Poe dedicated *Eureka*.[1] John T. Irwin suggests that for Poe, Champollion, "in his role as a decipherer of cryptic writing, had the greatest personal significance."[2] In October 1837 Poe published a laudatory review of John Lloyd Stephens's *Egypt* in the *New York Review*. Indeed, Poe's imagination delighted in using the Near East. Out of twenty-five tales in his collection *Tales of the Grotesque and Arabesque*, only five do not have references to the Near East.[3]

Yet, although Poe was attracted to the power of Orientalist discourse, he was acutely aware of the historical nightmare of colonization and constantly parodied the culture's colonial use of the Orient (most notably in "The Thousand-and-Second Tale of Scheherazade"). At the same time, he positioned himself as a Southerner who was ambivalently attached to the inherently raced idea of a Southern nationhood. Poe offers a particularly interesting case of Near Eastern Orientalist writing, because in his works, a parodied Orientalist discourse, critical of imperial nationalism, intersects with raced discourses on Southern nationalism, resulting in epistemological crises of the gendered and raced hierarchies of imperialism.

We know much of Poe's politics through his journalism. Sidney Kaplan notes that while nationalism was being articulated by many Northern writers through a support for abolition, Poe felt "called upon to say that slavemasters had violated no law divine."[4] Kenneth Silverman writes that Poe opposed abolition and "identified with the slaveholding interests in the South, whom he felt Northern writers misrepresented."[5] Because Poe was a Southern writer, his defense of slavery should come as no surprise.[6] Southern nationalism, which was predicated on the culture of slave ownership, was at its peak in the 1830s due to the tariff crisis. There were also calls for a distinctive Southern literature.

Northern nationalism, which was projected as the paradigm for the nation at large, was projected in images of providential nation, enterprise, and heroic manly bodies and was linked to ideas of expansion both within the Americas and beyond. The sheer geographical reach of the rhetoric of expansion culminated in the 1840s and 1850s with calls for drives into Asia, both to civilize it and to reap benefits from trade.[7] For Poe, Spofford, and Melville, the idea of hermeneutical power over the Near East, an imperial epistemology, was most significantly related to conceptions of nation and race and therefore needed to be critiqued.

Because Poe is often thought of as an apolitical writer, it is important to emphasize that his literary imagination was deeply sensitive to questions of national (racial) self-definition. Although *The Narrative of Arthur Gordon Pym,* for instance, is often read simply in symbolic or psychoanalytic terms, it is clear that the novel dramatizes the uncertain state of nationhood through the economy of ship as nation.[8] The allegory of the antebellum South striving to create a nation is all too clear. Fears of slave empowerment are played out through Seymour, the black mutineer on the *Grampus,* who is finally overcome by the simulated rebirth of a dead seaman, a role played by Pym, the lone white boy seeking to restore order on the ship/nation. It would be surprising if Poe were not aware of the totally wishful nature of the racial politics (where the white hero survives all) played out in *Pym.* Indeed, Poe deliberately creates this politics and then deconstructs the idea of westering white heroism (and substitutes for it a barbaric whiteness) by making Pym commit a crucial racial slip. When the *Jane Guy* is destroyed by black natives and Pym escapes with the Native American ("hybrid") Peters, Pym records that he and Peters "are the only living white men upon the island."[9] The slip through which the Native American, an individual from among the races decimated in the name of nationalism and westward expansion, is turned into the race of the colonizer is a means by which the Native American is treated as not black, a nonthreat, an ally of the white man, and therefore an imaginary comfort for Pym, rather than a thorn by his side. In the context of antebellum racial polarization, the relabeling of Peters as white is also a liberal move that indicates a desire to include racial others in the construction of national identity. The entire episode suggests Poe's complex involvement with and awareness of issues of race and conquest.

Questions of empire and Western colonization frequently arose in Poe's tales. Poe had read Macaulay's review of *The Memoirs of Warren Hastings* and used some of the material in his story "A Tale of the Ragged Mountains."[10] The story recounts the mental breakdown of Augustus Bedlo upon vividly hallucinating a scene from colonial India

in which he, along with other Europeans, is being chased into dark
alleys by a rabble of natives who refuse to be controlled by the native
policemen.[11] The harried Bedlo, it is suggested, is an incarnation of a Mr.
Oldeb, an officer of the empire killed during a native insurrection in
Benares in 1780. But Bedlo and Oldeb, as the twinning of their names
suggests, are not temporally or bodily distinct characters. Poe homo-
erotically links one to the other so that the pleasurable consumption of
Oldeb's life by Bedlo results in the latter's death. Bedlo enacts the role of
colonial Orientalist but is unable to master the Orient by creating it as
his text. Instead, the Orient overpowers him as he loses all sense of
agency and self.

Bedlo's contact with the Orient begins with his reenacting the trope
of discovery, both of the New World and of the Orient, the ostensible
goal of Columbus's quest. Through this relationship between the New
World and the Orient, Poe makes an important ideological connection
between colonization and the history of USAmerica. As Bedlo saunters
to the site of his Oriental vision, he believes "that the green sods and the
gray rocks upon which I trod, had been trodden never before by the foot
of a human being."[12] Poe's representation of Bedlo's vision begins like a
narrative of pioneer exploration, a discovery of "empty" lands; however, the city ahead of him is Oriental. A glimpse of an Eastern city rises
before him, and Bedlo attempts to defuse its difference by writing about
it as part of an easily recognizable cultural repertoire, "an Eastern-look-
ing city, such as we read of in the Arabian Tales." The city has "a wilderness of balconies, of verandas, of minarets, of shrines, . . . silks, muslins,
the most dazzling cutlery, the most magnificent jewels."[13] But as Bedlo
changes from being empowered observer to forced witness of native
will, he flounders. Terrified as he watches the native uprising, he loses
all sense of selfhood as the imperial body literally dissipates: "I had no
bodily, no visible, audible, or palpable presence." Only as this colonial
vision recedes does he regain "the sense of weight, of volition, of substance" and become his "original self."[14]

Despite the ease with which he used European settings in many of
his tales, Poe chooses not to do so here. Instead, he sets this tale of British
colonialism in Charlottesville, Virginia, in 1827. Charlottesville was
important to Poe because he attended the University of Virginia there
and because it was the residence of Thomas Jefferson, the founder of the
university. In his career, Jefferson combined a rhetoric of freedom with
a personal practice of slavery. But surely Poe must have also had in
mind the Jefferson who authorized USAmerican expansion by sending

out Lewis and Clark; we know from his "Journal of Julius Rodman" that Poe was interested in their expeditions.[15] By situating the tale in Charlottesville, Poe suggests a parallel between the culture of Southern slave plantations and colonialism, the moral burden of which will remain for generations to bear. The "gentleman" bodily exterior of Bedlo, whose "amiable manners and many virtues" have endeared him to the citizens of Charlottesville, is contoured by an exclusion of native suppression.

"A Tale of the Ragged Mountains" undermines both the discourse of colonialism and that of Orientalism. The Orient, instead of being easily available for Western consumption and a means of defining nationhood, literally consumes the Westerner. A more farcical subversion of Western cultural imperialism occurs in "Some Words with a Mummy," where a mummy that scholars attempt to study comes to life and delivers a harangue on the inferiority of contemporary USAmerican civilization. The spectral body of the Oriental becomes more powerful than the real bodies of USAmerican men. The Egyptian (mummy) finds the Capitol at Washington, D.C., insignificant in comparison to the palace at Karnac; he considers the railways ill conceived as compared to the iron-grooved causeways on which Egyptians transported temples and obelisks; and finally he sees the USAmerican democratic experiment as a failure, albeit well intentioned. The mummy's arguments produce a radical historical revision of USAmerican conceptions of epistemology, time, and space. Instead of USAmerica (the latest westerly nation) embodying rationality and scientific progress, Egypt now embodies it. In an inversion of the Columbian and westerly visions of civilization progressing to the New World, USAmerica represents the past and Egypt represents present and future progress.

In "Ligeia," signifiers of the Orient and Southern womanhood intersect to generate an epistemological crisis about nationalism and empire. It has been obvious to readers of the tale that at the constative level, Ligeia and Rowena represent contrasting types of womanhood—the dark and the light. It is also clear that at the performative level, Poe clearly deconstructs this traditional symbology. The dark, passionate Ligeia also has a low, sweet voice and a cold, marble touch; the fair Rowena has the capacity to become a Ligeia and, through her rebirth, to question boundaries between life and death. But Ligeia and Rowena are more than abstractions of womanhood. Ligeia clearly represents Near Eastern Oriental knowledge, the control over which was a defining feature of USAmerican nationhood in the early and middle years of the nineteenth century.

"Ligeia" begins with an entry into a dreamlike state, which for Near Eastern Orientalist writers signified either the East or the harem, which was a metonym for the East. In Ballou's *The Turkish Slave*, the sultan of the harem is in a constant "dreamy, half intoxicated" state.[16] Meredith, the hero of Cummins's Oriental novel, feasts, wines, and smokes a soothing opium pipe before attaining the "elysium of the Oriental."[17] "Ligeia" anticipates the trope of the East in its opening, where time, space, and causality are all held in abeyance: "I cannot, for my soul, remember how, when, or even precisely where, I first became acquainted with the lady Ligeia."[18]

The physical description of Ligeia also clearly confirms her embodiment of the Near Eastern Orient. Ligeia's hair is "raven-black" with "glossy," "luxuriant and naturally curling tresses." Her eyes are described as "far larger than the ordinary eyes of our own race." They are even "fuller than the fullest of the gazelle eyes of the tribe of the valley of Nourjahad." The color of her eyes is the "most brilliant of black," and over them are "jetty lashes of great length." Her beauty appears to the narrator to be otherworldly, comparable to nothing other than "the beauty of the fabulous Houri of the Turk" (80). And like the "Orient," which with the popularity of Egyptology was revealed to have an ancient language and culture—indeed it was perceived to be a challenge to the centrality of Western civilization—Ligeia is well learned. Her eyes have a profundity unmatched anywhere other than in the well of Democritus (81);[19] she is proficient in many classical languages and deeply immersed in metaphysical studies.

Ligeia's vast knowledge, combined with her Near Eastern looks, associates her with the culture and learning of the region. Egyptology, as we know, revealed the existence of a civilization and culture that predated the West. Epistemological control over this culture (which was not necessarily coincident with possession of lands and peoples, although indirect possession in terms of control of trade cannot be ruled out) soon began to be seen as an index of the power of a nation. Knowledge of the Orient meant not simply discovering what was there but knowing it in its totality better than the natives and mastering it. Writers of missionary-colonial novels, such as DeForest and Cummins, used the figure of the male archaeologist precisely to parody this attempt at control.

Poe's dark Ligeia, like the Near Eastern Orient, is also a possessor of knowledge beyond that of the West. She is proficient in "classical tongues" and knows more of "moral, physical, and mathematical science" than any other person known to the narrator—male or female (81, 82). Her learning is so vast that it sets her at a distance from the narrator and re-creates, as Jay B. Hubbell puts it, the Petrarchan ideal of the lady that Southern writers, Poe included, particularly delighted in commemorating.[20] With Ligeia, Poe signifies on this Petrarchan ideal and maps onto it the idea of the Orient, lands that were deemed to be similarly inaccessible. Poe's narrator, like the Orientalist, is anxious to fully understand Ligeia's repository of knowledge. He is epistemologically positioned very much like the voyager-archaeologist of the mid–nineteenth century who was later figured in the novels of Cummins and DeForest. He ruminates: "What was it . . . which lay far within the pupils of my beloved? What *was* it? I was possessed with a passion to discover" (81).

Discover, which comes from the Latin words *dis* (apart) and *cooperire* (to cover), carries in its meaning both the will to knowledge and the unveiling or the revelation of a hidden source, as if for the first time. The trope of discovery is the site where Orient and woman intersect. In "Ligeia," the desire of the narrator to discover Ligeia's knowledge is presented in tones that are wild, exclamatory, and highly sexualized. The narrator recollects, "And thus how frequently, in my intense scrutiny of Ligeia's eyes, have I felt approaching the *full knowledge* of their expression—felt it approaching—*yet not quite be mine*" (emphasis mine). And as if recording an act of complete empowerment, the narrator states, "Ligeia's beauty passed into my spirit, there dwelling as in a shrine" (81).

But Poe could not simply accept the imperialist myth of control through which the United States was defining itself both in missionary activities and in popular writings, such as William Ware's. Poe positions the narrator as "discoverer" of Ligeia—and thus as the potential embodiment of the nation as an empire—only to upset the gendered power dynamics between observer and observed, West and East, male and female. Cynthia Jordan, in fact, sees Poe's stories about women as means of demonstrating the repressiveness of androcentric culture and giving voice to the otherness represented by women.[21] I suggest that Poe also gives voice to the otherness of the Near Eastern Orient and that in "Ligeia," as I will discuss later, he also attempts to confront the gendered otherness of homosexism. Ligeia's superhuman struggles against death, the intensity of her desire for life, and her agency are beyond the narrator's powers of observation or discovery. Long after her death, the narrator remembers this manifestation of will in Ligeia and suffers bodily agitation. Her quest for life goes beyond the limits of the Oriental subject position and of her subject position as a woman (the narrator recalls her "more than womanly abandonment to . . . love") and creates an undefined space that the narrator finds difficult to map linguistically: "It is this wild longing—it is this eager vehemence of desire for life—but for life—that I have *no power to portray—no utterance capable of expressing*" (82–83; emphasis mine). The narrator also finds words "impotent" in conveying her wild desire for life, because this desire cannot be interpreted simply through the reason/emotion and mind/body dichotomies offered in Western metaphysics, and on which traditional Oriental representation also depends. Ligeia upsets the traditional dichotomy between Western reason and Oriental passion by embodying both. As the narrator recalls, neither "solace" nor "reason" work in trying to deal with Ligeia's death throes (82).

Poe also sets up the narrator's relationship with Ligeia in terms that parallel, yet subvert, traditional discursive relations between the Orient and the New World. While the Near Eastern Orient, for the most part, was gendered in terms of knowledge to be mastered or an illicit, often threatening sexuality that needed control, the Far East, a generation later, was pictured either as essential woman or as the mother to whom the Western subject desired to return. Walt Whitman, in "A Broadway Pageant," contrasts "America," the "Young Libertad," with "venerable Asia, the all-mother."[22] In "Facing West from California's Shores," he looks on India as "the house of maternity" to which the poet, a "child" of the New World, would go, "seeking what is yet unfound."[23] Whitman constructs the Orient as mother but simultaneously repeats the colonialist trope of discovery by suggesting that the Orient is "unfound" (not there) until it is found/discovered by the West. Ralph Waldo Emerson similarly looked to the East as the past, drawing a contrast between the "devout and contemplative East," which one could learn from, and America, which was the present.[24]

Poe's representation of Ligeia as engaged in studies of transcendentalism calls to mind early transcendentalist use of the East as a site of feel-good colonialist retrieval of knowledge.[25] In the face of Ligeia's "gigantic" and "astounding" knowledge, the narrator resigns himself "with a childlike confidence" to her guidance. But unlike the transcendentalists' Orient, the Orient of Poe is not simply an abstraction to be retrieved at will. So great is Ligeia's power that even her memory consigns the narrator to silence. Poe even inserts a certain ambivalence in the narrator's statements about his grief over Ligeia's death: "How poignant, then, *must have been*, the grief with which, after some years, I beheld my well-grounded expectations take wings to themselves and fly away" (82). The use of the phrase *must have been* instead of the verb *was* suggests both an ambiguity in the narrator's relations with Ligeia and an uncertainty in representation that questions the traditional orientalist stance of hermeneutic power and control.

The "death" of Ligeia ends the first part of the story; the second part concerns the narrator's move to an abbey, his fantastical decorating of it, his marriage to Rowena, her death, and Ligeia/Rowena's coming back to life. In this section the discourses on imperial Orientalist self-definition, slavery, and Southern nationalism (as embodied in the ideal of Southern womanhood) intersect. At a most fundamental level, the narrator's decorations of his future bridal chamber question and parody the fetish for exotic Oriental decor in the mid–nineteenth century. The increased trade with the East, particularly in New England, created and sustained a demand for Eastern goods.[26] Part of the impulse behind this Eastern craze was the domestication of the exotic, a manner of asserting what Bill Ashcroft calls "the ability of the superior European civilization which was 'on the side of history' to absorb and surpass their achievements."[27]

Poe's narrator, however, furnishes his quarters with such a surplus and endless piling of oriental artifacts and does so with such self-consciousness that his actions parody those of Egyptologists seeking control over their subjects, though his efforts fall under the guise of "civilization" and "taste." The abbey has "gorgeous and fantastic draperies," "solemn carvings of Egypt" (83); the ceiling is "elaborately fretted with the wildest and most grotesque specimens of a semi-Gothic, semi-Druidical device"; there are "ottomans and golden candelabra, of Eastern figure," and "massive-looking tapestry" in the "richest cloth of gold, with arabesque figures"; and in "each of the angles of the chamber stood on end a gigantic sarcophagus of black granite, from the tombs of the kings over against Luxor" (84).

More important than the surplus of Oriental artifacts collected by the narrator is their particular location. It is surely significant that the narrator houses his fantastical Oriental furnishings in an old, gloomy, deserted abbey—a place of worship, asceticism, and faith. The abbey's "gloomy," "dreary," and "savage" aspects suggest the moral degeneration of Christianity, the supreme signifier of Western civilization. But the abbey here functions as more than a metaphor for Western civilization/Christianity. In the story it is also a gendered space, the place that the narrator deliberately demarcates as Rowena's bridal chamber, decorating it and preparing it for her arrival. It is the place where Rowena dies and where Ligeia makes her mummified appearance. Performatively, then, the abbey recalls not just the monastery but also the convent (it houses Rowena, the fair woman) and the harem (it houses Ligeia, the dark, Oriental woman).[28]

The idea that the abbey functions as a harem is actually not surprising if we remember the frequency with which the Near East and particularly Near Eastern women were associated with harems. In "Ligeia," the abbey, like the harem of the Western imaginary, is decorated in Eastern splendor; just as harems were seen as enclosed spaces (from which Eastern women had to be rescued), the abbey, with its sarcophagi, is associated with enclosure; Rowena's "bridal chamber" is situated in a high turret, again suggesting a haremlike inaccessibility; and the "trellis-work of an aged vine" over part of the window recalls the latticework architecture of harems. Most importantly, the bridal chamber, like the harem, houses not one woman but two—Ligeia and Rowena.

Western interest in harems emanated from the two kinds of illicit sexuality associated with them. The first, more popular kind was the idea of male sexual access to more than one woman. In this fantasy, the harem had functioned as a site onto which Western travelers could project their erotic fantasies and act out their desires for domination. It was the final enclosure, into which (visual) entry signaled victory for the Western voyeur. In the context of harem as enclosure, Poe's deliberate mapping of the harem onto the abbey signals an intent to call attention both to the commonality of gender concerns across cultures and to questions of power and control. In fact, French travel writers as early as the late seventeenth century had compared harems and convents. In a discussion of the recurrence of convents and harems in French fiction, Ruth Thomas points out that "[t]he convent and the harem are obviously both prisons for women." In each, Thomas continues, "the woman is viewed within a moralistic framework," and in each case the authority "has a similar origin and nature."[29] Just as the harem is organized around the single male figure to whom all the women belong, the convent is similarly polygamous, housing all the brides of the absent master, Christ.

The second kind of illicit sexuality associated with harems enriches our understanding of the tale as a critique of male imperialism and of the embodiment of nation as a powerful, exploring male. As Susanna Rowson demonstrates in Slaves in Algiers, harems were places specifically marked for women, where women could critique the world of men and form strong bonds among each other. The lesbian possibilities of this space had long fascinated Westerners, and USAmerican Orientalist writers like Rowson and Cummins had explored the potential of the harem to subvert traditional gender constructions. In "Ligeia," the dramatic movement of roughly the last quarter of the story revolves around the narrator trying to suppress his visions of seeing Ligeia and Rowena simultaneously as one, because his (bodily) identity depends on being able to construct the world according to dualities. But performatively, the text enacts the bonding of the two: Ligeia becomes Rowena, who becomes Ligeia, and so on. The text thus questions not simply androcentric culture but also the heterosexist culture that the narrator embodies and that is threatened in the narrative.

More broadly, then, "Ligeia" raises questions of power, identity, and gendering that are furthered by the story's images of enclosure, confinement, and multiple women. But surely we cannot overlook the significance of the preponderance of these images in the work of a writer who defended the institution of slavery, an institution that enslaved and confined slaves as instruments of material labor and created a system of polygamy where the white plantation owner had access to the bodies of black women.[30] In this structure the Southern white woman was located at the interstices of high culture and slavery. The Southern lady, like the slave woman (though by no means in the same position of powerlessness), was a part of the polygamous system, a part of the harem of the master. At the same time, she was upheld as an exemplar of values and virtues and an embodiment of the best of the Southern tradition.

Anne Goodwyn Jones has suggested that the idea of Southern womanhood became "a central symbol in the South's idea of itself." She writes, "The southern lady is at the core of a region's self-definition; the identity of the South is contingent in part upon the persistence of its tradition of the lady." "More than just a fragile flower," she continues, "the image of the southern lady represents her culture's idea of religious, moral, sexual, racial, and social perfection. . . . She embodies virtue, but her goodness depends directly on innocence—in fact, on ignorance of evil. She is chaste because she has never been tempted; in some renditions she lacks sexual interest altogether. Because it is unthinkable for her to desire sex, much less sex with a black man . . . her genes are pure white. . . . Finally, she serves others—God, husband, family, society— showing in her submissiveness the perfection of pure sacrifice."[31] Jones's work provides interesting insights into the cultural uses of the image of the Southern lady, making explicit the connection between nationalism and gendering. Jones shows how the female embodying the region is dissociated from the sexualized body. The beautiful, innocent, submissive, pure Southern lady, an icon to be protected and worshiped, literally represented Southern white identity.

Poe himself was not immune to the attraction exerted by this ideal. His own journalistic writings about women often reveal a striking similarity to idealistic descriptions of the Southern lady. Addressing the question of female education, for instance, Poe lauds the roles of wife and mother and ends with a plea against women entering the public domain, in which he invokes the spiritual status of women: "Her name is too sacred to be profaned by public breath."[32] Poe's representation of Rowena metonymically recalls this phantasmagorical ideal of Southern womanhood. I say that it does so metonymically because Rowena is not completely represented as the Southern lady; however, the parts of Southern identity that describe her are drawn from an assumption about the reader's familiarity with the whole.

The narrator of "Ligeia" prefaces his recollection of Rowena by calling attention to his deranged state of mind and his addiction to opium, suggesting the dreamlike nature of Rowena. Significantly, Poe's only use of the term *slave* in "Ligeia" occurs here: "I had become a bounden slave in the trammels of opium" (84). Although the word *slave* in the preceding sentence refers to the narrator's servitude to a drug that overpowers and controls him, its use in the context of the narratives of confinement and escape in the story signifies more than simply the narrator's vulnerability. Because this narrator single-mindedly creates a double enclosure—the harem mapped onto the abbey—into which he virtually entombs Rowena and from which the body of the woman (Rowena/Ligeia) will struggle to free itself, it is surely ironic that he thinks of himself as a slave. However, if we remember that in relation to Ligeia the narrator both subverts and appears as the Orientalist voyeur type, we can see that in his relation to Rowena he similarly plays on the role of the Southern white male. In treating the Southern white woman as if she were a phantasm or pure signification, the Southern male enslaved himself in the myth created by her.

Just as Southern womanhood was constructed against (and in opposition to) the womanhood of the slave woman, Rowena is represented as an antithesis to another type of womanhood—in this case woman as Orient or Orient as woman. Rowena is first represented in the story through signifiers of race. Unlike Ligeia, she is "the fair-haired and blue eyed." She belongs to a "haughty family" and is referred to as "Lady Rowena Trevanion, of Tremaine" (84). In contrast to Ligeia, whose paternal name the narrator cannot remember, Rowena belongs to the aristocracy. Like the ideal of Southern womanhood, Rowena suggests tradition and continuity. Her name itself, as Clark Griffith suggests, might be drawn from *Ivanhoe;*[33] and she is described in the language of chivalric tradition so popular with Southern romance writers, as "a maiden and daughter so beloved" (84). Unlike Ligeia, whose love was passionate and idolatrous, Rowena loves the narrator "but little" (85).

Poe also amply suggests that the world of the Southern national-istic imagination is askew by putting anachronistic details in the rep-resentation of Rowena. Just as Poe's detective, Dupin, was an aberrant, eccentric aristocrat without wealth or position, Rowena's family is haughty and titled but poor;[34] it is suggested that they allow Rowena to be imprisoned in marriage in the abbey/harem because of their "thirst of gold" (84). The narrator, instead of worshiping the image of womanhood that Rowena represents, loathes it "with a hatred belong-ing more to demon than to man" (85). Rowena dies, but only provi-sionally, and in her dying she questions the boundaries between life and death. She comes back to life, ripping apart the bandages that bind her (no doubt recalling the corsets that women had to wear to conform to an image of womanhood), but she does so only to startle the narra-tor and shake him from his musings. The moment he attempts to liter-ally revive her (by rubbing her face or calling to her), she lapses back into the image of death.

The representation of the fair-haired, blue-eyed Rowena of aristo-cratic stock incarcerated in the harem/abbey points both to the ideolog-ically confining nature of the image of Southern womanhood and to the actual incarceration of slave bodies within the Southern plantation sys-tem. Poe's apparent need to imaginatively wrestle with the image of Southern womanhood, the icon of Southern nationalistic desire, is per-fectly understandable given the rise of discourses on Southern national-ism in the 1820s and 1830s. Prompted by the crisis over the tariff in South Carolina, the ideology of Southern nationalism first appeared in the 1820s; with the launching of William Lloyd Garrison's *The Liberator* and the nullification crisis of the 1830s, this ideology was crystallized and at its peak.[35] Poe, although sympathetic to slavery, interrogated and deconstructed in his fiction the various discourses of nationalism, including that of Southern nationhood, which was at its height during the time he was writing.

The ending of "Ligeia" enacts a crisis of nationalism and of the heterosexism that underlies ideas of nationhood and the Orient, as the various icons of nationalistic discourses (as embodied in different types of womanhood) intersect and question each other. The fair-haired and blue-eyed Lady Rowena Trevanion of Tremaine—bandaged around mouth and body, like her corseted and supposedly voiceless sisters—appears to grow taller. At this point the picture of the Oriental woman (though no longer simply objectified) is mapped onto the image of Rowena. Rana Kabbani suggests that the contradictory demands made of women in Victorian England culminated in a fantasy of womanhood embodied in Jane Burden, who suggested an ethos: "When she came into a room, in her strangely beautiful garments, looking at least eight feet high the effect was as if she had walked out of an Egyptian tomb at Luxor."[36] Ligeia/Rowena resembles this alternative ethos that emerged from the perceived orientalizing of the ideal of beauty. The transformation of Rowena into Ligeia or the bonding of Rowena and Ligeia enacts a similar shift to the ideal of the Orient.

But while the images of the two discourses of nation—Southern womanhood and the idea of USAmerica conquering the Orient—succeed each other, they intersect with another racialized voice that undermines them and puts both of them under question. As Toni Morrison has so powerfully suggested, Poe was one of the most important writers to respond to the Africanist presence.[37] The aspect of the transformed Rowena/Ligeia that is emphasized the most is her blackness. Her hair, the narrator recalls, *"was blacker than the raven wings of midnight,"* and her eyes were the "black and the wild eyes" of his love Ligeia (88). The metamorphosed woman here signifies a blackness that can be nothing short of racialism in the American South. The blackness of the African slave, on whom rested the peculiar institution of slavery, could not be simply dismissed or justified. It would come back to haunt the very conceptions of nationhood that attempted to launch a discourse of pure origins, conceptions of the nobility of the Southerner and the benevolence of plantations.

The blackness of Rowena/Ligeia recalls the racial discourse with which *The Narrative of Arthur Gordon Pym* ends. In *Pym*, Poe calls attention to the dangers of creating a racial alterity by having the *Jane Guy* destroyed in the Antarctic by metaphysical blacks—complete with black teeth and joined by black seabirds—who are terrified of anything white, including eggs and flour aboard the ship. The mysterious writings at Tsalal, which the narrator identifies as mixtures of Ethiopian, Arabic, and Egyptian words, and which read, "To be shady," "To be white," and "The region of the South," clearly link the (USAmerican) South with dualistic racial politics.[38] The narrative concludes with Pym and his mate sailing on milky white water toward a perfectly white human figure, an image that is a strong critique of the consequences of creating cultural identity on the basis of racial/cultural purity. The bodies of Pym and his mate virtually dissolve into whiteness, into narcissistic images of themselves. "Ligeia" ends on a cautionary note, a critique of the discourses of nationalism designed to consolidate an imperialistic self by conquest of the Orient or a Confederate self by creating an idealization of Southern womanhood.

Like Poe, Harriet Prescott Spofford, in "Desert Sands" (1863), dramatizes the dangers of imperialistic appropriation of the Orient, mediating questions of power and control through questions of aesthetic appropriation. In her story, the imperial body of the male Orientalist artist literally depends on the suppression of woman/other. The story centers around the efforts of the narrator, Sydney, to find aesthetic inspiration and to produce his masterpiece painting. As Sydney grows more frustrated with his inability to create an original artwork and makes more frenzied attempts to produce his masterpiece, he increasingly seeks inspiration from the Orient. He is fascinated by Vespasia, East Indian by birth and a patron of the arts, and he is scornful of his "pale" wife, Eos. As Sydney travels to the Orient in search of inspiration and begins to paint with a new strength and energy, Eos's health steadily declines. The story ends melodramatically with the masterpiece complete, Eos dead, and the overreaching artist struck blind.

As the above synopsis suggests, the plot structure of "Desert Sands" parallels, to a great extent, the structure of "Ligeia." The two women, Eos and Vespasia, are the light and the dark, the angelic and sexily demonic, the West and the Orient, respectively; Sydney finds Eos, the "pale phantom of a woman," repugnant but is strongly attracted to Vespasia, the "Oriental creature of fire and strength."[39] Like "Ligeia," Spofford's tale begins with the narrator recalling the events of the past and ends with him repenting the folly of his actions.

In "Desert Sands," Spofford rewrites the aestheticization of the Orient and demonstrates the simultaneous subordination of women and the Orient in the discourse of Near Eastern orientalism. "Desert Sands" centers around the feverish attempts of the narrator-artist to gain enough inspiration to paint his masterpiece. As he journeys from one Near Eastern country to another, dragging his ailing wife, Eos, with him, he at last completes the perfect picture that captures the Orient: "There lay the desert before me again, its one moment of dawn, when the sands blanched, the skies blenched, and the opposite quarter dreamed of rosy suffusion to cast it again yet more faintly on the white dromedary and the white-wrapped Arab beside him" (214). This is the final moment of triumph in the story, as the New Englander captures on his canvas the enigma of the Near Eastern Orient; the Arab literally becomes part of the landscape, and the narrator revels in this construction. But Spofford's representation of this artistic victory critiques the imperialistic use of the Near Eastern Orient as simply an objectified territory, serving the imagination of the narrator.

Sydney attempts to suppress Eos's talent by associating her with familiar Near Eastern oriental images. Eos's landscape painting is perfect, but the narrator in his jealousy does not want it exhibited. "She was mine, not theirs," he claimed, adding that if he had "kept her apart and hidden, veiling her when she went out, always accompanying her," she would not be so "slime[d]" with other men's praise (183). In the narrator's vision, the woman, like the East (which is veiled and needs unveiling), is his alone to possess. Indeed, Sydney's control over Eos is so complete that he is asked by Vespasia "in what seclusion she is cloistered." Vespasia asks him, "Is she from Stamboul? Do you keep a seraglio?" (189). Notwithstanding the perpetuation of the stereotype of the imprisoned Eastern woman here, what Spofford critiques through Vespasia's questions is the suppression of women's right to expression. That the discourses on woman and the East intersect here points to the masculinist nature of imperialist ideology.

Spofford, like DeForest and Cummins, critiques the idea of the westering hero for whom the Orient is simply available as fodder for the imagination. Just as DeForest's Huberstein DeVries plans to excavate entire regions, the narrator of "Desert Sands" needs limitless expanses. For Sydney, the Orient simply becomes an extension of the frontier of the United States. He needs to go to the East, he explains to Eos, because "[t]here is nothing left me here . . . the great rivers, prairies, everglades, I have sucked them all dry. . . . Besides, they have no storied sanctity, the pyramids do not begin nor the blameless Ethiops end them" (201). The metaphor of nourishment suggests that the imperial body of the narrator depends on a feeding off of "new" territory. For Sydney, the Near

East is a site readily available for aesthetic consumption and awaits him like the open West of the United States.

Sydney's journeys through the East are attempts to avoid its historical specificity and otherness and to capture on canvas a representation of an Oriental imaginary, one which can easily be mastered. Sydney's descriptions of his travels are deliberately vague. The steamer, we are told, touches the shores of Africa, and the couple initially stay "within the precincts of the old historic town—alien and fantastic—that received [them]" (202). Sydney recalls his complete satisfaction when "some city—whose strange, sweet name savored of dates and palm-wine, and 'lucent syrops tinct with cinnamon'—veiled itself behind us" (203). Names, places, and sights are deliberately vague in this totally discursive and syncretic Orient that Sydney, in his encounter, wishes totally to aestheticize and appropriate. The faceless Arabs, in turn, "circled round the dying fire [and] made groups where *chiaroscuro* could do no more" (203).

By the mid–nineteenth century, the Near East had become familiar in the popular imagination both through literature and through discourses on Egyptology. Racial debates on Egyptology resonated more in the United States than in Europe because of concern with the racial composition of the Egyptians. As I discussed earlier, the anxiety felt by abolitionists and Southerners alike at the thought of Egyptian culture being African in origin resulted in a series of essays, monographs, and books about ethnography and Egyptology. Many people in the United States considered themselves the hermeneutes of the Near East. Spofford critiques this use of knowledge as an attempt to empower a male, westering national identity and represents it as a deadly masculinist ideology. In "Desert Sands," Sydney's increasing empowerment over his environment is coterminous with Eos's gradual physical decline. The narrative ends with the completion of the painting as Eos thanks Sydney for "having made and felt [her] a part of yourself" and then sinks to her death (215). As in "Ligeia," the discourse on Orient and woman become one. Vespasia, the fascinating Oriental woman, simply disappears into an undefined East, and Eos is literally transmuted into the artistic product, the painting of the East.

Susan Gubar has argued that historically the model of the male writer using his pen/penis to write on the virgin page has resulted in the creation of the female as a passive creation. Women, consequently, have viewed themselves as texts and artifacts to be viewed, used, and created by men.[40] "Desert Sands" is a perfect allegory of woman becoming text; but it is also an allegory of Orient becoming text. Sydney literally wants to erase the sociopolitical Orient and veil it with the anonymity of desert sands, on which he can then inscribe his own text. Spofford's conflation of woman and Orient, as well as the retributive ending of "Desert Sands," in which Sydney is struck blind after he completes his painting, suggests a critical awareness of the issues of power and control that developed as the United States was increasingly thought, in the Columbiad vision, to be the culmination of *Translatio Imperii*, the seat of a new empire, albeit without outright colonization and with an altruistic sense of mission.

Writing contemporaneously with Spofford, Melville further complicates the idea of the Near East as the new frontier by dramatizing the resistance of the Near Eastern Orient to the hermeneutic mappings of the New World hero. The Near East, particularly the Holy Land, exerted an attraction on Melville much as it did on the writers of missionary narratives. But while Ballou, Ware, DeForest, and Cummins contained, to an extent, the racial-cultural hybridity of the Near East by using the missionary-conversion narrative as an organizing structure, thus positioning the USAmerican imperialistically, Melville, in *Clarel*, fictionalized instead the doubts and hesitancies of the New World hero seeking religious regeneration through a pilgrimage to the Holy Land. The hero embodying the nation is sent on a journey that involves a questioning not only of his faith but, more importantly, of his gender and race identity, both of which define him as imperial subject.

Clarel, the eponymous hero of Melville's long, rambling poem, goes through a cycle of religious doubt, despair, and learning. Yet, as many critics have suggested, the religious plot is only one of several important motifs in the poem. *Clarel* is Melville's critique of nineteenth-century Egyptological attempts to manage the racial-cultural alterity of the Near East through hermeneutic mastery or by re-creating the Near East as part of the imperial imaginary, an Eastern culture in need of missionary conversion from the New World. As with Poe, with Melville mastery takes the form of desire for the Other. Through Clarel, a young theological student journeying the Near East, Melville eroticizes the relationship between the New World and the Near Eastern Orient and demonstrates how the racial-cultural difference of the Near East cannot be contained by a creation of race hierarchies or by adopting male/female and mind/body dichotomies; instead, Melville's poem questions the raced and gendered oppositions between the New World and the Near East through the circulation of homoerotic desire.

The Near East as a representation of difference, resisting mastery by the West, had long been a source of fascination for Melville. Unlike popular Egyptologists and archaeologists who wanted an imperial mastery about ancient cultures, and unlike phrenologists who used Egyptological information to confirm the inferiority of nonwhite races, Melville, like DeForest, Cummins, Poe, and Spofford, emphasized the problematic nature of these attempts at mastery and control. Melville's interest in the process of Near Eastern Oriental definition can be seen as early as "Bartleby, the Scrivener: A Tale of Wall Street," first published anonymously in *Putnam's Magazine* in 1853. Ostensibly, "Bartleby" is presented as a story of Wall Street. The basic drama of "Bartleby" involves the repeated attempts of the well-connected, though unnamed, narrator to decipher the mystery of his scrivener, Bartleby, who persists in preferring not to humor his boss. Much more than a daily nuisance, Bartleby, like the Near Eastern Orient, is a hermeneutical nightmare for his boss. The narrator cogitates about Bartleby, "I now recalled the quiet mysteries which I had noted in the man. . . . that he never went any where in particular that I could learn; . . . that he had declined telling who he was. . . ."[41] Bartleby's refusal to explain his behavior not only disarms the narrator but "unman[s]" him as he loses control over this mysterious subject.[42] When Bartleby is taken away to the "Tombs," the New York prison, as a vagrant, he is housed in a Near Eastern structure that the narrator describes thus:

> It was not accessible to the common prisoners. The surrounding walls, of amazing thickness, kept off all sounds behind them. The Egyptian character of the masonry weighed upon me with its gloom. But a soft imprisoned turf grew under foot. The heart of the eternal pyramids, it seemed wherein, by some strange magic, through the clefts, grass-seed, dropped by birds, had sprung.[43]

Here Bartleby's hermeneutical impenetrability, as it were, is explicitly tied to the resistance of the Near Eastern Orient to Western inquiry. Inaccessible to sight or sound, Bartleby repulses the textual/sexual (penetrative) advances of the narrator, who now feels "weighed" by Bartleby's opaqueness. Although the narrator, the prodigy of New World power and control, in his indefatigable optimism fancies he has found the key to Bartleby, "the heart of the eternal pyramids," in the discovery of Bartleby's heart-wrenching work in the Dead Letter Office, the very simplicity of the explanation puts under question, or at least under ironic scrutiny, its interpretive validity. The attempt to conclusively explain Oriental artifacts and cultures can yield little other than arguments that mock the ability of the New World to master the Orient.

In 1856, three years after the publication of "Bartleby," Melville published a humorous piece called "I and My Chimney." Here, Melville satirized the vogue for Egyptology and lay archaeology popularized by travel writing. The story is dominated by the pyramid-like chimney over which the narrator marvels, a structure that his wife considers simply unsightly and unnecessary. "The architect of the chimney," the narrator fancies, "must have had the pyramid of Cheops before him."[44] Like the Pyramids, the chimney possesses a multivalence that defies comprehension, because "by the mere eye . . . only one side can be received at one time."[45] To the more mundane wife, who is like the popular tourist of the Near East, the chimney assumes importance only because of a possibility that it contains hidden treasure, which, in turn, demands its archaeological excavation. However, the narrator prevails: the chimney/pyramid remains untouched and undeciphered.

Thus, by the time Melville began the travels that would lead to the publication of *Clarel* several years later, his critique of popular Near Eastern orientalism was well established. In the fall of 1856, Melville traveled to Europe and made a seven-month journey through Greece, Turkey, Egypt, Italy, and Palestine, all of which he documented in his journal of the period. In *Clarel*, the racial and cultural issues raised in the journal find clearer poetic expression. While the journal records the narrator's confusion and his sense of being overwhelmed by the cultures of the Near East, *Clarel* crystallizes this loss of an active, imperial, male agency of the New World into a racialized dynamics of desire that renders gender differences fluid and underscores the anxiety about mastering the Orient.

Melville's need to enter into a productive, critical dialogue with the textual palimpsest that the Near Eastern Orient had become is evident in many of his journal entries. Like Poe, Melville deconstructs one of the most popular tropes of the Near East, the harem, by linking the sensual harem of the Western imagination with the West's most revered image of women—the cloister. Melville writes: "Harem (sacred) on board steam boats. Lattice division. Ladies pale, straight noses, regular features, fine busts. Look like nuns in their plaine dress, but with a roundness of bust not belonging to that character. Perfect decorum between sexes."[46] The demarcations between sacred and profane and between asceticism and sensuality that are central to Western conceptions of womanhood and whose diffusion defines culture and respectability are disturbed in Melville's journal. Similarly, while travel writers were fictionalizing the expanding U.S. missionary efforts in the Near East as courageous, Melville viewed these efforts as hopeless and unwarranted to begin with. In one of his impassioned outbursts, Melville remarks: "Mr & Mrs Saunders, outside the wall, the American Missionary.—Dismal story of their experiments. Might as well attempt to convert bricks into bride-cake as the Orientals into Christians. It is against the will of God that the East should be Christianized."[47]

In addition to the critiques of popular Egyptology and missionary activity, the journal also questions the privileged status of observer that is accorded the USAmerican tourist in popular Orientalist writing. Instead of the powerful, male body exploring and defining the Near East, the journal is replete with images of confusion, bewilderment, and terror that question the very agency of this body. In the great bazaar of Istanbul, the observer is literally subject to disintegration. The bazaar is "rotten & wicked looking," "as if a suicide hung from every rafter," a place where "[y]ou suffocate for room."[48] Similarly, the Egyptian pyramids evoke in him feelings of powerlessness: "A feeling of awe & terror came over me. Dread of the Arabs."[49] Like Meredith, the hero of *El Fureidis*, who chafes at being the object of the Oriental gaze, Melville, when in Jerusalem, records "offering [himself] up a passive subject," "pent in by lofty walls obstructing ventilation."[50] While one could argue that such images of constriction replicate an imperial New World narrative based on such binarisms as (frontier) openness versus (Oriental) restriction, I would say that the affective nature of Melville's descriptions, wherein the narrator is acted on by what he sees, as was Meredith, reverses the activity/passivity dichotomy of traditional Orientalism and undermines the very idea of the New World hero deciphering the Near East.

In *Clarel*, the epistemological confusion about the Near East and its hybrid cultures continues, mediated through the circulation of desire and the fluidity of gendered dichotomies. The plot of *Clarel* involves the Near Eastern journey of its eponymous hero, a divinity student, who travels to Jerusalem to pacify his religious doubts. Arriving in Jerusalem, he falls in love with a Jewish woman, Ruth. When Ruth's USAmerican father, Nathan, is murdered by Arabs, the mourning period forbids Clarel from seeing Ruth, so Clarel decides to leave on a pilgrimage with a motley group of travelers. This pilgrimage comprises the bulk of *Clarel*. On his return to Jerusalem, Clarel finds Ruth and her mother dead, and his own religious doubts remain unanswered.

Although *Clarel* omits direct representation of Egypt and Turkey, limiting itself instead only to Palestine and ostensibly following the structure of a religious journey, its cultural concerns—in particular, the racial borderlands of the Near East—are paramount. Recent commentators of *Clarel* have been quick to note that despite its surfeit of biblical allusions, the metaphysical aspect is only one part of the poem. Nina Baym makes a case, for instance, for the importance of the love plot, noting that Clarel's "abandonment of love becomes part of the plot itself." Baym argues: "The events of the pilgrimage . . . are elaborated against, and referred back to, the motivating event: Clarel's flight from Ruth. Thus the intellectual and erotic dimensions of the situation are integrated."[51] Similarly, Warren Rosenberg finds that in *Clarel* Melville finally treats the erotic theme fully, integrating it with the philosophical through the use of the "dichotomous feminine myth" of woman as virtuous and evil simultaneously.[52] But although gender is now recognized as central to an understanding of the poem, its simultaneous negotiations of racial-cultural difference have not received much attention. Despite Dorothee Metlitsky Finkelstein's exhaustive study of Melville's use of Near Eastern material in his works, critics have downplayed the Oriental racial-cultural concerns of *Clarel*.[53] As my analysis demonstrates, however, issues of race and gender intersect powerfully in *Clarel*, linking the breakdown of heteronormativity and the raced dichotomies between the United States and the Near Eastern Orient with a positive desire for the raced other.

Melville's fascination with the racial-cultural hybridity of the Near East is evident in *Clarel* from the start. The first character presented in *Clarel* is Abdon, the host at the inn in Jerusalem where Clarel stays. Abdon is called the "Black Jew." As Walter Bezanson suggests, Melville probably derived the idea of the character from Eliot Warburton's *Travels in Egypt and the Holy Land* (1859). Warburton speculates that one of the lost tribes of Israel might be found in Cochin, India, where two races of Jews are said to have settled: the black and the white.[54] Melville's decision to use Warburton's *Travels* as a source for his character is clearly more than an attempt at historical verisimilitude. Developing a black Jewish character obviously allowed Melville to mediate the anxieties about racial origins that were exacerbated by the mixture of races in the Near East, as well as the racial anxieties of postbellum USAmerica. Melville subjects Clarel, the embodiment of New World naïveté, whose identity depends on an exclusion of racial impurity, to an intimacy with the hybridity of the Near Eastern Orient. Newly arrived to the Holy Land, Clarel must negotiate the undefinable mixture that Abdon represents. About Abdon, Clarel meditates, "so strange his shade / Of swartness like a born Hindoo, / And wizened visage which betrayed / The Hebrew cast."[55] Combining Hebraic, Asian, and African (as *black* Jew) simultaneously, Abdon signifies a racial impurity that both fascinates and unnerves Clarel, who, in turn, attempts to rewrite Abdon as an exemplar of cultural continuity, uncontaminated by contact with cultural others. Clarel muses, "This seems a deeper mystery; / How Judah, Benjamin, live on— / Unmixed into time's swamping sea" (I.ii.48–50, p. 9). The key word here is *unmixed*, a term that evokes the paranoia of racial identity during Reconstruction as well as the anxieties about the racial-cultural mixtures in the borderlands of the Near East.

For Melville, the Near East provoked questions about racial alterity and national ideology, both of which took gendered form. In the section titled "Nathan," Melville critiques the imperial impulse to view the Near East as a frontier to be mastered and as a raced other; instead, *Clarel* redefines the border as porous and permeable. Melville begins the section by tracing Nathan's lineage back to early New England immigrants whose lives parallel traditional historiography's version of New World settlement. The first pilgrims weather the hardships of travel and carve out a settlement; these original immigrants are followed by others who push westward, each leaving behind an ampler legacy in more prosperous cities. However, this literal lineage of Nathan is less important than the collective, figurative, self-congratulatory version of New World history that it represents. The original pioneers, "austere, ascetical, but free," "[hew] their way from sea-beat rock," putting in train new emigrants who press farther westward, "At each remove a goodlier wain" (I.xvii. 2, 3, 13, p. 57). At once mimicking the rhetoric of New World westward expansion and calling to mind the millennial expectations of the Second Kingdom that were attributed to Jews in the mid–nineteenth century, this genealogy is fraught with national and religio-symbolic significance.[56] In addition, the narrative of subduing the frontier depends on absolute racialized distinctions between the wild and the settled and is insistently gendered as male. It is a story, as Melville puts it, of "landing patriarchs" and of the "sire" of Nathan (I.xvii, 35, 40, p. 58).

However, Melville critiques this favored national narrative of westward expansion by powerfully foregrounding the racial alterities it attempts to suppress. Nathan's father, the stalwart patriarch who subdued the frontier to carve out his domain, lies in death "forever stilled /

With sachems and mound-builders old" (I.xvii.45–46, p. 58). The identities of Western settlers, Melville suggests, were formed through an
exclusion of (and thus intimately bound with) the Native Americans
they attempted to suppress. Nathan is born into an anxious awareness
of this racial alterity that he obsessively attempts to manage.

> . . . Three Indian mounds
> Against the horizon's level bounds
> Dim showed across the prairie green
> Like dwarfed and blunted mimic shapes
> Of Pyramids at distance seen. . . .
>
> (I.xvii.57–61, p. 58)

Here, Melville links together the racial borderlands of the USAmerican
West with that of the Near East. Nathan is constantly confronted with
signs of the Native American past—for example, mounds and bleached
skulls—that unsettle his (religious) ideological foundations. Converted
to Judaism through the love of Agar, a Jewish woman, Nathan attempts
to reenact the settlement narrative of his ancestors by literally creating a
New Israel in the Near East. This displaced version of pioneer history,
which evokes the genealogy of the New World as a new empire, insistently locates racial paranoia at the center of New World settlement and,
by implication, in Near Eastern ventures. Melville describes Nathan's
efforts to carve out a pure Judaic space in images that suggest rigidity
and absolute demarcation. Nathan is described throughout the poem as
"walled in," "Defensive," "resolute," within the "stronghold" of the
town, surrounded by "wandering Arabs." Nathan's Zionist outpost
thrives on racial othering as did western settlements in USAmerica:
"His fathers old those Indians deemed: / Nathan the Arabs here
esteemed / The same—slaves meriting the rod" (I.xvii.309–11, p. 65).
The racial Other continues to assert itself, transgressing and erasing the
border, even as the patriarchal, westering male attempts to control that
Other. Melville critiques the impulse to racial purity and normative
masculinity in Clarel by figuratively linking these with separation,
power, and destructive impulses to control.

Even though the character of Nathan occupies little space in the
poem, I have focused on him at some length because he plays a significant role in the development of the plot and serves as a vehicle through
which Melville mediates nineteenth-century anxieties about racial-cultural mixing, anxieties particularly apparent in the borderlands of the
Near East. Critics who have argued for the primacy of the erotic dimen-

sion of *Clarel* over the philosophical one have seen Clarel's decision to leave Ruth (and go on a pilgrimage) as a major causal event in the poem.[57] However, in their attempt to privilege the erotic theme of the poem, they have overlooked the original factor causing Clarel's departure: Nathan's death and the Judaic custom of bereavement that forbids Ruth from interaction with Clarel. Nathan's death marks the end of the phallocentric attempt to manage the racial other through hierarchical demarcation and separation and makes way for Clarel's explorations of the borderlands of the Near East.

Clarel's departure from the inn is marked by a racial difference that Melville specifically signifies as that of the Orient. Awaiting departure, the pilgrims hear sounds of "mongrel Arabs—the loud coil / And uproar of high words they wage" (I.xliv.8–9, p. 137). The Orient— Melville uses the term *Orient* here—seems to be characterized by a stereotypical irrationality and inertia: "'Tis special—marks the Orient life, / Which, roused from indolence to toil, / Indignant starts, enkindling strife" (I.xliv.11–13, p. 137). In and of itself, this characterization of the Orient is not particularly significant: indolence and unreason were often seen as markers of a syncretic Orient. Important, however, is Clarel's response to the sights and sounds that mark the difference of the Oriental others.

> The mountain mild, the wrangling crew—
> . . . why should these indue
> With vague unrest, and swell the sigh?
> Add to the burden? tease the sense
> With unconfirmed significance?
>
> (I.xliv.28–32, p. 137)

The proliferation here of sensualized terms suggests that Clarel's early response to the Arab is eroticized. The picture of "the Orient life" acts on the body of the hero with an agency of its own, "teas[ing]" his senses, disrupting his idea of racial-cultural difference, and reversing the traditional dynamics of the New World hero mastering the Orient. The racial difference represented by the Orient, unlike the figures on the urn in John Keats's "Ode on a Grecian Urn," refuse to simply be transformed into a vision of the viewer, into an aestheticized stillness.

It is significant that this Oriental encounter occurs just before the beginning of part II of the poem, in which Clarel leaves with the motley crew of pilgrims and Arab guides to begin his travels through the Holy Land. Clarel's journey through the Holy Land, it is clear, will be not simply philosophical and metaphysical but also cultural. Djalea, the Muslim head guard of the pilgrims, for instance, is a constant object of speculation and inquiry for all the pilgrims. Rumored to be the son of an Emir, physically imposing, and yet serene, Djalea, in his almost perpetual silence, signifies to the pilgrims the "inscrutable Orient" that Clarel and other pilgrims attempt to read. To the narrator, Djalea's status serves as a reminder of the inexplicable capriciousness of Oriental society: ". . . Abrupt reverse / The princes in the East may know: / Lawgivers are outlaws at a blow" (II.vii.17–19, p. 163).

As the pilgrims journey on, Djalea calmly staving off a possible attack by robbers, it is clear that the impulse to define and decipher the Near Eastern Orient is a major part of *Clarel,* as it was of Melville's journal. In *Clarel* this impulse takes the form of mapping the racial over the erotic. Vine, to whom Clarel is increasingly attracted, is described in terms similar to Djalea, the mysterious Oriental. Like Djalea, Vine rides apart, "estranged" from the rest, lost in inscrutable reverie (II.xiv.52, p. 187). Indeed, as Clarel notes, Djalea uses a "courtesy peculiar . . . / In act of his accosting Vine" (II.x.85–86, p. 172), a sign that denotes a special affinity and confounds Clarel's view that "The pilgrims [are] an equal band" (II.x.92, p. 172). Clarel's attraction to Vine is thus also a displaced attraction to Djalea and the cultural difference of the Near East that he signifies, a fact that becomes clear in "Vine and Clarel," the most overtly homoerotic section of the poem.

Because of the emotional intensity of this section, most commentators have rightly seen it as central to an understanding of *Clarel.* Yet discussions of the section focus only on the few select parts dealing with Clarel's response to Vine. If we view this section in light of Clarel's responses to the racial-cultural difference of the Near East, however, our picture of this section—indeed of the erotics of *Clarel*—changes significantly. By reading this section as part of a triptych, in conjunction with the section on Nathan and Clarel's reading of Abdon, we see how Clarel's attraction to Vine is a displacement of his desire to overcome the otherness of the Near East through a hermeneutical understanding that denies the separation between self and other. Melville's embodiment of Clarel thus resists the imperial paradigms of Near Eastern Orientalism that operate through a need to exclude the Other. Although distantiated, Clarel's desire for Vine questions the separations and demarcations between the New World and the Near East on which the construction of the imperial body rests.

Nathan's attempt to insulate himself from racial others takes the form of a frontier settlement, patriarchally organized, with the border marking an absolute separation. Clarel's Near Eastern venture, in contrast, is marked from the beginning with images of permeability and transgression. It is appropriate, therefore, that "Vine and Clarel" begins with a fluid construction of gendered identities as Clarel configures Vine: "He espied him through a leafy screen, / Luxurious there in umbrage thrown, / Light sprays above his temples blown—" (II.xxvii.11–13, p. 235). Partially hidden amid vegetation and thus associated with nature, the picture of Vine here subverts traditional gender differences and serves as a prelude to the transgression of both raced and gendered boundaries later in the section. Almost every critic of *Clarel* has focused on Clarel's attraction to Vine, beginning, most notably, with Walter Bezanson, who interpreted it as Melville's portraiture of his own tormented, yet intense, relationship with Hawthorne.[58] However, although homoeroticism is of particular importance here, the focus on gender alone neglects the racial dynamics of the Near Eastern Orient that are an integral part of the section.

It is significant that Clarel and Vine's encounter takes place against the backdrop of an Oriental entourage that constantly serves as a reminder of the racial-cultural other. This is the point at which the section begins: "While now, to serve the pilgrim train / The Arabs willow branches hew . . . Or, kneeling by the margin, stoop / To brim memorial bottles up" (II.xxvii. 1–2, 4–5, 235). Spatially, the scene is framed with Clarel and Vine at the center and the raced other, the Arab, at the periphery. As the section progresses, however, the Near Eastern Oriental moves steadily to the center of the picture, becoming part of the interaction between Clarel and Vine themselves. Structurally, "Vine and Clarel" is organized around Vine's musings and the increasing intensity of Clarel's overtures toward him. The substance of Vine's reflections, however, so important in an understanding of the section, has been neglected.[59] While Clarel is regarding Vine fondly, Vine is elaborating a discourse on the Arab. Beginning with a short sally along the lines of *carpe diem*, Vine changes direction and continues:

> "Look; in yon vault so leafy dark
> At deep end lit by gemmy spark
> . . . .
> The sheik on that celestial mare

Shot, fading.—Clan of outcast Hagar,
Well do ye come by spear and dagger!
Yet in your bearing ye outvie
Our western Red Men, chiefs that stalk
In mud paint—whirl the tomahawk.—
But in these Nimrods noted you
The natural language of the eye
Burning or liquid, flame or dew,
As still the changeable quick mood
Made transit in the wayward blood?
Methought therein one might espy,
For all the wildness, thoughts refined
By the old Asia's dreamful mind;"

. . . .

Of true unworldliness looked Vine,
Ah, clear sweet ether of the soul

. . . .

O, now but for communion true
And close; let go each alien theme;
Give me thyself!
                    (II.xxvii.39–40, 43–56, 64–65, 69–71, pp. 236–37)

Seen as part of a triptych, along with the Nathan and Abdon sections, Vine's musings reflect an anxious need to define and thus imaginatively control the Oriental other. Through Vine, Melville mediates the raced anxieties generated by Egyptology and the contact with Near Eastern cultures. To Vine, the Arab represents an ontological puzzle. Magnificent in his bearing on the "celestial mare," biblically typified as the wandering other, and seemingly savage with "spear and dagger," he defies clear definition. Yet this attempt to classify the Arab from a vantage point of New World hermeneutical certainty evokes the long history of narratives of Native Americans, as well as Melville's familiarity with popular Near Eastern travel writers, such as George William Curtis, who had invoked a similar parallel.[60] Such comparisons were fraught with ideological tensions. By the time Melville was writing Clarel, the forced removal of Native Americans through the Indian Removal Act had already become history, while Wounded Knee loomed ahead. Melville's representation of Native Americans through Vine here, as "Our . . . Red Men . . . that stalk / In mud paint—whirl the tomahawk," implicitly free to roam, thus ironically comments on the brutal politics

of settlement at the same time as it suggests Vine's desire to claim a kinship with the Other. This initial mapping of the Near Eastern Oriental
ends with Vine's attempt to consolidate both the Arab and the Native
American in the figure of the deep-thinking native.

At this point Clarel's desire for Vine intensifies. The attempt to
claim the raced other is thus triangulated with the circulation of homoerotic desire. Clarel tries to deny his own investment in reading the Oriental, however, by simply ignoring the substance of Vine's musings, a
move replicated in critical readings of the section. Clarel instead constructs Vine acontextually, as unworldly and above and beyond the
racial politics that absorb him and muses: "Of true unworldliness
looked Vine / Ah, clear sweet ether of the soul / (Mused Clarel), holding him in view" (II.xxvii.64–66, p. 237). Yet, as the dramatic movement
of the section suggests, Clarel's attraction for Vine involves a displaced
desire for the Oriental.

This pattern of Oriental definition, punctuated by Clarel's overtures to Vine, continues in the rest of the section. The focus of Vine's definition shifts to the lost nobility of the Arabs, drawing on the theme of
historical degeneracy familiar in discourses of the Near East. However,
unlike the novels of DeForest and Cummins discussed earlier, in which
the Near East ultimately needs the agency of the New World to become
civilized, in Vine's construction the Near East and the New World are
both frontier societies attempting to create a rudimentary culture.

> Some tribesmen from the south I saw,
> Their tents pitched in the Gothic nave,
> The ruined one. Disowning law,
> Not lawless lived they; no, indeed;
> Their chief—why, one of Sydney's clan,
> A slayer, but chivalric man;
> And chivalry, with all that breed
> Was Arabic or Saracen
> In source they tell. But, as men stray
> Further from Ararat away
> Pity it were did they recede
> In carriage, manners, and the rest;
> But no, for ours the palm indeed
> In bland amenities far West!
> Come now, for pastime let's complain
> Grudged thanks, Columbus, for thy main!

> Put back, as 'twere—assigned by fate
> To fight crude Nature o'er again. . . .
>
> (II xxvii, l83–100, pp. 237–38)

Melville's twinning here of the New World and the Near East undermines and questions distinctions between old and new, past and present, degeneracy and innocence that were structuring popular U.S. Orientalisms. Clarel, the New World hero, responds with attraction to the
subversion of raced boundaries in Vine's narrative, just as he was
attracted to the racial enigma represented by Abdon. The section of the
poem on Nathan reinforces boundaries between settlement and wilderness and between good and evil, embodying them in the figure of the
patriarch and in the patriarchal union (with Nathan's daughter, Ruth)
that is promised to the wandering hero. In "Vine and Clarel," the transformation of raced boundaries into permeable borders is accompanied
by a breakdown of heteronormative gender difference. Clarel longs to
"wed / Our souls in one:—Ah, call me brother!— / So feminine his passionate mood" (II.xxvii.108–10, p. 238).

The breakdown of heteronormativity in this section is closely
linked to the racial dynamics of the poem. Melville sets up the interac-
tions of the section so carefully that Clarel's homoerotic desire for Vine
is mapped onto Vine's desire for the oriental other. When Clarel reveals
his longings to Vine, Vine does not actually chastise him. A shadow
glides across his face, and Clarel interprets this as a rebuke of his
"dream of love / In man toward man" (II.xxvii.126–27, p. 238). And
even as Clarel tortures himself with self-recrimination and imagines
Vine's judgment on him, he looks up to see "serious softness in those
[Vine's] eyes / Bent on him" (II.xxvii.134–35, p. 239). While Clarel continues to battle with his guilt, Vine, in an almost uninterrupted motion,
shifts his attention to an Arab guard in prayer and directs Clarel to do
likewise.

> But a sign
> Came here indicative from Vine
> Who with a reverent hushed air
> His view directed toward the glade
> Beyond, wherein a niche was made
> Of leafage, and a kneeler there,
> The meek one, on whom, as he prayed,

> A golden shaft of mellow light
> Oblique through vernal cleft above,
> And making his pale forehead bright,
> Scintillant fell.
>
> (II.xxvii.145–55, p. 239)

Fascination with Arabs (particularly Djalea) in prayer is scattered intermittently throughout the poem. It is personalized here through Vine's
angle of vision.[61] Alone, partially hidden by the foliage, and illuminated
by the sunlight, the figure of the Arab evokes that of Vine at the opening
of the section, as he was seen "through a leafy screen / Luxurious there
in umbrage thrown" (II.xxvii.11–13, p. 235). Structurally, Melville
replaces Vine with the Arab as Clarel's object of desire; the act of Oriental definition produces a narrative of homoerotic twinning, not only of
Clarel and Vine, but also of Vine and the Arab and of Clarel and the
Arab.

"Vine and Clarel" is Melville's most complex response to the nineteenth-century discourses about cultural origins popularized by ethnographers like Morton and Gliddon and to the racial borderlands of the
Near East. At once a repository of an ancient culture yet frontierlike, the
Near East defies temporal-hermeneutic fixity as it does the poles of civilization and savagery. The process through which the New World hero
saves or defines the Near East, either as missionary or archaeologist and
in both cases attempting to demarcate the Oriental as other, gives way
in *Clarel* to a more pronounced process of desire and identification, an
attempt to deny any separation between self and Other. Melville was
too aware of the powerful, male, heteronormative, and raced discourses
of imperialism, however, to completely naturalize or idealize this merg-
ing. Clarel's fascination with the Oriental/Vine is tempered, and to an
extent Othered, with reminders of his "normal" allegiance to Ruth and
the patriarchy of Nathan's New Israel. He is rebuked by Vine in his
attempted intimacy, and the end of the poem finds him lamenting his
decision to leave on the pilgrimage, a decision that has apparently
caused Ruth's death by mourning.

Poe's exaggeration of Oriental fads in "Ligeia" and his farcical representation of Egyptology as naive chauvinism in "Some Words with a
Mummy," Spofford's representation of Oriental appropriation as death,
and Melville's dramatization of the confusion of racial epistemologies
within the Near East all critique the embodiment of nation as powerful,

masculinized, and ready to uplift or define the Orient. That the satiric and tragic impulses were so integral to Near Eastern Orientalist literature is testimony to the multiple ways in which writers resisted the ideologies of a hegemonic, expanding nationalism, even as they evoked the dominant ideology through the deployment of such tropes as the westering hero and the discourses of missionary conversion.

5

The Culture of Asian Orientalism: Missionary Writings, Travel Writings, Popular Poetry

In 1829, G. and C. and H. Carvill, a publishing company in New York, issued a volume of poems by Lucretia Maria Davidson of Plattsburgh, New York. The 172-page volume contained some sixty-odd poems rang-ing from the very personal "On the Birth of a Sister" to the religious "The Guardian Angel" and the historical "On the Execution of Mary Queen of Scots." Most of the poems were relatively short, running at most eight or nine stanzas; however, the longest poem in the collection, running almost thirty pages, was a verse romance set in Kashmir, India, called "Amir Khan," which Davidson's biographer, Samuel Morse, chose as the title poem of the collection called *Amir Khan and Other Poems.* What is interesting about this collection in a consideration of U.S. Orientalisms is not simply the author's almost obsessive fascination with the topology of the Far East, although that in itself warrants atten-tion, but the fact that the book was a posthumous publication of a girl who had died four years earlier at the mere age of sixteen.

Davidson was obviously a precocious child, having written her first poem at the age of nine. As would have been the case of any other gen-teel New England girl of her time, her excessive preoccupation with writ-ing was diagnosed as the cause of her poor health. For several months she languished without pen and paper, but her mother, sensing her dis-tress, counseled writing again. A wealthy patron sponsored her educa-tion at the Troy Female Seminary until her stay there was cut short by her fatal illness. In short, there was nothing in Davidson's environment to excite an unusual interest in the Far Eastern Orient; yet that is precisely what occupied her imagination. The long narrative poem "Amir Khan" is about an improbable ill-starred romance between Amir Khan, a king of Kashmir, and Amreta, a captured Circassian woman. Yet Davidson uses standard features of the Indian landscape—bulbul and, plantain—with a familiarity that suggests an easy availability of Orientalist literature of the Far East and an interest in India in particular.

Davidson's interest in the Far Eastern Orient might at first seem purely abstract and imitative of European Orientalism, particularly if we contrast the contacts of the Far East both with the closer political contacts of the United States with the North African Orient in the late eighteenth century and with U.S. cultural and commercial contacts with the Near East a generation later. The capture of USAmerican slaves by Algerians, for instance, provided an immediate impetus for embodying the nation as free and moral; similarly, the advent of Egyptology and the raced anxieties of origins that it generated, as well as the rush of popular travel to the Near East, created the impetus for archaeological and missionary Orientalism. The Far East, in contrast, neither provided occasion for militaristic engagement nor was a popular tourist destination. Yet it was trade with the Far East that was most heavily invested with visions of the westerly movement of empire and with imperatives of national destiny, fulfilling Columbus's original mission. This vision, along with the European scholarly-imperial investment in the Indic Orient, affected not only aspects of public policy regarding the Far East but also the interests of travel writers, poets, and essayists.

This fascination with the Far East culminated in the 1850s and 1860s, in the works of such writers as Ralph Waldo Emerson, Walt Whitman, Henry David Thoreau, Henry Wadsworth Longfellow, James Russell Lowell, and Bret Harte. Even as early as 1821, when Emerson was only seventeen, he had written a long poem called "Indian Superstition" for the Harvard College Exhibition. The sheer magnitude of interests in the Far Eastern Orient suggests that the literary Orientalism of the mid–nineteenth century was more than simply a secondhand imitation of European Orientalism. The same Harvard College Exhibition for which Emerson wrote his poem, for instance, included numerous works on topics concerning the Far Eastern Orient, such as "Whether the Prevalence of Despotism in Asia be occasioned principally by Physical Causes," " On the Indian Astronomy," "The Institutions of the East Indians," "Prospects of Christianity in India," and "The Roman Ceremonies, the System of the Druids, the Religion of the Hindoos, and the Superstition of the American Indians."[1] By the late nineteenth century, it was obvious that the very mention of the East would help sell litera-ture. Richard Henry Stoddard, for instance, called his collection of poems published in 1871 *The Book of the East and Other Poems,* even though poems about the East filled only a little over thirty of that vol-ume's nearly three hundred pages.[2]

The New England intelligentsia thus had an indigenous interest in the Far East and wanted to create its own Far Eastern Orientalist dis-course. Part of the interest in contributing to this discourse might be the desire of New England writers to be part of what Raymond Schwab describes as the Oriental Renaissance. Schwab sees Anquetil Duperron's arrival in India in 1754 and William Jones's arrival in 1783 as important events that were to change the intellectual climate of the West. The pub-lication of *Zend Avesta* in 1771 by Anquetil-Duperron marked the begin-ning of the time when a complete world that Schwab says could be "placed alongside the Greco-Roman heritage" entered the Western con-figuration of the universe.[3] Schwab describes the effect of the arrival of Sanskrit texts in Europe as a second Renaissance, creating repercussions as important as those produced in the fifteenth century by the arrival of Greek manuscripts.[4] Unlike the first Renaissance, however, which con-firmed the centrality of Western civilization, the Oriental Renaissance opened up a world of new languages and ideas of which the Greco-Roman heritage was but one strand. Schwab writes, "The closed circle of languages, within which the false problems, impotent intuitions, and crippled enterprises of monogeneticists such as Postel and Leibniz had always come to naught, burst open, posing new problems, problems in reverse, on the infinity of languages."[5]

Not only Europe but the United States too participated in this Ori-ental Renaissance. But although Schwab's monumental study stresses the scholarly, productive effects of nineteenth-century Orientalism, it does so with an almost complete disregard for the age of empire during which this scholarship took place.[6] Linguists, social and literary histori-ans, and anthropologists were after all attached in one way or another to institutions whose Oriental affiliations were affected by interests of empire. U.S. Far Eastern literary Orientalism, like European Oriental-ism, was likewise intimately connected with the economic, political, religious, and racial discourses on the Far East, all of which found expression in celebrations of the westerly vision of empire.

The cultural construction of the Far Eastern Orient, particularly

India (which I will focus on as the primary Oriental example in this section), was thus highly contradictory. India was revered as the land of scriptures and literatures, the birthplace of civilization; yet to be accommodated within the westerly vision of empire, in which civilization was seen as moving west and culminating in the New World, it had to be either constructed as degraded or as transhistorical past. The acquisition of both material and cultural goods from India could be seen as the rightful fulfillment of Columbus's original dream or as an idealized and redemptive journey of the newest empire to the old. In either case, the contemporary material reality of colonial India had to be excluded. This chapter examines the persistence of the westerly vision of empire in both commercial and intellectual contacts with Asia, briefly analyzes the Asian Orientalist works of a few popular poets and travel writers, and traces the genealogy of Emerson's and Whitman's highly contradictory sacralization of India as absolute, spiritual past. The following analysis of some popular avenues of contact between the United States and the Far East is thus intended not as an authoritative or exhaustive history but as a rhetorical intervention aimed at reconfiguring a discourse that heretofore has been seen in purely abstract/philosophical terms.

Although popular travel to Asia was limited, trade was well established and was associated with more than just economic considerations. Ideological imperatives of race and nation intervened. The national significance of commercial contacts with India had been seen as early as 1787, when Jefferson stressed the need for a North American road to India.[7] Much later, William Henry Seward stated more grandiosely that he expected the United States to embrace Canada, Mexico, and Alaska and, from its continental base, to dominate the markets of Asia, "the chief theater of events in the world's great hereafter."[8] The United States had joined in the competition for Chinese trade soon after independence. In the 1790s, Amaso Delano, the great-grandfather of F. D. Roosevelt, was already capitalizing on Chinese demand for fur, and by 1842, the leading U.S. firm trading with China reported a net profit of $130,000 for the year.[9] U.S. trade with India was similarly expanding. Even as early as the 1820s, the *Boston Daily Advertiser*, for instance, featured imports from India on almost every page.[10] For many politicians, however, trade with Asia signified more than simply economic benefit: it signified imperial might. Thomas Hart Benton, a senator from Missouri and later a congressman, made trade with India (and the necessary development of the West and the Pacific) his personal crusade. Indeed, after his death Benton was memorialized through his connection to the cause of Indian trade. The inscription on his statue in St. Louis read, "There is the East; there lies the road to India."[11]

Of course, the U.S. scramble for Asia in the mid–nineteenth century was an inevitable economic prelude to the great increase in U.S. influence by the end of the century. In Europe, as Lenin had seen, the growth of monopoly capitalism, the need to export capital, and the need for cheap labor led to the aggressive search for colonies in the mid–nineteenth century.[12] The United States had itself embarked on a period of speculative boom in the 1830s, and by midcentury it was well on its way to phenomenal industrial growth.

Yet, in the United States, trade with the Far East was invested with more than simply economic concerns. It was linked to utopian visions of the nation's imperial destiny, a fulfillment of the westerly vision of empire, cast in bodied terms. The account of historian William B. Weeden, at the end of the nineteenth century, is symptomatic of the raced, imperial ideologies associated with Asian trade. Weeden writes:

> Always, since the Aryan hordes swarmed out from the mother continent, spreading over Europe, then over the new Americas, Oriental trade had attracted the boldest and most venturesome spirits. . . . Here silks, jewels, and spices, with aromatic tea and coffee, waited for the Aryan cousin voyaging back from the cold climes. Now, the last outgoers from the Aryan stream, the Americans from the last-subdued continent, were about to join the eager throng of visitors.[13]

For Weeden, New England's entry into trade with Asia in the seventeenth and eighteenth centuries was a sign of the cultural and racial continuity of the New World with Europe. The idea of "civilization" coming full circle is here exemplified by the Aryans' constitutional change from "hordes" to bodied, bold "spirits." An indistinguishable pack of beings, the initial swarming hordes of Aryans leave Asia, the mother country, for Europe, where they are transformed into bold, fearless individuals. The movement from Asia to Europe is one from infancy to adulthood, from undifferentiated being to an autonomous, masculinized individualism. Their return to the Orient through trade is a sign of their conquering spirit, the newest version of which is evidenced in New England. Weeden's linkage of trade with the idea of the culmination of civilization in the New World reflects the strength of the latter idea in the nineteenth century.

The popularity of the idea of the westerly movement of civilization, as well as the contradictions it created for constructions of Asia, can be seen in many of the scholarly interests in Asia, particularly India. The American Oriental Society, formed in midcentury, had as its object the study of languages, customs, and religions of Eastern countries. Yet, as we know, the attempt to seek knowledge was related to national self-definition. The society saw itself as representative of the reach of the new, potentially expanding nation and in competition with the powers of Europe. Missionary activity, the traditional outpost of colonial ventures, was similarly prioritized by the society in its search for knowledge about the Orient. The society promoted the learning of Indian languages not simply for scholarly ends but also as a sign of the cultural-moral influence of the New World. In its journal in 1847, for instance, the society noted with pride the U.S. missionary presence as compared with that of England. There were about a hundred U.S. missionaries in the countries east and west of the Ganges, and they had command of such languages as Tamil, Telugu, Punjabi, and Maratta.[14]

But Sanskrit scholarship posed problems for theories of the westerly movement of civilization. Because Sanskrit rivaled most languages in antiquity, its existence questioned the primacy of other languages and cultures and the centrality of Greco-Roman civilization. Yet India could not easily be accommodated within the temporal paradigm of westerly theories of empire. About the civilization of India, Bayard Taylor wrote:

> In Egypt, you are brought face to face with periods so remote, that they lie more than half within the realm of Fable; yet there the groping antiquarian has pierced the mystery, and leads you down from dynasty to dynasty, on the crumbling steps of hieroglyphic lore. But in India,—the cradle, as many believe, of the Human Race—we have no such helps, and while we gaze upon the tokens of faith which was no doubt pre-existent to that of the Pharaohs, science sits down baffled and leaves us to wander in the dark. . . . The whole backward vista of Time is thrown open.[15]

Taylor's comparisons of the problems posed by Egyptology and Indology are symptomatic of the need of Western scholars to maintain the binaries of center/margin even as they looked to the East in search of knowledge. The difference between approaching Egyptology and Indology, according to Taylor, is that Egyptology has been explicated in the recent past whereas Indology (without such help) belongs to a remote, inaccessible past.

In reality, however, the reverse was true. While Egyptology had revealed the existence of a written language predating Christianity, nobody for centuries before Jean-François Champollion had actually read the hieroglyphics. The Westerner as archaeologist-missionary could therefore, without much historical reappropriation, be used as an imperial-hermeneutic figure in Near Eastern Oriental literature, both recovering lost culture for the natives and bettering their present condition. In India, however, writers were presented with a civilization where the ancient language, although limited to the priestly class, was actually in use.[16] Hieroglyphic interpretation could be totally appropriated as a Western knowledge, but Sanskrit writings could not. Faced with a non-Western culture with a fund of knowledge from which the Western world had hitherto been exempt, and which therefore questioned the Columbiad vision of civilization and empire moving to the New World, writers attempted to represent India's scriptures and writings as a Western discovery.

In his long essay on Oriental poetry, William Rounseville Alger described the extraordinary range of subject matter and metrical traditions of Hindu and Persian poetry, marveled at the ancient history of these traditions, and described the work of the Indic scholar William Jones thus:

> Sir William Jones was the Vasco de Gama who first piloted the thought of Europe to these Oriental shores. It was on one of his earliest expeditions into Sanscrit-land, that the divining-rod of his sensitive genius, fluttering in response of an irresistible attraction towards the veiled and un-imaginable mines of Indian poetry, fastened at last, by magnetic instinct, upon Sakuntala. . . .[17]

In Alger's drama of discovery, there are two players alone: the scholar as imperial explorer and the texts awaiting explication. The male scholar/explorer, armed with phallic genius, penetrates the veiled poetic treasures of India. The unabashed eroticism and hierarchical gendering in the preceding passage reflects Alger's appropriation of commonplace colonialist tropes. What stands out in Alger's representation of the Western discovery of Indic texts, however, is the complete absence of contemporary India in the negotiation between the Western scholar and the texts of the remote past.

Between the Western scholar/explorer and the India of the remote past was, of course, colonial India, the materiality of which, particularly in the continued use of Sanskrit and scholastic traditions, questioned, to an extent, the idea that civilization and culture had moved west. The historical-material existence of India posed a problem for many writers, and they sought simply to avoid it by avoiding the present. In a sense, the status of India was similar to that of the North African states, which loomed large in the popular imagination at the end of the eighteenth century. The North African states, although not under foreign dominion, had a system of slavery that was vastly different from U.S. slavery but that powerfully signified on it. The rhetoric of empire thus involved rewriting the present through distinct oppositions between USAmerican freedom and Algerian slavery. The British colonization of India, however, involved questions not only of freedom and servitude but also of raced hierarchies of West and East and of white and native, all of which evoked the racial schisms of the country at midcentury. The embodiment of the nation as strong and unified, heading the westerly movement of civilization away from India, demanded therefore that India be located in the absolute past. The construction of the imperial body thus involved excluding the historical-material reality of India and rewriting India as spiritual (past) alone. It is not surprising, therefore, that in much of the Orientalist fiction, poetry, and essays related to India—even by such writers as Emerson, who claimed to have been most influenced by Indian thought, and Whitman, who glorified India as the dawn of civilization—there is a painful, self-conscious elision of the social-material reality of India itself, an elision not apparent in most Algerian or Egyptological Oriental writings.[18]

This omission of contemporary history in literary Orientalist writing of the mid–nineteenth century cannot be seen as anything but strategic. One cannot simply assume, for instance, that the contemporary status of India was of no consequence in the United States or that popular writing paid no attention to the politics of the country. Missionaries routinely presented pictures of degraded natives who might be roused to a better existence under the tutelage of England. Rev. Isaac Taylor, revolted at the hundred million peoples of India "given up to so false, debasing, and destructive a religion," noted with satisfaction that Great Britain had, by the 1820s, increased its dominion in India; he wrote, "at least twenty million of the inhabitants acknowledge the power, and it is hoped will derive benefit from the protection of England."[19]

Many travel writers paid particular attention to the raced politics of colonialism. Bayard Taylor, in his immensely popular *A Visit to India, China, and Japan* (1862), devoted an entire chapter to analyzing the methods of British colonial rule.[20] Although he concluded that with few exceptions, order and security reigned in India under the British, he reported that he was "disgusted and indignant" at the "contemptuous manner in which the natives, even those of the best and most intelligent classes, [were] almost invariably spoken [to] and treated."[21] In *Central Asia: Travels in Cashmere, Little Tibet, and Central Asia* (1874) Taylor again returned to the question of British rule. He now concluded: "the English rule in India is based simply upon force, and by force sustained. Notwithstanding the comparative order and security which have been established . . . the native population has learned no loyalty to the Government under which they live."[22] One cannot be certain whether Taylor had the mutiny of 1857 in mind in mentioning the use of force, but his analysis suggests a close parallel to that key moment of native rebellion and colonial suppression. Not only does Taylor's analysis serve as a point of historical accuracy but rather that of a consciousness of colonialism as oppression in the USAmerican cultural imaginary.

Some of Taylor's critiques of British rule stem from the indignation he felt, as a patriotic citizen, when nations that were themselves perpetuating oppression harshly criticized the United States on the subject of slavery. Writing again of the treatment of the natives by the British, Taylor expostulates:

> I have heard the term "niggers" applied to the whole race by those high in office. . . . And this, too, towards those of our own Caucasian blood, where there is no instinct of race to excuse their unjust prejudice. Why is it that the virtue of Exeter Hall and Stafford House can tolerate this without a blush, yet condemn, with pharisaic zeal, the social inequality of the negro and the white races in America?[23]

Taylor's racial beliefs were no doubt at variance with most nineteenth-century theories of race that separated Asians from Caucasians. However, the interesting aspect of Taylor's response to British subjection is how it brings to the surface issues of racial conflict within the country, thus linking EuroAmerican colonialism with internal colonization within the United States.

But while travel writers and missionaries increasingly dramatized the contemporary political events of India, most poets, fiction writers, and essayists simply excluded the present. This strategic omission, despite the wealth of knowledge about India, is at the heart of much

U.S. Orientalist discourse on India in the latter part of the nineteenth century. But to dwell on colonialism as well as on Indology, a product of colonialism, would be to acknowledge in some way the complicity of power and knowledge and also to confront issues of slavery and expansionism. As Bayard Taylor's comments compellingly point out, Indian colonization could not be thought about apart from issues of racial conflict that challenged theories of the westerly movement of civilization, and on which, in turn, the construction of nation as imperial body depended. I am not suggesting that writers of Indic Orientalism ignored questions of race. As I will discuss later, most of them participated, in varying degrees, in the abolitionist movement. However, they rarely questioned theories of racial evolution that prioritized Caucasians. The status of Indology as a construction of India was, therefore, highly contradictory. Participating in the discourse of Indology meant, on the one hand, venerating the Sanskrit scriptures of India and, on the other hand, denying any materiality to the Indian culture and peoples.

The politics of Asian Orientalism thus contributed to features that are commonly associated with transcendentalism—mysticism, spirituality, and a transcending of this world. Such a discourse, I will argue, was not divorced from history. It was, in fact, historically informed, being a product of the periods of colonization and slavery even though it was ahistorically framed—and strategically so—in its insistence on getting beyond history. The Asian Orientalist discourse of the mid–nineteenth century insistently constructed the Orient as passive, spiritual, and fatalistically tied to the past, in comparison to a vibrant, active, present-centered United States. Such a curious inversion of the hierarchical mind/body split of Western metaphysics has radical implications for revising the gendered dynamics of Orientalist discourse, which, as Said suggests, links Orient/body/woman. In U.S. Asian Orientalism, however, the association of the Orient with the soul works as an erasure of historicity, the bracketing of which is the enabling condition for the construction of the imperial body. The Orient appears either as absolute spirituality, a needed complement to the West, or as the mother with whom the New World prodigal needs to be united.

Such binary cultural configurations were not simply unthought appropriations of an available symbology but conscious constructions created to accommodate the Orient within ideologies of unified nationhood and empire. U.S. Orientalism as a discourse could not be free of the technologies of race so dominant in the mid–nineteenth century, but these technologies were accompanied with various kinds of resistances.

Many writers rhetorically propagated the raced idea of a spiritual/inactive Orient but based it on arguments that questioned the overt rhetoric. Let us examine two such arguments at some length.

In his "Memoir on the History of Buddhism," presented to the American Oriental Society, Edward E. Salisbury wrote about Indian character as follows:

> With the luxurious climate of that country, imagination has associated a national character of entire passivity, such as is neither prone to take up influences from without, requiring any moral or physical effort on the part of the recipient, nor inclined to exert itself actively abroad. Yet the more we know of the East by critical investigation, . . . the more evident does it become, the wide East, as well as the West, is under obligations, to a greater or lesser extent, for civilizing impulses, to the peculiar manner of thought and expressions in language, which belonged originally to the Sanskrit people of India.[24]

Salisbury begins by outlining the stereotypes of Indians developed through imperial technologies of race. Indology, Salisbury argues, resists these technologies because a passive, unresponsive, circumscribed, lazy people could not have created the literature venerated by Indologists. Yet Salisbury's critique of raced imperial constructions itself relies on the binaristic dichotomy of Eastern past and Western present. Indeed, Salisbury's argument problematically excludes the sociopolitical present of India, even though his paper attempts to redress the problem of racial Othering. The author's conflictual relationship with imperial technologies of race, in which the present belongs only to the West, continues in the second sentence of the preceding quotation. Salisbury could not have been unaware that his use of the word *civilizing* in this sentence—not to identify an attribute of the West, as was customary, but in relation to India—was highly charged. Yet even Salisbury qualifies this association of civilizing with India by suggesting that the "civilizing impulses" are part of India's antiquity. Despite the noblest of intentions, Indology, as constructed by such practitioners as Salisbury, effectively enabled the functioning of the technologies of race in the mid–nineteenth century.

A similar conflict between Indology and nineteenth-century technologies of race can be seen in Emerson's account about the effects of reading the *Bhagavad-Gita*. In his journal entry of October 1, 1848, he noted: "I owed . . . a magnificent day to the *Bhagavat Geeta*. It was the first of books; it was as if an empire spake to us, nothing small or unworthy, but large, serene, consistent, the voice of an old intelligence, which in another age and climate had pondered and thus disposed of the same questions which exercise us."[25] The most charged word in the above entry is *empire*, which both echoes theories of the westerly movement of civilization, locating India as the empire of the past, and calls on expansionism to fulfill the destiny of the New World as an empire. As in most Indic Orientalist writing, there is a clear binaristic separation between the India of the past and the new empire of the present. Yet, in the very moment of creating hierarchical dichotomies, Emerson's narrative questions the idea of Western progression by giving an originary ontological status to the intellectual complexities of the Eastern past.

Although literary U.S. Orientalist writers profusely acknowledged their debts to the literature and culture of the Far East, they attempted to avoid its contemporary, material reality. The nineteenth-century sacralization of India, in particular, resembles multiculturalism's present-day sacralization of "native" cultures, which are monologically revered and commodified for containing values of the past.[26] Just as the 1990s when the focus on the present-day raced and sexed identities of peoples is avoided because it would rupture the happy pluralist vision of ethnic mosaics, nineteenth-century Orientalists, such as Emerson and Whitman, bracketed the idea of a contemporary Oriental civilization. An inclusion of their present, I will argue, would have interrupted the construction of the imperial body and undermined discourses of the westerly vision of empire. In addition, the reality of colonization foregrounded issues that recalled too closely the racial schisms of the nation and questioned visions of spirituality/wholeness that Indology strove to construct. Ultimately, both these questions were linked to the discourses of race in the nineteenth century.

The nineteenth century witnessed a culmination of scientific theories of race that were obsessed with classifying human species into different physical-moral-intellectual categories. The first systematic classification of races by Johann Friedrich Blumenbach in 1776 was followed by James Cowles Prichard's in 1808. Both works were closely followed in the United States.[27] Blumenbach denied the inherent inferiority of a particular race but did see the Caucasians as the most beautiful race.[28] Nineteenth-century USAmerica closely followed and commented on these theories. "In the first decades of the nineteenth century," Reginald Horsman writes, "Englishmen and Americans increasingly compared the Anglo-Saxon peoples to others and concluded that blood, not environment or accident, had led to their success."[29] In 1830, Dr. Charles Caldwell, a USAmerican, published his *Thoughts on the Original Unity of the Human Race* and argued vehemently for polygenesis. God, he said, had created four original races—Caucasian, Mongolian, Indian, and African. Although Caldwell criticized slavery, he gave slave owners all the ammunition they needed to justify the practice. The Caucasian race, he said, has made "all the great and important discoveries, inventions, and improvements"; he concluded that the black resembled the ape, particularly in his genital organs.[30] By the 1850s, theories that different races, including orientals, had varying mental abilities were simply accepted as fact.

Treatises on race and racial classification became immensely popular. Josiah C. Nott and George R. Gliddon's *Types of Mankind,* an expensive book published in 1854, sold thirty-five hundred copies in four months and went through ten editions by 1871.[31] By the time of the U.S. Centennial Exposition in Philadelphia in 1876, theories of racial evolution were routine. Showman P. T. Barnum capitalized on this easy association of the West with civilization and of Africans, Native Americans, and Far Easterners with bestiality, by starting the popular freak shows in which "primitives" were exhibited. One must emphasize that Asian cultures were not exempt from these displays of freakishness. One freak show, for instance, included "Krao, the Missing Link," "Jo-Jo, the Dog-Faced Boy," and a "Hindoo Hairy Family."[32]

It would hardly seem possible for nineteenth-century Orientalist writers to be unaffected by scholarly racial theories that were so much a part of the cultural discourse of the period and that were manifested in all areas of popular culture. Although none of them expressed opinions resembling that of the British colonialist Macaulay, who simply dismissed Indian contributions to learning as "less valuable than what may be found in the paltry abridgments used at preparatory schools in England,"[33] they found it difficult to reconcile the Columbiad vision with the idea of a contemporary non-Western culture. Thus, while the geographic space between the Atlantic and Pacific was being rapidly overcome, and while ideas about a Pacific route to India were being energetically discussed, writers grappled with the complexities of Asian cultures and emerged with two persistent imaginative tropes. In the first, Asia was associated with the remote past and commodified as a land of untold wealth and miracles that awaited the vigorous New World. In the writings of Emerson and Whitman, however, a far more complex version of Asia as Orient emerged. For Emerson, the Orient became an absolute, spiritualized Other; for Whitman, the Asian Orient, also associated with knowledge, figured as primal mother/parent. In both Emerson's and Whitman's texts, the Orient was repeatedly revealed to be a stabilized construct that contained anxieties about racial difference and the masculinity and heteronormativity of the imperial body of the New World.

In many U.S. Orientalist works, Asia was simply a place of unlimited wealth, that is, a fulfillment of sensual lack. While many policymakers and political commentators were energetically espousing different means of having access to the markets of the Orient, poets were describing the wealth of the Orient in its sensual detail. In Lucretia M. Davidson's "Amir Khan," the Khan's palace is filled with "Rich vases, with sweet incense streaming / Mirrors a flood of brilliance beaming . . . And marble pillars, pure and cold, / And glittering roof, inlaid with gold, / And gems, and diamonds. . . ."[34] As in the works of Tyler and Cummins, the Orient mirrors the sensual desires of the Westerner. Similarly, riches and the desire for riches form the theme of Longfellow's "The Kalif of Baldacca" (1864). In that poem, peace reigns in the city of Kambalu, where "The miners are sifting the golden sand, / The divers are plunging for pearls in the seas."[35]

The metonymy of the Orient as riches is of course common in European as well as U.S. Orientalism. But the distinctive feature of Far Eastern Oriental discourse in the United States in the mid–nineteenth century is the construction of the Asian Orient as decrepit, old, and tied down by superstition and outdated belief systems; in the Western mind, precisely such an Asia invites the regenerative capacities of the New World and legitimates a narrative of replacing the old with the new. Distinctions between the New World and the Orient involve raced and gendered distinctions between present and past. In James Russell Lowell's "Dara" (1850), Persia is an old, uninspiring empire, described in images of rot and sexual impotence. It is a "decaying empire," "wilted by harem-heats."[36] The narrative of the poem involves the moral reinvigoration of this empire by a simple, athletic shepherd called Dara, who, even though given the opportunity for corruption, remains pure. Significantly, once Dara's virtue is recognized by the king, the kingdom of old is energized. In the context of European colonization in the nineteenth century and of the Columbiad vision, the poem reads as an allegory of transformation. Dara, the agent of change, represents the power of youth, maleness, and entrepreneurial energy that defined the world of the market in mid-nineteenth-century USAmerica.

Lowell's poem "An Oriental Apologue" (1849) similarly dramatizes the theme of the old, irrational Orient in need of youth and change.
The poem, set in India, narrates the constant religious arguments and
intolerances between a Muhammadan dervish and a Hindu gym-
nosophist. The lives of both men reflect the passivity and lethargy of the
race: "Their only care (in that delicious clime) / At proper intervals to
pray and curse."[37] Events suddenly change when the two men are visited by a handsome white stranger, the embodiment of the West, whom
the two holy men take to be God incarnate: "The strange youth had a
look as if he might / Have trod far planets where the atmosphere, / (Of
nobler temper) steeps the face with light, / Just as our skins are tanned
and freckled here."[38] This stranger chastises the two priests for adhering
to outdated beliefs and brings about a destructive end to the feud.
Bayard Taylor, in comparison, simply eulogized the past glory of Asia
in his collection of poems called *Poems of the Orient:* "Asia stands / No
more an empress" but the land where the "sun of Empire set."[39]

Most Asian Orientalist literature of the mid–nineteenth century
seized on the topos of the ancient past as a metonymy of the Orient.
Interestingly, Lowell's "An Oriental Apologue" was published in the
abolitionist newspaper *The National Anti-Slavery Standard,* an organ of
current political thought. But even though "An Oriental Apologue"
uses the occasion of religious strife in India as an allegory for the feud-
ing abolitionists and slave owners, the India of the poem has little materiality. Indeed, the character of the white god who can save both the
Union and the natives evokes both ideas of a united nation and of
British colonial rule. However, Lowell's parodic use of stereotypes of
the Orient (such as religious fanaticism) suggests a consciousness about
the discourse on the Orient that emerges at the same time as the stereotypes are being most prolifically used.

This type of self-consciousness is particularly evident in Bayard
Taylor's poem "An Oriental Idyl" (1854), which uses the Orient as a site
for the childhood imaginary and also employs such tropes as the spiritual Orient and the Oriental mother, tropes used by Emerson and Whitman. In the Orient, the unnamed speaker of the poem is near bazaars
but closes his ears to the world around him and declares, "I scarcely
hear the hum of trade."[40] The Orient is a site conducive to "the sweet,
unconscious life." But the speaker makes clear that his childlike fascination with the Orient is a deliberate posture intended to dematerialize the
Orient and render it always at a second remove from reality: "Upon the
glittering pagentries . . . I look / As idly as a babe that sees / The painted

pictures of a book."[41] The act of relapsing into childhood necessitates that the Oriental other be no more than a picture-book version of Western fantasy.

Taylor both critiques and acknowledges the power of a trope that was consistently appropriated, particularly by those eager to sacralize the Indic Orient; his poem serves as a powerful reminder that it was possible to be critically self-consciousness of the imperial position even as the United States was rushing to open up the markets of the East. Thus, while some popular writers participated in the construction of the East as riches waiting to be mined, and while missionary writers represented the East as an area of degradation needing U.S. intervention, significant resistances to these paradigms suggest the multivalenced nature of the Orient in the popular imagination. In the works of Emerson and Whitman, however, the Asian Orient became a central, enabling trope for formulating conceptions of a vigorous, young, expanding nation, and a discursive site within which the vexed relationships of empire, masculinity, and race could be articulated.

6

"Mine Asia": Emerson's Erotics of Oriental Possession

The contrast between missionary and travel writings about India and Ralph Waldo Emerson's representations of Asia/India, particularly in his later essays, is stark. Missionary writing, because of its proselytizing purpose, focused on the filth, squalor, and depravities of Asia, detailing in particular the follies of heathen superstition. Travel writers, depending on the degree to which they romanticized the Asian Orient, noted local customs and commented on political systems. Most of Emerson's writings about Asia/India, in contrast, focused on ancient philosophies and scriptures and sacralized a spiritual India of the past.

Of all the transcendentalists, Emerson read Orientalist texts most extensively and wrote at great length about what knowledge of the Orient meant to him. While he read Persian poets and the writings of Confucius, his interest was geared mainly toward Indic texts, which became, for him, signifiers of the Orient.[1] Emerson's interest in India, however, was far from purely academic, philosophical, or spiritual, if we see these areas as separate from issues of power and ideology. The more Emerson read Indic texts, the more he began to use the Orient to stand for an absolute spiritual past, against which a whole and unified New World nationhood as the latest seat of the westerly, Anglo-Saxon movement of civilization could be formulated. This construction of Asia as unproblematic spiritual territory, dissociated from materiality and power relations, was also a political necessity for Emerson, because it allowed him to co-opt the idea of unified space in order to negotiate the idea of a fragmented nationhood. The construction of Asia/India as feminized, disembodied spirit (particularly after the 1850s, when Emerson's own involvement with racial issues deepened) enabled the exclusion of the raced bodies of India and facilitated the creation of the imperial body as an athletic male. Yet, as we examine Emerson's discourses on Asia, we see how sexuality and sex-gender configurations insistently disrupt the narrative of wholeness in which the nation is gendered as an athletic and powerful male. At significant moments in Emerson's construction of the Indic Orient, the heteronormativity of this maleness is questioned and it becomes increasingly evident that the idea of a powerful (heterosexual) male nationhood depends greatly on a homoerotic nationhood that needs to be suppressed.

The interrelationships of race and gender in Emerson's construction of Asia become clearer as we examine the shift in his writings after the 1850s. The assertions of male nationhood emerge most forcefully in his writings at this time, during a period that marks both a distinct increase in his writings about Asia and the beginning of his engagement in the abolition movement. The Fugitive Slave Act of 1850 involved Emerson in the abolition movement as never before and created many conflicts in his thinking about race. At this moment, Asia began to serve as a trope for both containing and deflecting domestic racial concerns. Thus, representations of the Asian Orient as passive, spiritual, and incapable of action also work as mystifications of the uncertain gendering and paralysis of will in the body politic of the New World. Emerson's spiritual Indic Orient was thus raced through the very exclusions it participated in and generated.

In fact, Emerson's early readings about India clearly exemplify that the distribution and production of knowledge about India in the United States was necessarily linked to power relations. Much of the information about India came, for instance, from the Asiatic Society of Bengal, which was formed by the British to better govern the natives. One of Emerson's earliest readings about India was Hugh Pearson's *Memoirs of Rev. Claudius Buchanan;* Buchanan, the vice provost of the College of Fort William in Bengal, routinely presided over scholarship that would promote missionary colonialism.[2] Then, in 1819, Emerson read volume 1 of Lord Woodhouselee's *Considerations on the Present Political State of India,* a book concerned with the delinquencies and depravities of contemporary India.[3] Most scholarship on India reinforced the dualistic conception of contemporary depravity and past spiritual plenitude.

Thus, it is not surprising that when his aunt Mary Moody Emerson wrote to him asking his opinion of Rammohan Roy, Emerson's response was terse. Rammohan Roy, a reformist Hindu and brilliant scholar, had stirred much interest in Unitarian circles, not least because he had converted British Trinitarians. Emerson's response to his aunt in 1822 reveals more than lukewarm interest in Roy: "I know not any more about your Hindoo convert than I have seen in the *Christian Register*, and am truly rejoiced that the Unitarians have one trophy to build upon the plain. . . ."[4] Despite Roy's considerable commentaries on Unitarianism, Hinduism, and several philosophical texts, Emerson found it difficult to see in Roy anything more than a potential convert. By 1834, however, Emerson had included Roy in a list of representative men and noted in his journal about him, "It is a faithful saying worthy of all acceptation that a reasoning Man conscious of his powers and duties annihilates all distinction of circumstances."[5]

The assertion that such "circumstances" as race and culture were irrelevant to representative men runs counter to theories of racial evolution. Yet, particularly in his later writings, Emerson characterized the Asian Orient as a passive other and asserted the westerly move of civilization culminating in the idea of Columbia as the new empire. As my analysis of Emerson's Asian Oriental pieces demonstrates, Emerson's increasingly totalized visions of the Orient became much needed constructions through which he sought to maintain faith in what he saw as an increasingly fractured and rapacious New World.

In his early works, Emerson did not in fact totalize Asia as a passive Other or the United States as an empire. However, he used the Asian Orient as a site to construct definitions of nationhood. "Indian Superstition," written less than a decade after the 1812 war with Britain, is a fascinating poem in which the discourses of revolutionary nationhood, Oriental alterity, and empire contest and question each other. The poem sets up the United States and India as polar opposites, the latter to be redeemed by the former, a configuration that is fairly predictable given the fact that the topics in the Harvard College exhibition were explicitly missionary-colonial in nature. India is a land mired in superstition, its peoples degraded by the senseless mortification of such rituals as the "juggernaut;" the United States is figured as Columbia, the new nation that promises freedom to its peoples and hope to the world.[6]

The poem begins with an invocation of Prospero's book in *The Tempest*. This appropriation of the British mythologizing of exploration and conquest signals the importance of imperial histories, here naturalized as the "discovery" of the New World. India becomes the site where the New World offers sustenance and guidance to the natives. The poem ends with an almost complete substitution of the United States for Britain, with the former positioned as the guardian angel of India. But the United States, personified as Columbia, around whose brow "laurelled lightnings" are woven, is also the revolutionary nation inspiring all nations to freedom (line 102).[7] The nation is represented as a woman, valiantly clad with armor, defending the rights of her people: "Wide through the nations is her watchword known, / Her spear uplifted, and her bugle blown" (lines 149–50). As a revolutionary nation, Columbia is part of the historical progress toward radical change sweeping the world. The strong nation, at the forefront of change and leading the world, is figured as a woman. Yet gender does not work oppositionally here. As Rey Chow points out in her discussion of gender in the context of imperialism, issues of power break down the oppositional binaries of the sex-gender system.[8] Thus, Columbia is a woman only literally; discursively Columbia is not constructed as a contrast to man but as a figure for freedom and revolution to which other nations may aspire. Later, however, in the midst of heated questions about slavery, when the anxiety to maintain a whole, unified national body is stronger, the nation is gendered as a powerful male, one not simply guiding but also conquering the world.

In "Indian Superstition," the representation of Columbia as a strong, virtuous woman and a guardian angel over India demanded that India be constructed as degraded and vice-ridden. But perhaps the very circumstances of the writing of the poem suggest a reverse causality. Harvard, in exhibiting its knowledge of various Orients, as various British societies were doing, and in instructing Emerson, then a junior at that institution, to write on Indian superstition, was implicitly demanding a representation of Oriental degradation in relation to an enlightened and enlightening culture. Emerson provided the representations demanded by his assignment, but he also simultaneously questioned the ethics of colonialism through which, paradoxically, such representations were generated. "Indian Superstition" does indeed present India as a land oppressed by violent religious practices and a caste system dictated by "the stern Brahmin armed with plagues divine" (line 70). But while most Orientalists focused on the present degradation of India and evoked a past golden age in which the Indic texts were generated (and thus implicitly supported the colonial imperative to "save" the country), Emerson, in this early poem, focused intensely on the colonized status of the country. Images of current degradation are suggestively double-voiced and invoke both native and British brutality.

> Far o'er the East where boundless Ocean smiles,
> And greets the wanderer to his thousand isles,
> Dishonoured India clanks her sullen chains. . . .
>
> (lines 11–13)

The images of enslavement refer both to the superstitions that are the ostensible subject of the poem and to the oppressive nature of British colonial rule under which India is put in chains.

The importance of a historical-material construction of India is also evident in the poem's calls to past glory, which recall a past free of Western dominion: "How long shall anxious ages roll away / .... Ere India's giant genius strongly wake / Stretched in dark slumber oer Oblivion's lake / Snatch from his heaven, aspiring to be free" (lines 79, 81–83). The poem ends with a prediction that Columbia's chant of freedom will be passed on to India: "Wide through the nations is her watchword known, / .... To rend the idol and the royal robe / India hath caught it " (lines 149, 152–53). Emerson's India in this poem is not simply a site of pre-Enlightenment irrationality but a historical and historicized nation with a movement and revolutionary agency of its own (albeit inspired by the New World). Indeed, in an earlier version of the poem, Emerson made the link between the United States, which had thwarted British control, and India, which needed similar revolution, even clearer.

> Britain withdraw her legions from the land
> Her thirsty despots & their fierce command
> And Hindoo heroes rule their native shore
> And heaven the long lost boon of peace restore.[9]

Perhaps Emerson excised these lines from the final version of the poem because he knew that the condemnation of Western colonialism that they expressed was too strong even for a revolutionary nation. Despite the omission of these lines, the poem retained several images of enslavement related to the colonial status of India. Columbia, personifying liberty and empire, enjoined a shackled India, imaged earlier as a female slave, to rise in revolt.

More than a decade intervened between this heavily allusive poem, written in restrained heroic couplets, and the launching of Emerson's career as an orator and essayist after leaving the ministry of the Unitarian Church in 1832. In those years Emerson read more oriental works and prepared to write the essays that have been canonized as integral to the tradition of liberal individualism: "Nature," "Self-Reliance," and the "Divinity School Address." Although these essays have been read mainly in the light of transcendental aesthetics and have been seen as manifestos of self-construction repudiating the burgeoning industrial world of the nineteenth century, it is important to emphasize that concerns of the embodiment of nation remain in them.[10] Emerson states in "Self-Reliance," "Every true man is a cause, a country, and an age." This declaration does not simply mean that Emerson is dissociating the concerns of the individual from those of cause and country; on the contrary, the very fact that "cause," "country," and "age" are aligned with the "true man" suggests that individual and nation were very much correlated in Emerson's thinking. In these essays, Emerson is embodying an idealized nationhood through the "true man." As Emerson says, also in "Self-Reliance," "A man Caesar is born, and for ages after, we have a Roman Empire."[11]

Beginning with the 1830s, then, the figure of nation in Emerson's works undergoes a gender shift, not simply literally, but also figuratively. The "true man" begins to embody the nation, and as interpellated subject he is insistently marked by the strength and masculinity he embodies. Indeed, the definition of the masculinity of the idealized Emersonian male becomes a major focus of these essays. Emerson's own poem placed as an epigraph to "Self-Reliance" demonstrates this anxious concern with masculinity, defined through and against a vision of the maternal/woman.

> Cast the bantling on the rocks
> Suckle him with the she-wolf's teat:
> Wintered with the hawk and fox
> Power and speed be hands and feet.[12]

The masculine subject defined by Emerson derives his phallic power not from the world of competition and speculation of the mid-nineteenth-century United States but from the wilder elements of nature.[13] The identity is distinctly phallic, nonetheless, though drawing on a frontier rather than an urban tradition of masculinity. "Nature," Emerson's transcendentalist proclamation, was characteristically in the frontier-colonial tradition: "There are new lands, new men, new thoughts." Nature in the United States meant new territory and westward expansion. At the same time, nature as material, the not-me, is maternal. The speaker starts, "embosomed for a season in nature" and declares he has a "child's love to it," his "beautiful mother."[14]

But, for Emerson, the proclamation "new lands, new men, new thoughts" was not simply a figure for the nation. It was intimately related to the role of the United States in relation to the world. The new nation was embodied in the strong, virile male whose mission it was to morally regenerate the world. It is not surprising, therefore, that one of the earliest representations of this athletic male embodying the nation and renewing the world appears in an 1824 journal entry in a transnational context. Emerson writes:

> the Spirit of Humanity finds it curious & good to leave the armchair of its old age . . . & go back to the scenes of Auld Lang Syne, to the old mansion house of Asia, the playground of its childhood, the land of distant but cherished remembrance. That spot must needs be dear where the faculties first opened, where youth first triumphed in the elasticity of strength & spirits & where the ways of Civilization & thought . . . were first explored. It brings the mind palpable relief to withdraw it from the noisy & overgrown world to these peaceful primeval solitudes. . . . Asia, Africa, Europe, old, leprous & wicked, have run round the goal of centuries till we are tired and they are ready to drop. But now a strong man has entered the race & is outstripping them all. Strong Man! youth & glory are with thee. . . . Europe is thy father—bear him on thy Atlantean shoulders. Asia, thy grandshire, regenerate him. Africa, their ancient abused . . . bondman. Give him his freedom.[15]

This passage demonstrates the complex connections between Emerson's representation of Asia, the construction of the United States as an athletic male, and the persistent anxiety over lost or potentially lost, vital sexual energy. Asia, as represented in the preceding passage, serves a number of ideological functions. It is the progenitor of knowledge and the birthplace of civilization, yet it is a world of pre-Enlightenment rationality, a world of "primeval solitudes," a place where the Western world can seek refuge, it is implied, in a nonintellectual way. The ancestral image of the estate, "the old mansion house," is a nourishing, nurturing one against which the EuroAmerican appears as a child. Yet, in comparison to the youthful body of the New World, Asia appears as part of the weary, diseased, and defiled body, "leprous and wicked"—

the body without athletic vitality—while the United States appears as the strong, athletic male, potent enough to regenerate the world. The overdetermined contrasts between youth and age and between vigor and decay point to the mutual implication of the dichotomies. Possibly influenced by Emerson, Walt Whitman would later make these images central to his personification of the body of the nation.

The embodiment of the New World as Atlas is also a significant ideological shift from its embodiment as Columbia. The nation as Columbia was cast in the city-on-the-hill tradition as an example to the world and as part of liberation movements everywhere. It was an image that worked by moral exemplar, even though it was figured as all-powerful; Columbia's rays extended everywhere. Atlas, in contrast, is embodied through images of physical power. Atlas is clearly a mover, the sole site of regenerative action, an imperial figure needed everywhere. And this robust image of the nation is clearly formed in relation to the rest of the world. As in nineteenth-century arguments about the westerly movement of empire and civilization, there is a genealogical progression from Asia to Europe to the United States.

It is also significant that Emerson includes Africa in his ruminations about the westerly course of empire. Although there is considerable ambiguity in the pronoun *their* in the phrase "Africa, their ancient abused . . . bondman," there is a clear recognition that the moral disease of the imperial body can too easily be mystified by the embodiment of the United States as a youth with the ability to change and grow (and easily "give" the African his freedom). It is in the context of the active, athletic, potent male that the dual construction of Asia in the preceding passage is significant. Asia is both the nurturer and the diseased body, a site that needs intervention from the New World and the site that can make the New World whole. In both cases it lacks its own agency, but it also points to the incompletion and diseased body of the New World. The healthy, phallic, male body depends on the image of the diseased body. Henceforth, the nation as strong, virile male would be constructed through its exclusions, a figure in crisis.

Asia often appeared to Emerson clearly gendered as a woman. Emerson called his wife "mine Asia," an interesting endearment in light of the coldness of their courtship, and one that perhaps explains Emerson's reworking of the traditional mind/body dichotomies in his Oriental writings where Asia is dissociated from the body and materiality. In an 1837 journal entry, Emerson noted how, in the midst of his scholarly ruminations about genius, "mine Asia came in and wrote her name, her son's and her husband's to warm my cold pages."[16] Asia/Lydia here represents faculties of emotion as opposed to the faculties of intellect that Emerson (the West) represents. Many of Emerson's essays rest on binary distinctions between the West and the East, activity and passivity, dynamism and fate—distinctions that are often maintained to shore up a vision of the nation as a powerful imperial body.

Traditional feminist and psychoanalytic criticism has viewed such oppositions as unmistakable male-female binary distinctions. Hélène Cixous writes, for instance:

> Thought has always worked by opposition. . . . A male privilege, which can be seen in the opposition by which it sustains itself, between activity and passivity. Traditionally, the question of sexual difference is coupled with the same opposition: activity/passivity.[17]

Cixous's point about the widespread use of hierarchical binary oppositions is an important one that has been echoed by many poststructuralist theorists.[18] However, as recent feminist and gay and lesbian theorists have suggested, the sex-gender equation needs to be rigorously scrutinized.[19] Such binaries as activity and passivity might well be based on an othering of a gender, but they might also be based on an othering of aberrant sexualities. In terms of ideologies of nationhood, too, the othering of sexualities plays an important role. The early nineteenth century saw both the rise of nationalism in the West and the medicalization of homosexuality.[20] It is no wonder, then, as George L. Mosse points out, that maleness as a metonym for nation demarcated the homosexual as unnational and as a threat to the nation.[21] Emerson's binary oppositions similarly serve not simply to reify sex-gender distinctions but also to define normative masculinity.

Increasingly in his writings, Emerson constructs Asia as an almost absolute, transhistorical and transcontextual category that stands in opposition to the representation of Europe and America as male. Asia is variously positioned as ornament, sentiment, spirituality, passivity, fatalism; the New World/man is substance, materiality, activity, will. But just as these representations are increasingly reified, it is apparent that they are also being deployed as conscious constructions to shore up and unify an increasingly fragmented nation envisioned as an all-powerful male. Emerson needed a feminized discourse of the spirit to exclude the raced body and to embody the nation as an athletic male striding the world. For instance, the volume *Representative Men*, in which Emerson sets up Napoleon as a representative Westerner to be emulated, is written almost at the same time as his three major antislavery addresses. The image of the nation becoming Atlas, was, as we have seen, at odds with the nation being torn asunder and morally corrupted by slavery. At this juncture the reified constructions of Asia as a raced and sexed other become particularly important in sustaining the fantasy of wholeness. In "Fate," written a few years before *Representative Men*, the various ideological contradictions involved in the symbolic construction of Asia come to the surface and resist the imperial narrative of the Columbiad vision and the athletic male striding the world.

A journal entry of 1847 reveals Emerson formulating opposing ideological conceptions of the Orient and the Occident: "Orientalism is Fatalism, resignation: Occidentalism is Freedom & Will"; "We occidentals are educated to wish to be first."[22] The construction of the Orient as incapable of action and the assigning of will and agency to the Occident were means by which the nineteenth-century discourse of imperialism justified itself. Oriental passivity and fatalism invited New World will and action. Thus, it is not surprising that the more Emerson read Oriental philosophy and literature and himself wrote poems inspired by the Orient, the more he wished to keep the Orient and the Occident distinct. In 1857, the year after the publication of "Brahma," the most overtly Oriental of Emerson's poems, he noted in his journal: "We read the orientals, but remain occidental. The fewest men receive anything from their studies. The abolitionists are not better men for their zeal. They have neither abolished slavery in Carolina, nor in me."[23] Part of the desire to protect the Occident (here the United States) from contamination by Oriental passivity arises from the very real fear that the United States lacks the will to create its own history free of slavery.

Emerson attempted to resist the idea of history as a narrative of necessity by reconfiguring history as the will of strong men. Just as in "Nature," where he had embodied the New World male in the frontier-colonial tradition, he began to represent all conquerors as important movers of history. Already by 1841 Emerson was citing Napoleon as an example of will and agency: "There is properly no history, only biography."[24] Finally, in *Representative Men*, Emerson eulogized Napoleon as a man of genius who, although pitiless and bloodthirsty, carved out a brilliant career and agitated society.[25] In his essay on Plato, Emerson most fully developed ideological distinctions between the East and the West and linked them with the raced Columbiad vision of the westward movement of cultural evolution. Plato was the iconic figure representing this evolution. "The history of Europe," writes Emerson, is that of "immigrations from Asia, bringing with them the dreams of barbarians." He argues that Plato, having traveled to the East, "leaves with Asia the vast and superlative; he is the arrival of accuracy and intelligence."[26]

At this point in Emerson's writings, Asia also begins to figure as fate. Asia is associated not simply with passivity but with an acceptance of all events as necessity, a representation that had worked historically to justify Western colonial ventures. Emerson writes, "The country of unity, of immovable institutions, the seat of a philosophy delighting in abstractions, of men faithful in doctrine and in practice to the idea of a deaf, unimplorable, immense fate, is Asia." The West, in contrast, is "active and creative. . . . it is a land of arts, inventions, trade, freedom."[27] The oppositions between Europe and America, on the one hand, and Asia, on the other, strengthen as those between the known and unknown, the tangible and the intangible, dynamic movement and fixity, energy and passivity. These binary divisions echo the distinctions between the East and the West made in "The Superlative," published three years before "Plato." In the former essay, Emerson identifies the West as logical, bounded, and distinct and the East as pleasing, poetic, superlative. "The Superlative" ends with an echo of Bishop Berkeley: "it is too plain that there is no question that the star of empire rolls West: that the warm sons of the Southeast have bent the neck under the yoke of the cold temperament and the exact understanding of the Northwestern races."[28] The reconfiguration of Western metaphysical dichotomies of emotion and intellect through images of enslavement critiques, even as it recoups, the dichotomies of imperialism.

Similarly, in "Plato," Emerson admires Plato for imbibing "the unity of Asia and the detail of Europe; the infinitude of the Asiatic soul and the defining, result-loving, machine-making, surface-seeking, opera-going Europe."[29] Plato, in Emerson's view, learned from the East but, in keeping with theories of cultural evolution, returned empowered with the European will to know. In "Plato," Asia, in its mystery and unity, becomes the absolute threshold of unthinking dogma, which in turn validates the disciplinary power formations of the West: the Indian caste structure, for instance, invites the efforts of Europe to throw it off.[30] But Emerson also celebrates Indian philosophy for its emphasis on the fundamental unity of all things, for providing the imagination with vast horizons. Such contradictory formations of value attached to Asia should not be surprising given its insistent raced othering as Oriental.

The raced Other could be idealized both as a source of value (e.g., in the tradition of the noble savage) or as a threat to be controlled, but in both cases it remained outside hegemonic power.[31]

However abstract, mystical, or transcendental Emerson's Oriental interests might seem to have been, it is clearly no accident that his increased attention to Asia/India coincided with the decade of his first public antislavery addresses. Beginning in 1844 with his address "Emancipation in the British West Indies," Emerson spoke on the Fugitive Slave Law first in Concord in 1851 and then in New York City in 1854. In these essays, Emerson not only confronted the moral issue of slavery and the complex politics of abolition but also turned his attention more explicitly to questions of race and empire, both of which were also implicated in constructions of the Orient. In all three essays, Emerson argued forcefully for the abolition of slavery.[32] While the emancipation essay celebrates the anniversary of the West Indies emancipation, the other two essays present increasingly sharp critiques of the Fugitive Slave Law supported by Daniel Webster. The 1851 essay presents only an abhorrence against the encroachment of slavery in the free states; by 1854 the argument turns against all slaveholders and their unjust treatment of fellow humans. This apparent shift in Emerson's reasoning reflects his continual involvement with questions of race and empire, questions that were by no means settled by 1854 and that surfaced again in *English Traits* (1856). Because of the conjuncture of Emerson's increased interest in the Orient, particularly Asia, and his explicit considerations of racial issues, the latter need close examination.

The essay on the emancipation of the West Indies argues for a similar emancipation in the United States based on both moral and economic sense. Emerson expresses outrage at the inhuman treatment of Africans in the trafficking of slaves. Yet his representations of Africans reflect the disciplinary technologies of nineteenth-century theories of racial evolution. Presenting the economic merits of emancipation, Emerson writes:

> If the Virginian piques himself on the picturesque luxury of his vassalage, on the heavy Ethiopian manners of his house-servants, their silent obedience, their hue of bronze . . . and would not exchange them for the more intelligent but precarious service of whites, I shall not refuse to show him that when their free-papers are made out, it will still be their interest to remain on his estate.[33]

The Africans are represented here through signifiers that exemplify a dumb, animal-like character. Although picturesque, they move with a stupor and lethargy that point to their feeble mental faculties. The subscription to theories of racial evolution is then made amply clear when the service of whites is characterized as "more intelligent but precarious." Later essays by Emerson are equally clear about the comparative barbarity or culture of different races. His 1851 address on the Fugitive Slave Law, for instance, makes a case for the containment of slavery by arguing that such an action is warranted by the higher civilization of the West. Emerson writes: "Countries have been great by ideas. Europe is little compared with Asia and Africa; yet Asia and Africa are its ox and its ass. Europe, the least of all the continents, has almost monopolized for twenty centuries the genius and power of them all."[34] Indeed, as Len Gougeon points out, the obstacle to Emerson's more active participation in the abolition movement was his belief in "the basic inferiority of the Negro."[35]

Emerson's considerations about race did not cease with his antislavery addresses. Indeed, questions of race, empire, and colonialism became dominant concerns just as his apparently abstract and metaphysical Orientalist writings gathered momentum. *English Traits* is an extended inquiry into the culture of the British, often in relation to their role in settling the New World; an analysis of racial attributes and a comparative study of the histories of different races; and an examination of England as an empire. *English Traits* is an unabashed eulogy both to Britain as an empire maker and to the race that seized the colonial venture. It is also an attempt to validate the westerly movement of empire (figured in the cultural imaginary as the Columbiad vision) by drawing attention to the waning energies of Britain and the greater potential of the Anglo-Saxon race in the United States.[36]

English Traits abounds with facts and figures, political and cultural analyses of British colonial rule. Emerson writes:

> The British Empire is reckoned to contain (in 1848) 222,000,000 souls,—perhaps a fifth of the population of the globe. . . . The spawning force of the race has sufficed to the colonization of great parts of the world. . . . They have assimilating force, since they are imitated by their foreign subjects; and they are still aggressive and propagandist, enlarging the dominion of their arts and liberty. Their laws are hospitable, and slavery does not exist under them.
>
> What oppression exists is incidental and temporary.[37]

Emerson's admiration for Britain stems partly from its strength and ability to colonize, its energy to rule without (in his view) being despotic. The British are a manly, virile race, their procreation linked directly to their ability to rule. Emerson also makes clear that colonization is simply the historical-material evidence of racial evolution: "It is race, is it not? that puts the hundred millions of India under the dominion of a remote island in the north of Europe."[38]

Paradoxically, Emerson also felt that the very mixture of races from which the British had derived was responsible for their power.[39] The chapter entitled "Race" in *English Traits* attests to the mutual implication of the discourses of race and empire in the nineteenth century. Racial hybridity and purity vie for contention in Emerson's thinking. Emerson writes, "The English composite character betrays a mixed origin"; yet, in his description, the face of the Englishman is unmistakably marked as Saxon, the Englishman being "the fair Saxon man" who is molded for, among other things, "charities and colonies."[40]

It is obvious that Emerson's analyses of British character are linked to questions of New World national and racial identity. In a speech given at the annual banquet of the Manchester Athenaeum, Emerson declared, "That which lures a solitary American in the woods with the wish to see England, is the moral peculiarity of the Saxon race,—its commanding sense of right and wrong, the love and devotion to that,—this is the imperial trait, which arms them with the scepter of the globe."[41] Clearly, his fascination with the British character lies in Britain's role as an empire, a role destined for the United States as Atlas.[42] The New World, strong but solitary in its conquest of the frontier, seeks to appropriate for itself the imperial might of the Saxon race, of which the British are prime exemplars.

But this homage to racial might and empire, as well as the construction of the empire as a valiant male, betrays anxieties about both maleness and the legacy of empire. The manly, imperial character, Emerson writes, "lies at the foundation of that aristocratic character, which certainly wanders into strange vagaries, so that its origin is often lost sight of, but which, if it should lose this, would find itself paralyzed." What are these unethical vagaries of character that can make the imperial body dysfunctional/paralyzed? Emerson does not answer this question directly, but his next disquisition on the valued qualities of British character offers a possible clue. An admirable quality of the British is that of loyal adhesion, that habit of friendship, and homage of man to man, running through all classes,—the electing of worthy persons to a certain fraternity, to acts of kindness and warmth . . . which is alike lovely and honorable to those who render and those who receive it; which stands in contrast with the superficial attachments of other races.[43]

Emerson's prose here betrays a lingering, if anxious, homoerotic desire. Western manliness is defined by appropriate fraternal (nonbodily) relationships, which Emerson celebrates; but these in turn depend on a conscious exclusion of the deviant, fleeting (bodily) attachments among men of non-Western races. It is clear that Emerson's conceptions of empire and Anglo-Saxon superiority are complicated by the mutual implication of boundaries between heterosexuality and homosexuality, the distinctions between which define Western constructions of masculinity.

Nonetheless, during this period Emerson continued to view Asia/India as a repository of abstraction and principles of unity that the West needed. The East was the complement to the power and energy of the West and the New World. But if we politicize the conjunctures between the antislavery essays and essays about race with the valorization of the East, we see that the East functions not simply as an admired or ornamental complement to the West and the New World but as a necessary supplement to it. In "Plato," for instance, the continual admiration of conceptions of the "fundamental unity" of the East need to be seen not only in the light of cultural difference but also within the politics of national space. Ideas of unity were vital at a time when differences over the question of slavery were threatening to tear the nation apart. Emerson's explanation of the philosophies of the *Vishnu Purana* as "The Same, the Same: friend and foe are of one stuff" could well serve as a rallying cry of Unionists.[44]

It is in this context that we need to situate Emerson's supposedly abstract Orientalist poems, some of which, like "Brahma," were mercilessly parodied in popular journals.[45] The constant refrain in "Brahma" is the reconciliation and identity of what one might think of as opposites. Although the particulars of the poem were heavily influenced by Emerson's readings of passages from the *Vishnu Purana* and the *Katha Upanishad,* its final structure has an undeniable appeal for the turbulent years of the antebellum United States: "If the red slayer think he slays, / Or if the slain think he is slain, / They know not well the subtle ways /

I keep, and pass, and turn again."[46] The title of the poem identifies the "I" as Brahma, in transcendental terms the oversoul; however, the "I" also reads historically as the Union. Asia/India is appropriated, but this appropriation resists simply being imperial by becoming a necessary supplement to gendered conceptions of nationhood. As in the works of Algerian Orientalists, such Royall Tyler, and Near Eastern Orientalists, such as John DeForest and Maria Susanna Cummins, moments of gender anxiety question and resist the narrative of imperialism. And unlike in these Orientalist works, Emerson's Indic Orient seems unambiguously sacralized. Yet we cannot ignore how Emerson's construction of Asia ends up impoverishing the very subject it is intended to valorize. India/Asia is so completely identified with an East that signifies unity that it exists in a historical vacuum, far removed from the realities of colonialism that were preeminently determining its future in the mid–nineteenth century or from any sense of agency.

In "Fate," the most complex essay in Emerson's discourse on the Orient, questions of racial evolution, the westerly vision of empire, and the status of the Asia as cultural other are complexly positioned to both question and reify the construction of the nation as an imperial body. Even though the essay overtly celebrates the cause of empire, the narrative voice itself undermines the association of the West with phallic power and thus with imperial might. Delivered in the 1850s and published in 1860, shortly before the Civil War, it anticipates much of the bloody carnage that ensued. Here Emerson reformulates his earlier belief in the benevolence of nature or the capacity of people to control and harness nature to their ends. The essay is choked full of images of death, disease, and destruction brought about by pitiless nature.[47]

Yet Emerson's analysis of fate is still tied to culture and cultural practices. Belief in fate and passivity (as opposed to will) is still seen as a feature of the past or of what is synonymous with the past, the East. The Calvinist belief in the insignificance of individual will, writes Emerson, is similar to "the Turk, the Arab, the Persian, [who accept] the foreordained fate." He adds, "The Hindoo under the wheel is as firm."[48] As Emerson attempts to understand and define fate, he is helped most by Hindu scriptures that are illustrative of the concept. The changing forms of Vishnu and Maya, for instance, exemplify the idea of limitations/fate at all levels: "The limitations refine as the soul purifies, but the ring of necessity is always perched at the top."[49]

But if fate in the context of the East signifies an assent to events as destiny, for the West it means the destiny of empire. In a strong declaration of Anglo-Saxon high destiny, Emerson writes: "Cold and sea will train an imperial Saxon race. . . . All the bloods it shall absorb and domineer."[50] The contrasts between the abilities of Western and non-Western races are overt and clear. Emerson marvels, for instance, at the "tense geometrical brain, apt for . . . vigorous computation and logic," in the great astronomers of the West. In contrast, he hypothesizes that just as "in every barrel of cowries brought to New Bedford there shall be one *orangia*, so there will, in a dozen millions of Malays and Mahometans, be one or two astronomical skulls."[51] The Anglo-Saxon race is identified not only as powerful but as gifted with the intellect and character that makes it worthy of empire. And this race has planted itself "on every shore and market of America and Australia" and is "monopolizing the commerce of these countries."[52]

This faith in the morality and will of the Anglo-Saxon race, of which the New World is a culmination, is doubly ironic in Emerson's "Fate," however, given his definition of nature as fate and the preoccupation with slavery that lurks behind many of the racial speculations in the essay. "The German and Irish millions, like the Negro," Emerson writes, "have a great deal of guano in their destiny. They are ferried over the Atlantic and carted over America, to ditch and to drudge, to make corn cheap and then to lie down prematurely to make a spot of green grass on the prairie."[53] Emerson's conflation of German, Irish, and Negro might well be seen as a need to mystify the horrors of slavery. The very inclusion of the Negro in the analogy, however, suggests that slavery is a barely suppressed absence. Indeed, slavery in the United States, the newest seat of empire, is perhaps the clearest example of the workings of Fate: "How shall a man escape from his ancestors, or draw off from his veins the black drop which he drew from his father's or his mother's life?" asks Emerson.[54] And even though Emerson later asserts that intellect annuls fate, he makes this assertion in the context of debates about abolition—the "crowing about liberty by slaves"[55]—and in an effort to minimize the crisis of slavery.

In the face of this crisis, an often feminized, yet spiritualized, Asia figured as fate, immobility, unity, and passivity allowed the nation to be embodied as will, action, and present-oriented dynamism. Emerson clearly figured the New World as a vigorous young empire, a destiny forecast in theories of racial evolution and in the narrative of the westerly vision of empire that fascinated Emerson and many people of his generation. Yet the process of reifying these oppositions betrays an anxiety about boundaries between normativity and deviance, maleness and otherness. And in such essays as "Fate," in which concerns about racial evolution and New World empire intersected with questions about slavery, the status of the United States as young, resilient, and potentially powerful is undermined. Thus the very imperialist construction of Asia/India as abstract fate, free of the historical realities of colonialism, surfaces in the essay to rip apart the fiction of the United States as a new empire propelled by will and dynamism.[56]

7

Whitman, Columbus, and the Asian Mother

Unlike Ralph Waldo Emerson, Walt Whitman did not engage in a long and sustained study of Indic texts. However, he shared the cosmopolitan outlook of the United States at midcentury and was fascinated with the Oriental cultures the country was increasingly coming in contact with. Asia—in particular, India—appealed to Whitman's imagination both as a figure symbolizing the farthest reaches of empire and as a maternal imaginary through which the New World could be seen as youthful and dynamic, with empire being the natural outcome of the amative poetic persona, who, embodying the nation, would embrace the world. Just as in Emerson's writings, where the passive, spiritual, immaterial, Indic Orient enabled the embodiment of the nation as a vigorous imperial body, in Whitman's poems the Indic Orient as maternal and originary, exclusive of history, contours the embodiment of the nation as a youth/child. This ahistorical Orient, is, however, a recuperation of unified space in the face of a materiality that Whitman's poems do not escape. Whitman's Asia, far from simply being an abstraction, is constructed against and through particular historical-material realities that form a major part of the poems.

As with Emerson, however, critical questions about Whitman and the Orient have been concerned with the resemblances between Whitman's philosophical (i.e., nonideological) ideas and those of Asian, specifically Hindu, thought. The controversy over the intellectual origins of Whitman's poems began with Henry David Thoreau's visit to the poet in Brooklyn in 1856, a year after the publication of the first edition of *Leaves of Grass*. Thoreau had called Whitman's poems "wonderfully like the Orientals" (by which Thoreau meant Hindu poems in translation) but when he asked Whitman if he had read any Indian literature or Hindu scriptures, Whitman replied, "No: tell me about them."[1] Emerson, too, had described *Leaves of Grass* as "a remarkable mixture" of the *Bhagavad-Gita* and the *New York Herald*.[2] Yet, in 1857, despite his proclaimed ignorance about Hindu scriptures, Whitman defended Emerson's poem "Brahma" by attempting to explain the status of Brahma as a deity.[3] Later, in "A Backward Glance o'er Travel'd Roads," Whitman admitted reading the Hindu poems before writing the 1855 edition of *Leaves of Grass*.[4]

Totally ignoring the constructions of the Indic Orient in Whitman's poems and the ideological significance of these constructions, criticism has participated in the dematerialization of Asia by focusing simply on the sources of Whitman's so-called mysticism. And even episodes in the history of this mystical criticism are curiously imperialistic. Gay Wilson Allen, for example, lauded V. K. Chari's study of Whitman and the Vedantic tradition for using Vedantic examples only to "clarify and illuminate Whitman's meaning" (i.e., not to demonstrate the importance of the Vedantic tradition).[5] Chari himself apologetically explained that calling Whitman a Vedantic mystic was not a denial of him as a democratic bard and indeed was not a study in literary indebtedness.[6] In any event, ever since Malcolm Cowley's introduction to the 1855 edition of *Leaves of Grass*, in which he argued that "Song of Myself" could be understood in conjunction with a number of mystical writings, including the *Bhagavad-Gita* and the Upanishads, criticism has participated in the creation of a mystical Asia that the transcendentalists repeatedly used.

Yet the sites of Whitman's poems of the Orient were often concrete historical-material situations, such as the parade on Broadway and the installation of the Atlantic cables. We cannot also assume that Whitman did not know anything about Asia and that the association of Asia with some undefined mysticism was simply unconscious. Whitman was an omnivorous reader and an obsessive recorder of details. His notebook jottings of the 1850s show him fascinated with the cultures of China and India. In a lengthy entry on China in June 1857, Whitman noted details about Chinese forms of worship, Chinese tea, the physiognomy of the people, the climate, the manner of executions, and, finally, the status of the United States in China.[7] The late 1850s find him comparing the numbers of different races in Asia, including Tibetans, Hindus, Chinese, Baluchis, and Afghans.[8] During the same period, he noted with amazement that from time immemorial, Asia had contained more than half the population of the earth.[9] And like many of his peers, Whitman was keenly interested in U.S. trade with Asia. After reflecting on the customs of the Chinese in his notebook, Whitman jotted down Chinese exports and noted, "The Americans are in very good repute in China—the English and French very bad."[10]

Whitman's interest in Asia was part of his vision of the United States as a vigorous, polyglot nation with interests and influences everywhere and comprised of peoples of all lands and races. In his poems and prefaces to the different editions of Leaves of Grass, Whitman frequently addressed an international audience and assumed that the world was watching the new country with interest. "To Foreign Lands," for instance, represents the United States as an enigma that the world is intently watching and puzzling over. In this context, his job as poet, the speaker declares, is to "define America, her athletic Democracy."[11] Like Emerson, Whitman embodies the nation through the muscular and manly body.

But although Whitman constantly reiterated ideas of universal fraternity and comradeship, he envisioned the world itself in terms that seem problematically exclusive if we take literally the chants about universality, though they do not seem so in view of nineteenth-century racial typologies. In a preface Whitman had intended for a foreign edition of Leaves of Grass, he wrote that "the peculiar glory of These United States" lies in its "splendid COMRADESHIP, typifying the people everywhere, uniting closer and closer not only The American States, but all Nations, and all Humanity."[12] Stating his present purpose in 1876 as that of starting "international poems," he comments that although his earlier poems were "addressed to democratic needs," he cannot "evade the conviction that the substances and subtle ties behind them and which they celebrate . . . belong equally to all countries."[13] He then offers his poems to "the English, the Irish, the Scottish, and the Welsh . . . to the Germanic peoples—to France, Spain, Italy, Holland—to Austro-Hungary—every Scandinavian, every Russ."[14] Given the Eurocentric technologies of race in the mid–nineteenth century and their popularity in the United States, we cannot expect Whitman's list of "all countries" to be any more inclusive. Yet it is obvious that despite Whitman's reading and knowledge of Asia, all Asian, African, and South American countries are conspicuously absent in this list of potential readership.

Racial ideologies alone, however, do not suffice in explaining Whitman's maternal Asia. To better situate Whitman's Indic discourse, we need to understand the dynamics of his concept of the nation becoming an empire, linked as it is with his concerns about the individual subject and concepts of amativeness and adhesion. For Emerson, the idea of nation as empire was based on theories of racial evolution, the westerly movement of civilization, and the youth and energy of the New World. Whitman, too, had an investment in theories of the westerly vision of empire. For Whitman, however, the concept of empire was intimately linked with his concerns with the individual subject. Empire was a natural outcome of the poetic persona, who, embodying the nation, would embrace the world.

In Whitman's poetry, the embodiment of the United States as the new, democratic nation spreading its influence over the world coalesced with the celebration of the figure of Columbus and his quest to find a sea route to Asia. Amos Bronson Alcott in fact praised Whitman as "the American Columbus."[15] Although Whitman's specific poems eulogizing Columbus appeared late in life—"Prayer of Columbus" in 1874 and "A Thought of Columbus" in 1897—poems envisioning a similar joining of countries under new Columbia had appeared much earlier. For instance, "Our Old Feuillage," parts of which were composed as early as 1856, presents an expanded nation consequent on amativeness. The poem lovingly details the geographic breadth of the United States from Florida to California and, without interruption in the cadences listing different places, includes other (embraced) countries in distinctly erotic terms: for example, "soft-breath'd Cuba" and "Kanada" (line 3, 9; LG 171). In Whitman's early Columbiad vision, the United States is the "continent of Democracy," at once lovingly omnivorous and just. Whitman's substitution of the word *continent* for *country* suggests that nationalism and imperialism, no matter how naturalized, were by no means separate in Whitman's works. Indeed, Whitman's poetic endeavor in his early poems was an attempt to naturalize imperialism as democratic nationalism through the hypnotic, rhythmically regular cadences of his lists of happy peoples.

Later in life, when he wrote about Columbus in "Prayer of Columbus" Whitman did so in broken rhythms and empathized with the battered and shamed sailor of later years. Yet both of his poems about Columbus eulogized the sailor's colonization and omitted all reference to slaves: "By me the hemispheres rounded and tied, the unknown to the known" (l. 33 *LG* 422). Columbus had become a major hero in nine-teenth-century USAmerica, in large measure due to Irving's *The Life and Voyages of Christopher Columbus*, first published in London in 1828. Irv-ing's biography met with phenomenal success, reaching 175 editions by the end of the century. Whitman himself read the biography in the 1860s, following the publicity over the republication of Irving's works.[16] However, although Irving had presented Columbus as an important national icon, he also lamented Columbus's enslaving of Indians.[17] Con-cluding his biography with thoughts on Columbus's character, Irving surmised that charges against Columbus's avarice were simply unjust: "He aimed at dignity and wealth in the same lofty spirit in which he sought renown."[18] Yet Irving also wrote about Columbus: "It cannot be denied . . . that his piety was . . . darkened by the bigotry of the age. . . . In this spirit of bigotry he considered himself justified in making cap-tives of the Indians, and transporting them to Spain to have them taught the doctrines of Christianity, and in selling them for slaves, if they pre-tended to resist his invasions."[19] Whitman was also keenly interested in the different aspects of Columbus's character. In the prose notes for his poem, he had jotted down several phrases verbatim from the conclud-ing essay in Irving's biography. The decision not to associate Columbus at all with slavery was thus deliberate, motivated by a need to create a powerful cultural hero appropriate for a new, expanding nation.

Indeed, questions of nation, slavery, and race were closely related in Whitman's thinking, as they were in Emerson's. A thorough analysis of Whitman's thinking about race in the context of slavery would prob-ably require a book-length study. But to examine both the implications of Whitman's representations of the Indic Orient and his discourse on empire, some aspects of Whitman's attitudes toward different races need to be considered. As Betsy Erkkila explains, Whitman often accepted many of the nineteenth-century beliefs about black racial infe-riority but just as often refused to accept the idea of slavery as morally just. At a time when antiforeign societies were gaining votes in Massa-chusetts, Whitman, in "I Sing the Body Electric," celebrated the white and the black body.[20] Part of section 7 of the poem read like a present-day Benetton advertisement using multiracial posters: "Examine these limbs, red, black, or white, they are cunning in tendon and nerve" (line 99; *LG* 98). But eulogizing the black body (and other bodies of color) was one thing; recognizing races of color as equal to the white races was another. Whitman, like most of his contemporaries, avidly read

theories of racial classification and phrenology that "proved" the superior mental capabilities of the white races, and he did not seriously
question them.[21]

It was thus no contradiction for Whitman to simultaneously rejoice
vociferously at the end of slavery in the United States, envision a world
of equal human beings brought closer by modern scientific inventions,
and offer unqualified praise, as Emerson often did, for European colonization. In "The Eighteenth Presidency," a manuscript Whitman hoped
would be published and would help the cause of Republican candidate
John C. Fremont, Whitman wrote: "Freedom against slavery is not issuing here alone, but is issuing everywhere. . . . Landmarks of masters,
slaves, kings, aristocracies, are moth-eaten, and the peoples of the earth
are planting new vast land marks for themselves."[22] In the same tone of
strident optimism in the wake of egalitarian systems all over the world,
striking a powerful populist note, Whitman continues:

> Everything indicates unparalleled reforms. . . . Never was the rep-
> resentative man more energetic, more like a god, than to-day. He
> urges on the myriads before him, he crowds them aside, his daring
> step approaches the arctic and antarctic poles, he colonizes the
> shores of the Pacific, the Asiatic Indias, the birthplace of languages
> and of races, the Archipelagoes, Australia; he explores Africa, he
> unearths Assyria and Egypt. . . . On all sides tyrants tremble,
> crowns are unsteady.[23]

The idea of the strong "representative man" vigorously striding across
countries, creating his own order, clearly echoes Emerson's laudatory
biographies. But in Whitman's formulation the representative man had
to also be the common, average citizen, who, because he embodied
democracy, was always a threat to monarchic privilege. He made
tyrants tremble and crowns become unsteady. That this populist representative man is also the colonizer with unlimited power over the
natives is not seen as a contradiction. But Whitman could present colonialism as democracy only by dissociating it from questions about the
freedom of Asians and other people of color. The narrative both resists
and reifies this dissociation. Within the discourse of colonialism as
emancipation, the narrative of the godlike representative man exploring
Africa is oddly ahistorical. However, as a mystification of the issues of
slavery and power, the trope of exploration, thematized most often as
freedom, works well.

Whitman's discourse on the Far Eastern Orient employs a strategic language of political innocence. While the writers of Algerian Orientalism embodied the nation as manly and virtuous, and while Near Eastern Orientalists embodied it through the archaeologist/explorer/missionary with the power to define, Whitman makes his poetic persona, as representative of an expanding United States, simply a strong, earthy male with an omnivorous appetite and a desire to embrace all. He is an innocent striding the world. Whitman projects his poetic persona, whose palms cover continents, as a nonchalant, amative self, and he presents this persona as representative of his contemporary United States; in relation to this amative self, the Asian Orient appears most regularly as mother. But while the imperialistic implications of this loving, embracing self are clear, the very idea of the nation as a lover necessitates us viewing it as a subject that necessarily derives its identity from interaction with the Other.

"Salut Au Monde!" is an early internationalist poem that illustrates both how the national bard's appropriation of the Indic Orient is presented as amativeness and how the imperial body is contoured through an exclusion of nonwhite bodies. Walt Whitman, the poetic persona of the poem, hears, sees, and salutes the world and thus constructs his subjectivity through a seemingly nonhierarchical equalization and inclusion of different peoples.

> I hear continual echoes from the Thames,
> I hear the fierce French liberty songs,
> I hear the Italian boat-sculler the musical recitative of old poems.
>
> . . . .
>
> I hear the chirp of the Mexican muleteer, and the bells of the mule,
>
> . . . .
>
> I hear the Hindoo teaching his favorite pupil the loves, wars,
> adages, transmitted safely to this day from poets who wrote three
> thousand years ago.
>
> (lines 27–29, 32, 40; *LG* 138–39)

Note how, even in this process of easy equalization, the persona focuses almost entirely on the past—in the case of India, on a very distant past.

The cadences of the poem continue uninterrupted through the repeated opening phrase of each line, "I hear," which implies a democratic equality of all peoples. As we examine the particular geographic spaces and the specific races mentioned, however, we see that these

measured cadences work to unproblematically mystify the racial hierarchies that accompany Whitman's creation of a polyglot, yet ultimately
EuroAmerican, self. In the crucial section of the poem, section 8, where
the persona constructs himself in lines beginning with "I am," it is clear
that the racial self of the persona, no matter how eclectic, is EuroAmerican. "I am a real Parisian / I am a habitan of Vienna. . . . / I am of London, Manchester. . . . / I am of Madrid," the persona exclaims (lines
131–32, 134–35). And after this self has been consolidated, the persona
has the powers of unlimited sight: "I see vapors exhaling from unexplored countries"; "I see the savage types. . . . I see African and Asiatic
towns. . . . I see the swarms of Pekin, Canton, Benares, Delhi, Calcutta,
Tokio" (lines 138, 140; *LG* 144). The loving, indiscriminate self here is
discriminatingly Euramerican: he *is* a Parisian or a Londoner, a singular
person; however, he *sees* Asians in a mass. As if reworking a frontier tradition for the Orient, the amative self derives its expansive identity from
its survey of "unexplored countries" and the indistinguishable
"swarms" of Asian peoples.

"Salut Au Monde!" demonstrates both the subversiveness and the
limits of Whitman's politics of amative inclusion/imperialism. In the
mid–nineteenth century, when scientists, historians, and theologians
were constantly justifying the colonial rights of the white race, Whitman
wrote, "Each of us limitless—each of us with his or her right upon the
earth" (line 196; *LG*, p. 147). Yet the traces of nineteenth-century racial
discourses in Whitman's poetry are also undeniable. Despite Whitman's
commitment to equality, people of color are consistently represented as
exotified (if oriental) or brutish (if black). The poet, as watcher of
humanity, sees, for instance, "the Turk smoking opium" and the "picturesque crowds at the fairs of Khiva" (lines 144–45; *LG* 145). He wel-
comes on equal terms the "Hottentot with clicking palate," the "human
forms with the fathomless ever-impressive countenance of brutes!"
(lines 199, 201; *LG* 147). Hottentot women were objects of great curiosity
in the nineteenth century, often believed to be physiologically close to
apes and thus more primitively sexual. Such scientists as Georges
Cuiver dissected and exhibited Hottentot women's genitalia to a fascinated public.[24] Most whites held the view that Africans were subhu-
man, but not all wanted to deny them political equality. Whitman's representation of Africans thus projected a position held by many
well-meaning reformers in the mid–nineteenth century, one that supported equal rights for all races but maintained an inherent, moral and
cultural intellectual inequality among them.

Years later, Whitman continued to be acutely interested in questions of race and the oppressions perpetrated because of racial hierarchies. In "Ethiopia Saluting the Colors," a poem composed in 1867, Whitman sympathetically foregrounds the horrors of enslavement as an African woman recounts her capture: "*A little child, they caught me as the savage beast is caught, / Then hither me across the sea the cruel slaver brought*" (lines 8–9; *LG* 318). The poet-speaker enfolds the woman in bonds of sympathy, but she undeniably represents a "hardly human" alterity. The speaker of the poem asks: "Who are you dusky woman, so ancient hardly human?"; "What is it fateful woman, so blear, hardly human?" (lines 1, 13; *LG* 318, 319).

Given the recuperation of raced hierarchies in Whitman's poems, it is no wonder that his Oriental poems exclude the contemporary realities of Asia, for to include them would be to once again foreground issues of oppression and questions about the intellectual stature of different races. Whitman's poems of the Far Eastern Orient, like the works of Emerson, focus on the Orient of the past but consistently emphasize the need for the contemporary United States to amatively enfold the Orient within its borders. This loving, imperial embrace through which the Orient is drawn closer is further naturalized because, in Whitman's imagery, it becomes the return of the New World child to the Old World mother.

To understand the attraction of the maternal as a construction of the Orient, we need to look briefly at the relationship between the idea of the maternal and the development of subjectivity. The mother, according to Lacan, is the imaginary in which one's subjectivity is experienced as undifferentiated.[25] Kristeva and Chodorow similarly see the identification with the maternal as narcissistic. Chodorow explains this identification through the perspective of early childhood development.

> As long as the infant cannot get along without its mother—because she acts as external ego, provides holding and nourishment, and is not experienced by the infant as a separate person at all—it will employ techniques which attempt to prevent or deny its mother's departures or separateness.[26]

The mother, as the object of imaginary identification, does not have a distinct identity. Chodorow continues further, "the infant is cognitively narcissistic; its experience of self is an experience of everything else in its world: 'What is 'not I' is libidinally and cognitively perceived as part of 'I.'"[27] The child, in other words, defines the world in terms of itself.

Analyzing the cultural implications of the consecration of motherhood within the West, Kristeva writes,

> this motherhood is the fantasy that is nurtured by the adult, man or woman, of a lost territory; what is more, it involves less an idealized archaic mother than the idealization of the relationship that binds us to her, one that cannot be localized—an idealization of primary narcissism.[28]

Within the parameters of the maternal dyad, the mother is a projection of infantile fantasies, with little or no agency of her own. This idea of the mother—without agency, ever giving, located in the past—attracts Whitman the poet, for whom it is represented by Asia. But this configuration of Asia as maternal by Whitman and other nineteenth-century USAmerican writers has cultural and ideological implications beyond the idea of an invigorating journey (of the child) to intellectual origins. Annette Kolodny has demonstrated the persistent use of the New World landscape as maternal, particularly in early accounts of travelers. In promotional tracts intended to lure immigrants, the New World was invariably described as Eden, paradise, the Golden Age—in short, maternal. Kolodny sees the return to the maternal as a fulfillment of a basic instinctual gratification, "regression from the cares of adult life and a return to the primal warmth of womb or breast in a feminine landscape."[29] Kolodny's Freudian analysis is a brilliant demonstration of the importance of imaging potential colonial land as maternal body just before the female body became the arch signifier of both nationalist and imperialist discourses within postcolonial studies. Beyond Kolodny's analysis, however, we need to recognize that the idea of the mother not only suggests regression but also becomes a means of naturalizing colonization. The construction of Asia as maternal thus uses a familiar New World trope that is, problematically, transferred to Asia, the next "natural" colonial territory.

Whitman invokes a maternal Asia to which the New World, now amid the turbulence of industrialization, needs to return; like Emerson, he also characterizes the New World as youthful, energetic, strong, and ready to conquer. The maternal trope, involving the return of the New World to the mother, thus strengthens the Columbiad vision of the westward course of civilization. At a time when debates about the practice of slavery were strongly questioning civilized values of the New World and were threatening to fracture the wholeness of the nation, the embodiment of the nation as the ever expansive Columbia was particularly appealing. Thus constructed, the Orient was implicitly joined to the New World and also symbolized an evolutionary model that could be easily grasped by people influenced by theories of racial evolution.

The maternal trope located outside the New World was so attractive because it could be used to shore up a complete and whole vision of national identity inside. Paradoxically, then, the Orient was located as a site of certainty and knowledge, of "spiritual truths" that transcended time because the Orient was an Other and because only by being an Other could it satisfy the need of writers to create the totalized vision of the nation becoming an empire. Whitman thus appropriated the idea of a maternal Orient, one that excluded its materiality, and he attempted through the process to embody the New World as an uncorrupted, yet narcissistically focused child, the final prodigy of the westward move of civilization. But to see Whitman, the enunciating subject here, as whole and powerful would be to assume a unified subjectivity, an agency free of the splits and ambivalences that inevitably complicate imperial consciousness. Whitman's construction of the Orient and his exclusion of colonial politics evoke the very material disruption that the maternal trope was supposed to elide. In Whitman's postbellum Oriental poems, history emerges as the unrepressed, questioning maternal plenitude, splitting the imperial body.

An early poem that demonstrates Whitman's complex dialectics of Orientalist representation is "A Broadway Pageant," which was written to commemorate the parade on Broadway prior to the signing of a Japanese-U.S. trade treaty. The poem begins by situating itself in this contemporary event, as it mentions the "swart-cheek'd two-sworded envoys" from Niphon (Japan), "Leaning back in their open barouches" (lines 1–2; LG 242). But soon it becomes clear that the current occasion is a means for negotiating the relationship between the Orient and the New World. The march on Broadway is figured as a march of the westward movement of civilization, in which Japan begins to represent a generalized Orient and the United States is embodied as "Libertad."

While the poem begins by setting up the Orient and "Libertad" as binary oppositions, the nature of these oppositions resists singular definition, because the construction of the Orient as maternal is highly problematic. The Orient, which soon begins to specifically signify India, is represented as follows:

The Originatress comes,
The nest of languages, the bequeather of poems, the race of eld,
Florid with blood, pensive, rapt with musings, hot with passion,
Sultry with perfume, with ample flowing garments,
With sunburnt visage, with intense soul and glittering eyes,
The race of Brahma comes.

(lines 26–31; LG 243)

India, here, is clearly associated with maternal images. It is the birth-place of civilization, the early nurturer or "nest" of languages, and like a good mother, it bequeaths culture to the world. However, the Orient is not simply the mother on whom the child projects its demands for cultural gratification but also a highly charged, sexualized body that demands its own gratification. The change from the maternal to the sexualized body in the preceding lines is represented as one from passivity to activity, where the Indic Orient acquires its own agency.[30] Further, the superimposition of the sexual on the maternal marks the relationship between Libertad and the Orient as forbidden, incestuous, and charged with fear, a positioning that later in the poem surfaces to question the demarcations between the New World and the Orient.

The embodiment of the nation as an empire cannot, however, be overlooked. The poetic persona of Whitman, the lover who embraces everything, shifts readily and seemingly without ideological design to the poet as a child or the poet embodying the nation as a child. And the slippage between poetic persona and nation is presented as so natural that the ideology of the nation as a child desiring the world needs little justification. Indeed, a generation later, the very appropriation of this idea would be popularized in a more directly imperialist manner by Theodore Roosevelt, through the image of the United States as a childlike, yet powerful, nation with a big stick, beating up the world.

As the poet continues watching the parade on Broadway, he sees the "kaleidoscope" of people marching in as representative of the westward march of civilization. The poetic persona, who is watching the procession of the Orient, embodies the nation/Libertad, which is watching the group of nations from its Western shore. And just as the lover embraces the people from the Orient, so, it is implied, is the "natural" and innocent will of Libertad. The slippage from poet to nation initiates the naturalization of the right to empire.

From Thibet, from the four winding and far-flowing rivers of China,
From the southern peninsulas and the demi-continental islands,
    from Malaysia,
These and whatever belongs to them palpable show forth to me, and
    are seiz'd by me,
And I am seiz'd by them, and friendlily held by them,
Till as here them all I chant, Libertad! for themselves and for you.

For I too raising my voice join the ranks of this pageant,
I am the chanter, I chant aloud the pageant,
I chant the world on my Western sea,
I chant copious the islands beyond, thick as stars in the sky,
I chant the new empire grander than any before, . . .

                                        (lines 49–58; LG 244–45)

Clearly, the embodiment of the national bard as amative, appetitive, embracing the Orient, and chanting "the new empire grander than any before" recuperates dominant discourses on expansionism in the mid– nineteenth century. Simultaneously, however, this amative-imperial embrace of Asia also has the potential to question the centrality of the poet-speaker who embodies the nation. In the beginning, the nations of Asia seemingly invite the imperial gaze as they "show forth" them- selves to the omnivorous "I." Here Whitman eroticizes and naturalizes the imperial gesture by presenting the stance of the lover as an involun- tary one, in the passive voice, where all the peoples are "seiz'd by [him]." But, at the same time, the erotic embrace evokes the uncertain dynamics of power of the imperial situation, as the poet himself is "seiz'd by them, and friendlily held by them," and, as a result, trans- formed as a subject through them. The imperial embrace mutually transfigures self and other.

"A Broadway Pageant" powerfully eroticizes the racial-cultural mixture that many feared would result from the high tide of immigra- tion in the middle of the century. But while xenophobic whites favored a selectively European immigration to ensure homogeneity, Whitman expresses a supreme self-confidence that all polyglot nations will come together to chant for a new empire. The recognition of the doubleness inherent in the imperial embrace is simultaneously masked as the col- lective will to empire. Later in the poem, the chanting alongside with the marchers becomes a chant for the new empire, ever widening its

embrace as steamships of "America the mistress" "[thread] the archi-
pelagoes' (line 61; LG 245). And this construction of the new world as a
unified empire is accompanied by an exclusion of eroticism, so that in
the last section of the poem, the binaries between Asia as maternal, passive, and past and Libertad as a child/youth, active and of the present,
become stronger.

What is involved in this shift of the poetic persona from erotic
lover to youth/child? To examine the ideological implications of this
shift, we need to look very briefly at some of Whitman's maternal representations prior to "A Broadway Pageant." Many critics have seen
Whitman's deification of the role of childbearing, the iconic role of the
mother, as an indication that Whitman was not free of the sexual clichés
of his age and that he sentimentalized restrictive roles for women.[31] But
while it is true that Whitman celebrated women as mothers and bodies
of women as childbearing bodies, in many of his early poems the focus
on the maternal body is not a means of desexualizing women or making the body part of the nineteenth-century cult of true womanhood. "I
Sing the Body Electric," an exultant, erotic representation of male and
female bodies, constantly returns to catalog listings of women as nur-
turers and caretakers. He lists "Girls, mothers, housekeepers," "The
female soothing a child," "The sprawl and fullness of babes," and so on
(LG 94). But the maternal body is an eroticized body that has the power
to disrupt the male gaze: "It attracts with fierce undeniable attraction"
even as the poet joins "the mother's breast with the little child" (lines
54, 31; LG 96, 95).[32]

The appeal of early accounts of New World landscapes, as Annette
Kolodny has shown, was the complex commingling of the erotic and filial.[33] But when Whitman attempts to exclude the erotic and represent
the Orient/Asia as maternal, it is an asexual maternal, divorced from
the body. The maternal, to use Kristeva's formulation here, is an idealization of primary narcissism. Such a formulation allows Whitman to
exclude the Orient as geographical, physical, and material space and
naturalize the imperial embodiment of the nation in "A Broadway
Pageant" as "Libertad of the world," accepting the offerings of "the
nobles of Asia." (line 66, 68, LG 245)

Instead of simply re-creating the westward journey across the
Pacific to the regions of Asia, a journey that had occupied the imagina-
tions of travelers and politicians, Whitman envisions a new time when
Asian nations themselves will come to learn from the empire of the present. In "A Broadway Pageant," the contrast between the dynamic,

active, contemporary United States and the passive Asia of the past is made clear: "Young Libertad! with the venerable Asia, the all-mother" (line 74; *LG* 245).

As in William Rounseville Alger's frontispiece, which characterizes the West as "Young and enterprising" and the East as "Old and Meditative," the emphasis in "A Broadway Pageant" is on the difference between youth and age, a difference that goes beyond the rhetoric of newness and novelty (as against the corruption of Europe) created by beginning explorers like John Smith. The venerable Asian mother, fixed in the past, has no materiality or presentness. Asia both is and is not. In a similar kind of paradox, the poet sees a contemporary event, the kaleidoscopic march on Broadway, one whose symbolic overtones recall the entry of immigrants into New York harbor, as one that includes, curiously, images of death. As the poet records the march, he notes, "Lithe and silent the Hindoo appears, the Asiatic continent itself appears, the past, the dead" (line 35; *LG* 244). Here again we see the elision of the presentness of the mother/Other. This emphasis on an increasingly spiritualized Orient of the past is also evident in Whitman's revision of the poem. Until 1871 the poem contained the phrase "Lesson-giving princes" to describe the Orientals in the march; in the 1871 edition the phrase was simply omitted.

"Facing West from California's Shores" continues the dialectics of past and present and of the maternal and the child that for Whitman constitute Asian Oriental representation. Again we see how of all Asian countries, India held the most interest for Whitman. "Facing West," which first appeared in the *Enfans d'Adam* collection, had the title "Hindustan, from the Western Sea" in the manuscript version. In this short poem, we see the complex raced and gendered anxieties inherent in Whitman's construction of the maternal Asia/India. The poem begins with the poet facing Asia from California, the Pacific shore of the United States, and, in the tradition of the colonial quest, "seeking what is yet unfound" (line 2; *LG* 110). In this initial moment, the poem recalls narratives of early U.S. colonizers that routinely characterized the North American continent as a wilderness, a land that had not been found. But this colonial moment, which is associated with the idea of maleness and conquest, is immediately followed by a nurturing maternal image in which the poet-child looks across the waters "towards the house of maternity" (line 3; *LG* 111).

It is significant that Whitman included "Facing West" in the *Enfans d'Adam* collection, the series of poems about womanly love that formed the female counterpart to the Calamus poems. Read through the prism

Young and enterprising is the West;
Old and meditative is the East.
Turn, O Youth! with intellectual zest,
Where the Sage invites thee to his feast.

of womanly love, "Facing West" becomes a rewriting of empire as an act of love. As in "The Broadway Pageant," in this poem India is once again the spiritualized maternal that supports the idea of the westerly march of the Anglo-Saxons. The idea that empire was moving from Asia, through Europe, to the New World had, as we know, clear racial connotations in the mid–nineteenth century. But Whitman, more strongly than most of his contemporaries, was fascinated by the theory of the common ancestry of Europeans and Asians. In a notebook entry dated between 1857 and 1860 Whitman wrote: "the inhabitants of India and the descendants of the Keltic and Teutonic nations are all of one family and must have migrated from one country. Whether that country was Persia or Cashmir . . . is not easily determined—but it seems likely that, accordingly, the white man of Europe and the tawny man of India have a common ancestry."[34]

Oneness is the insistent theme of the poem. In "Facing West," the highly racialized and hierarchical westward move "from Hindustan, from the vales of Kashmere, / From Asia" is presented as one that culminates in the poet as a child situated at the shores of California. The return is presented both as evolutionary and as a natural part of woman's maternal sphere. And Whitman again complicates the web of discourses about the Orient at the end of the poem by rewriting the popular version of Columbus's quest. The Columbus Whitman recalls at the end of the poem is not the larger-than-life hero conquering continents and subduing wildernesses but a figure wracked by doubts, unsure about the efficacy of his mission: "But where is what I started for so long ago? / And why is it yet unfound? (lines 10–11; *LG* 111). The Orient, figured as maternal, again functions as the site of a narcissism through which it is denied any materiality, but the narcissism here turns on itself, as the poet of the nation looks on himself and cannot eulogize what he sees.

"Facing West" defines an important aspect of the transcendentalists' use of Asia—their reference to the philosophical Asia of the past as a moral touchstone through which the moral and spiritual degeneration of the EuroAmerican present could be measured. Asia began to function as the pantheistic equivalent of nature, which for the transcendentalists

FIG. 3. Frontispiece of William Rounseville Alger's *The Poetry of the East* (Boston: Whittemore, Niles, and Hall, 1856). The United States is represented by the youth with the gun, the East by the figure of the mother.

was the realm of the divine. Although this nature figured differently for each of the transcendentalists—narcissistically as the maternal not-me for Emerson in "Nature," as the world of brute nature for Thoreau, and as uncensored human-animal nature for Whitman—for all of them nature functioned in opposition to the world of thought. However, the case with Asia was different. Here an admittedly dehistoricized but nevertheless scholastic Asia came very easily, and without seeming contradiction, to occupy the space of nature. The transcendentalists very much wanted to be part of the intellectual community of Europe that was discovering Indic scriptures for the first time, or what Raymond Schwab has called the Oriental Renaissance. But the iconography of nation as the vanguard of a civilization moving west made the representation of a scholastic India problematic. The maternal trope served the purpose of connection, naturalized the Orient as nature and nurturer, and did not demand any attention to culture. Through this trope it became possible to paradoxically acknowledge the Eastern beginnings of intellectual life while characterizing the scholastic products of these beginnings as part of nature. As we examine Whitman's "Passage to India," his most well known Indic Orientalist poem, we see the uneasy means by which Whitman celebrates India as nature/mother and as cultural/material topos. Interestingly enough, the poem is also the most historical-material of transcendental Orientalist works. History emerges here as the unavoidable, even as the cadences of the poem attempt to elide it.

That Whitman's association of India with the past in "Passage to India" was conscious can be seen in his jottings in *Specimen Days*.

> THE EAST.—What a subject for a poem! . . . The East, answering all lands, all ages, peoples; touching all senses, here, immediate, now—and yet so indescribably far off—such retrospect! The East—long-stretching-so losing itself—the orient, the gardens of Asia, the womb of history. . . . Always the East—old, how incalculably old! And yet here the same—ours yet, fresh as a rose. . . .[35]

Whitman's exclamatory jottings capture the intellectual excitement of what Schwab has called the Oriental Renaissance. Asia is again seen through the maternal metaphor, as the "womb of history." What seems to repeatedly fascinate Whitman, as Egyptology did the Near Eastern Orientalist writers, is his fantasy of the absolute remoteness and pastness of Asia and the fact that he, in the present, has access to the knowledges of Asia. But while Egyptological knowledge, figured as hermeneutic control in the present, was often a subject of parody, for Whitman and Emerson the Indic Orient is quite simply the past offering its vistas of knowledge. In Whitman's jottings, the possibility of an Asian present lurks behind each sentence, in the hypnotic incantations of the words *here, immediate, fresh,* and *now.* Yet the narrative maintains a split between the Asian past (to be acted on) and the experiential EuroAmerican present (as agent and actor), a split naturalized by the poet, who revels in his amatory embrace of the past.

The unavoidability of the Asian present and the simultaneous need to exclude this present form the complex dialectics of Indian Oriental representation in "Passage to India." Like "A Broadway Pageant," "Passage to India" owes its immediate inspiration to contemporary events. Whitman pays tribute to three major accomplishments: the laying of the Atlantic and Pacific cables, which was completed in 1866; the junction of the Union and Central Pacific transcontinental railroads on May 10, 1869; and the opening of the Suez Canal on November 17, 1869. Ostensibly, these material achievements linking lands together are celebrated in the poem as a continuation of Columbus's original quest to find a passage to India, which the poem again refigures as a spiritual quest, a longing to be one with the Asian mother. This material-to-spiritual, body-to-soul reading is so compelling that most contemporary readers have simply repeated this rhetoric in their analyses instead of examining the political contingencies involved.[36] Whitman, after all, had started his poetic career by announcing a subversion of the mind/body Platonic split. A closer look at the poem suggests, however, that the spiritual rhetoric of this poem is so self-consciously employed and attempts to elide so many sociopolitical contradictions that it asks to be read against the grain. Whitman embeds in the poem his resistance to the spiritualizing trope that excludes history, even as he is compelled, by transcendental necessity and by nineteenth-century technologies of race, to utilize that trope for its efficacy to accomplish such exclusion.

The opening section of the poem deliberately sets up a seemingly naturalized opposition between the present of technological achievement, in which the poet lives bodily, and the India of the past, to which the soul seeks return. The poet celebrates "the great achievements of the present," "the strong light works of engineers," while it sounds a plaintive cry to the past, "the dark unfathom'd retrospect" (lines 2, 3, 10; *LG* 411). The technological definition of the present also inscribes its gendered discourse on the body of the poet, who, through his passage out

of the body, attempts to resist being so defined. T. J. Jackson Lears contends: "In the triumphant bourgeois culture of the nineteenth century, to
be engaged in practical affairs was to be in the world of men, where conscious control and autonomous achievement were most highly prized.
To withdraw from that realm was to enter the feminine sphere. . . ."[37] If
the world of engineering marvels was associated with the male world of
achievement and virility, Whitman's use of technological feats as occasion to celebrate the spiritual world undermines the power of maleness
so prized in nineteenth-century bourgeois culture. India's role becomes
that of a powerful spiritual imaginary questioning the bodily-material-
male power of the New World.

But although this spiritual Orient resists the technologies of maleness and power of the mid–nineteenth century, it also problematically
impoverishes the Oriental subject by excluding colonial politics and
thus enacts its own protoimperialism. Let us look at the complex manner in which Whitman's poetry creates the spiritual Orient as a conscious construction based on the exclusion of contemporary colonialism
in section 2 of "Passage to India."

> Passage O soul to India!
> Eclaircise the myths Asiatic, the primitive fables.
>
> Not you alone proud truths of the world
> Nor you alone ye facts of modern science,
> But myths and fables of eld, Asia's, Africa's fables,
> . . . .
> O you fables spurning the known, eluding the hold of the known,
> mounting to heaven!
> . . . .
> Passage to India!
> Lo, soul seest thou not God's purpose from the first?
> The earth to be spann'd, connected by network,
> The races, neighbors, to marry and be given in marriage,
> The oceans to be cross'd, the distant brought near,
> The lands to be welded together.
>
> (lines 16–20, 25, 30–35; LG 412)

Like Emerson, Whitman creates a spiritual Asia; but he wishes to be
connected to it much more than Emerson does. The spiritual-maternal
Asia promised both the oneness and unity that could heal national

wounds and the transcending of history. But, as we see in the poem, history problematically surfaces in the narrative and disrupts the spiritual imaginary. Most obvious in the preceding section is Whitman's deployment of a humanist rhetoric, the egalitarian politics of which pay equal attention to Asia and the United States. But what immediately stands out in this chant of fraternity, which seeks to view New World modern inventions and Asian myths with a democratic eye, is the mention of Africa.

No matter how much we buy into the transcendental rhetoric of the poem, which compels us as readers to view all material facts only through their spiritual significance, we cannot assume that the inclusion of Africa in this poem is irrelevant. Africa (excluding the North African Orient, which was generally not included under the category of "Africa" in the mental topography of the nineteenth century) did not figure in the nineteenth-century theories of the westward march of empire. (Indeed, later in the poem, India is identified as the "cradle of man," the land that the "Cooling airs of Caucasus" come from.) Africa either personified the brutish or, to the more paternalistic, was the land of slavery. And during the years of Reconstruction, the problems of former slaves were far from over. The inclusion of Africa, with its reminders of slavery, thus disrupts the rhetoric of spirituality, even as both the African and the Indian continents are associated with a pre-Enlightenment irrationality and transcendental nature that eludes the known.

The clash between the rhetoric of spirituality and the material facts of colonization and slavery becomes more evident as the poem continues. In wildly exclamatory tones, the poem celebrates

> The earth to be spann'd, connected by network,
> The races, neighbors, to marry and be given in marriage,
> The oceans to be cross'd, the distant brought near,
> The lands to be welded together.
>
> (lines 32–35; LG 412)

By the 1870s, most of Asia and Africa had actually been brought under EuroAmerican domination, a fact that Whitman, a former newspaper editor, could not have been unaware of. Oceans had been crossed, and lands had been brutally welded together through colonization. And in the context of antimiscegenation laws at home, the happy marriage of races, articulated as the marriage of neighbors, was a mystification of racial conflict. Whitman, however, continued to use the metaphor of marriage to describe the colonizer-colonized relationship, suggesting at once an eroticism of power that enacts a naturalized imperialism and a power of eroticism that critically democratizes hierarchical relations. The poem extols the "Year of the marriage of continents, climates and oceans!" in which "Europe to Asia, Africa join'd, and they to the New World," "As brides and bridegrooms hand in hand" (lines 118, 121, 123; *LG* 416). Even though the Suez Canal provided Europe a highly efficient route to Asia, trade between Europe, Asia, and Africa was hardly equitable, and the canal furthered advantages only to European trade. Thus, the imaginative representation of the relation between Europe, America, Asia, and Africa as a marriage is at once humanistic wishful thinking and a mystification of the materialities of colonization and slavery.

In the context of nineteenth-century colonialism and the Columbiad vision, the particular historical representations of India in the poem are also ideologically significant. India, as we have seen, is the venerable mother, the past, the cradle of history, and ultimately transcendental nature and spirit. But the poem does not simply mythologize a past in the abstract; the particular past chosen for representation is especially revealing in its historical omissions and elisions. As the poet from the "shores of America" beholds the mythical past of India, eulogizing it as the "most populous, wealthiest of earth's lands," he offers a quick survey of important moments in Indian history. Significantly, the survey includes both foreign invasions of India and native rulers and stops just short of British colonial rule.

The survey begins with the marches of Alexander to India in the fourth century B.C., the reign of Buddha in the fifth/sixth century B.C., Timur's (Tamerlane) raids on Delhi in the late fourteenth century, and finally the reign of Aurangzebe in the late seventeenth and early eighteenth centuries. It is significant that Whitman chooses to end his historical sweep with the rule of Aurangzebe, the last viable native ruler who had held together large portions of India, including Assam and the Northwest frontier. Aurangzebe's death marks the end of native rule in India and the beginnings of British colonialism. By the mid–eighteenth century, the East India Company was firmly established and had forced the now puppet rulers to recognize its rights to collect revenues.[38] Whitman's decision to end the historical survey of India with Aurangzebe is surely a deliberate move. In a notebook entry in the late 1850s, Whitman had made a notation about Tamerlane and the end of Mogul rule in India in the nineteenth century.[39] Immediately following the mention of

Aurangzebe, the poem proceeds to commemorate travelers and explorers, beginning with Marco Polo, the most famous of Western travelers to the East, then Batouta the Moor, and finally Columbus.

Among the various travelers and conquerors mentioned in the poem, the complete lack of reference to British colonial rule cannot be seen as anything but strategic. By the time Whitman wrote "Passage to India," British rule had been consolidated, and native rebellion had been ruthlessly squashed—for example, in response to the Indian Mutiny of 1857. Whitman, with his journalistic interests, could not have been unaware of the native turmoil in colonial India, the grim facts of which, if included, would have disrupted the seamless, hypnotic chant of history in the poem. New York, the hometown of Whitman, was, in the mid–nineteenth century, extremely cosmopolitan in its outlook. Even during the time when debates over different slavery bills were escalating into public crises, major New York newspapers paid great attention to international events, including events in Asia. On April 18, 1856, for instance, the *New York Daily News* carried a front-page news bulletin on the annexation of Oudh, the swearing in of Lord Canning as governor-general in Calcutta, and trading and exchange rates in Bombay and Calcutta.[40] On the next day, the newspaper had front-page coverage of events in China and Syria.

The point to be noted is that contrary to the view of the older generation of Americanists that the country in the mid–nineteenth century was focussed only on ideologies of Westward expansion or the view of the new historicist generation that only issues of slavery occupied the public mind, the United States was, in addition, extremely aware of its role as an emerging world power and often analyzed internal events in terms of its status as new empire. Whitman's attempt to exclude the historical present, the raced body of India, in his representation of India in a poem that derives its immediate inspiration from current events reflects the transcendental need for a spiritual (here figured as maternal) Asia that acts as both healer and nurturer of the (fractured) imperial body.

Transcendentalists attempted to recuperate India as a fetishized past while excluding its brutal colonization and, consequently, the humanity of its people. Yet this evasion, as we have seen, was never quite possible, because the very omission of history was the premise on which the concepts of the transcendentalist Orient and the New World imperial body were constructed. Whitman's inclusion of Africa in "Passage to India," for instance, suggests a pressing need to simply eulogize the contact zone as a maternal, spiritual space instead of recognizing the complex, often violent politics of contact.

In "Passage to India," India becomes the land of "primal thought," the birthplace of civilization, yet a transcendental pre-Enlightenment space of nature prior to reason. The journey to the venerable Oriental mother is one to "reason's early paradise, / Back, back to wisdom's birth, to innocent intuitions" (lines 172–73; *LG* 418). The passage to this spiritualized mother naturalizes the imperial circumnavigation of the world as an amatory return of the world-weary EuroAmerican soul. Yet Whitman, as we have seen, used the spiritual rhetoric with a full awareness of the material conflicts it was attempting to displace.

For Whitman, as for Emerson, the spiritual Indic Orient enabled the creation of the imperial body of the nation, even as the construction of this Orient brought to the surface the racial and gendered anxieties inherent in the fantasy of an imperial nationhood. While it would be historically inappropriate to deny the subversion of racial hierarchies in Whitman's tropes of the loving poet and the maternal Orient at a time when most Westerners glorified the civilizing missions of the West, it would be equally problematic to dismiss the fantasy of cross-continental unification as simply a spiritual/psychological imaginary existing in a pure philosophical space where "power relations are suspended."[41] Such a dismissal would deny the importance of this spiritualized rhetoric as part of cultural discourses and the power of the latter as prime movers in affecting national agendas. Precisely by viewing transcendental Orientalist texts in some pure spiritual space, apart from racial macropolitics, we lose their value as texts of resistance and as cultural texts.

Afterword: From Whitman to Updike

> In Japan, he'd known with a clenched and absolute certainty,
> he'd find his cure. In Chiba. . . . Synonymous with implants,
> nerve-splicing, and microbionics, Chiba was a magnet for the
> Sprawl's techno-criminal subcultures.
>
> He [Terzibashjian] arrived with a black Hilton tray arranged
> with three tiny, fragrant cups of thick black coffee and three
> sticky, straw-colored Oriental sweets. . . . "We must, as you
> say in *Ingiliz*, take this one very easy . . . In Turkey there is
> disapproval of women who sport such modifications."
> —William Gibson, *Neuromancer*

I choose to end my study of U.S. Orientalisms with the late nineteenth century, not because the discourses on various Orients no longer occupied the literary imagination, but because the increased militaristic interventions of the United States in Central America and the Pacific created the conditions for different kinds of narratives in the twentieth century. On the one hand, the unambiguously expansionist nature of U.S. foreign ventures from the 1890s onward elicited from Orientalist writers a critique of the idea of the nation as an empire. Unlike many of the Algerian and Near Eastern Orientalist works of the nineteenth century, the twentieth-century USAmerican venturing into the East was seldom portrayed as the righteous hero on a mission, but rather as an acquisitive speculator or cynical drifter. Yet, on the other hand, the very ubiquity of U.S. diplomatic and cultural power, as well as the access to imperial discourses, made possible an appropriation of the Orient as a trope for structure, tradition, and stability. The Orient could thus serve as the means for the self-realization of the increasingly technologized and adrift American.

Perhaps no work serves better as an illustration of public interest in the Orient and the implication of the Orient in discourses of imperialism at the turn of the century than "Madame Butterfly." Published first as a short story by John Luther Long in 1898, it was turned into a play by

David Belasco (with the collaboration of Long) and first performed on stage in 1900. Puccini's operatic adaptation made the play a worldwide success. Two years after the initial production of the opera in Milan in 1904, it was taken on a seven-month performing tour through major cities in the United States, a venture unprecedented among operatic productions in the country. Long's story is a complex mediation on the discourses of U.S. imperialism at century's end and the cultural resistance to these discourses in the Orient, particularly in Japan. Japan had responded to the U.S. move to open up Japan for trade in the 1850s with a counter-move designed to resist total cultural colonization. The cultural elite sought to imitate Western powers in the areas of technology and institutions so that Japan could stand up to the West; yet, simultaneously, this elite strove to preserve "an inner core of national culture" so that Japan's modernization was not "an expression of helplessness in the face of Western aggression but a means of furthering Japanese national goals."[1]

In "Madame Butterfly," Benjamin F. Pinkerton, the cynical and rapacious American naval officer, the embodiment of the imperial nation at its worst, sees it as his prerogative to amuse himself with a decorous, pretty, and faithful Japanese wife. In Pinkerton's eyes, Cho-Cho-San is commodified as "an American refinement of a Japanese product, an American improvement in a Japanese invention and so on."[2] While Pinkerton has no intention of taking his Japanese marriage seriously and marries a USAmerican woman, Cho-Cho-San, heeding Pinkerton's flippant remarks about unnecessarily large family ties in Japan, cuts herself off from most of her family and faithfully awaits his return. Long's story, as many reviewers realized, was thus highly critical of imperialism.[3] Cho-Cho-San's ritualized suicide maintains the culture of the Japanese elite but at the same time suggests the tragic fate of Oriental societies in the face of an encroaching Western cultural imperialism. Yet, as David Henry Hwang has so compellingly pointed out in his rewriting of the opera/play/story, the popularity of the operatic *Madame Butterfly*, in which the suicide scene is much longer than the version in Long's story, depends on stereotypical Orientalist assumptions about the docility of Eastern women, which the story reinforces.[4] Thus, Long's transgressive critique of USAmerican imperialism coexists with the dominant hegemonic construction of Oriental passivity.

By the twentieth century, the dominance of the United States as a major cultural and political power and the existence of large Chinese diasporic communities, particularly in California, created an even

greater interest in fiction set in the Asian Orient. Shortly after his explorations of racial otherness in *The Emperor Jones* and *The Hairy Ape*,
Eugene O'Neill published a little-known play called *Marco Millions*
(1927). Like Long's Pinkerton in Japan, O'Neill's Marco in China is
acquisitive, mercantile, and thoughtless. Marco, a highly satirized character, embodies the aggressive capitalist culture evolving in the country
in the early twentieth century. Marco accepts the kindness of Kublai, the
kahn of Cathay, and efficiently executes the official duties given to him
by the ruler, but he is unable to understand the morality that the wise
king represents. When placed in charge of a native province, Marco, the
entrepreneur, introduces paper money and gunpowder and arrogantly
orders everyone to be happy. Because the USAmerican hero is so
obsessed with making his millions, he is blind to the love that the kahn's
daughter, Kukachin, has for him. As in "Madame Butterfly," the
tragedy involves the unrequited love of the Eastern woman for the
Western man; Kukachin is dead at the play's end, as is Cho-Cho-San in
"Madame Butterfly." Yet O'Neill uses Kukachin to deliver a scathing
critique of a capitalist and imperialist United States. In a remarkable
moment of letting the Orient speak, as it were, Kukachin reverses the
male imperial gaze and delivers the definitive reading of Marco as "an
exquisite judge of quantity" and "an idol of stuffed self-satisfaction."[5]
Although the East is once again the repository of spirituality (in opposition to Western materialism), the representation of the Orient as an
object of Western opportunism complicates the narrative of spirituality
and points to the imperialist basis of Western conceptions of the Orient.

The appeal of U.S. Orientalist fiction in popular culture in the early
twentieth century is also evident in the works of John P. Marquand.
Known principally as the creator of Mr. Moto, a character that later featured significantly in television shows, Marquand authored over fifteen
novels, including three Orientalist ones: *Ming Yellow* (1934), *No Hero*
(1935), and *Thank You, Mr. Moto* (1936). Marquand's Orientalist novels
typically involve a U.S. expatriate or traveler, well versed in local customs, who gets involved in an intrigue or conspiracy of international
dimensions. The hero shows prowess in traveling comfortably from one
culture to another and finally succeeds, in admirable nineteenth-century
fashion, in his mission of ensuring the safety of other expatriates. This
standard plot relies on, and assumes, hierarchically raced and gendered
cultural constructions of the Orient (China/Japan) and the United
States. In *Ming Yellow*, for instance, ming serves as a metonym for Chinese culture, as a relic of a bygone age, delicate and intrinsically valu-

able, yet easily bought by the power brokers on Wall Street. Through a series of cultural dichotomies, the oppositions between China and the United States are seen as those between passivity and activity, status and movement, intricacy and clarity, ambiguous sexuality and virility, past and present. For Tom Nelson, the hero of *Thank You, Mr. Moto,* China is a place where "men lived and died according to fixed etiquette, where nothing mattered very much, except perhaps tranquility."[6]

Marquand's most interesting creation is the Japanese Mr. Moto. Calm, outwardly obsequious, ever smiling, yet scheming, Moto embodies the paranoid fears of a generation of Americans about the potential power of Oriental countries, especially Japan and China, as well as suspicion about the Orientals living in the United States, a suspicion that led to the forced incarceration of Japanese Americans in internment camps during World War II. Yet despite, or perhaps because of, the paranoia, Moto is presented as an effeminate character, particularly in relation to the American hero. Moto enters the scene with an "inscrutable" Oriental smile, dusting his delicate fingers with a white handkerchief, the gold fillings in his teeth glittering in the sunlight. For Tom Nelson, the U.S. expatriate, Moto is an object of both conquest and desire. Remembering a conversation with Mr. Moto, Nelson, the narrator, writes, "He had never seemed so delicate as he did when I stood there looking down at him, a miniature of a man, as small as the gardens and the dwarfed trees of his island."[7] Marquand's representation of the Oriental male as not quite male, yet desirable, simply replicates the stereotype of the Asian male as passive and effeminate; however, Nelson's attraction to Moto and his construction of Moto as desirable also creates an ambivalent engendering of Nelson and questions the maleness and power of the hero embodying the nation.

After World War II, U.S. Orientalist literature undergoes a major thematic shift. In contrast to most of the texts discussed earlier, the conflation of the hero with the nation is tenuous at best in postwar texts. The split subjects of postwar fiction are uprooted characters in a permanent state of intellectual expatriation or alienation. Some look to the Asian Orient for succor, much in the tradition of nineteenth-century predecessors like Ralph Waldo Emerson and Walt Whitman, but unlike those predecessors, they encounter a hostile territory not amenable to intellectual and emotional appropriation. Others present the very attempt to arrive at a unified subjectivity, by adopting Oriental cultural practices, as misguided and comic at best.

John Hersey's *A Single Pebble* (1956) is a representative example of the inability of the USAmerican hero to wrest meaning and derive a wholeness of subjectivity from the Orient. The narrator, who, significantly, remains unnamed throughout the text, reveals little about himself other than that he is an engineer whose interest in China is to examine the possibilities of building a dam on the Yangtze River. The dramatic action takes place on the junk, or ship, on which the narrator travels with a crew of Chinese rivermen, the owner of the junk, and the owner's wife, Su-ling. In an inversion of the pattern of most U.S. Orientalist texts, *A Single Pebble* does not validate the manliness and strength of the hero. Instead, the unquestioned exemplar of courage and skill is the Chinese head tracker, Old Pebble. For most of his time on the junk, the ailing narrator is being nursed to health by Su-ling, while Old Pebble directs the junk's course safely through the treacherous river, which metaphorically represents the perilous journey of life. The narrator is in love with Su-ling, but Su-ling is no Cho-Cho-San of "Madame Butterfly" or Kukachin of *Marco Millions;* unlike the heroines of previous Orientalist texts, Su-ling shows no romantic interest in the USAmerican male. In an attempt to define himself through the Other, the narrator tries to classify the natives in turns as indolent, contented, and instinctual and then as reasoned and skilled, but no construction is fully explanatory. As the narrator agonizingly realizes, what is undermined during his journey on the river is the assumption of Western hermeneutic power.

> I was most intensely disturbed by the sense it [the river] gave me of the gap between the Chinese on the junk and myself, between Su-ling and myself, between the head tracker singing his beautiful chanteys and myself, between those to whom I was supposed to provide modern wonders of engineering and myself. . . ."[8]

The novel ends with the narrator unable to postulate any clear racial-cultural paradigms and unconcerned with his original project to build a dam.

The Beats perhaps stand alone in the postwar period in investing redemptively in oriental cultures and religions.[9] Hinduism and Zen Buddhism became, for writers like Allen Ginsberg and Jack Kerouac, possible avenues for countercultural values. Yet, in *The Dharma Bums,* Kerouac's assessment of the Beat use of Asia for personal/political salvation was highly critical. For Japhy, the most enthusiastic of the Dharma Bums, the Asian Orient is both a pre-Freudian sexual fantasy and the answer to Western technologized materialism. As Japhy enthusiastically explains, "there was no question of what to do about sex which is what I always liked about Oriental religion. And what I always dug about the Indians in our country."[10] But Ray, the moral spokesperson of the novel, discovers, through a Thoreauvian period of solitude, that intense, private meditation is possible in the mountains of the Northwest United States. What Kerouac critiques through Ray, however, is the idea of the Asian Orient as a panacea to Western ills, not the act of cultural appropriation itself.

The self-alienated and culturally alienated subject, trying, albeit unsuccessfully, to wrest an identity from an inhospitable Orient, is more typical of postwar texts than is the Beat mythologization of the Orient. The hero of Jay McInerney's *Ransom* (1985), sick with loathing for his father's world of commercial success, longs to escape Hollywood culture and find a site through which he can re-create himself. McInerney holds Ransom at a distance and represents the latter's Oriental quest as misdirected and pathetic at best: "He vaguely imagined Japan as . . . a strange island kingdom at the edge of the world, a personal frontier, a place of austere discipline which would cleanse and change him."[11] Ransom envisions Japan much as did Beats like Kerouac, for whom Asian cultures were seen as avenues through which the Western subject could be cleansed of materialism and made whole.[12] The Asian Orient is the new frontier of the imaginary, the Other through which the hero desires completion. But McInerney seems to suggest that the Asian Orient resists such an appropriation. Ransom enters the tutelage of a respected karate master, or *sen sei,* and attempts to perfect the art and morality of karate. In the end, he dies an unnecessary, if heroic, death, because he has not been able to follow the sensible advise of his *sen sei* to run when in trouble.

The Orient continues to figure prominently in the works of many contemporary writers. The characters of William Gibson's *Neuromancer* move from real to virtual reality—from space to cyberspace—through a series of Oriental journeys and detours. In *S,* John Updike draws on contemporary newspaper reports about the community of super-rich USAmerican sadhus in Rajneeshpuram, Oregon (followers of the Hindu guru Rajneesh), to parody the contemporary attempt to locate Oriental cultures and religions as counterculture utopias. Updike's Sara, although she is linked to the bold and rebellious Hester Prynne, is represented as a caricature of her literary forebear. A bored, rich woman, tired of her monotonous life as a New England doctor's wife, Sara seeks enlightenment from an ashram initiated by arhats in Arizona. Renamed

Kundalini by the arhat, Sara begins her new life of hard work, prayer, vegetarianism, and ascetic group sex, punctuated by visits to the ashram mall to buy arhat T-shirts and buttons. Only too late does she discover that the ashram is run by an Arthur Steinmetz, a USAmerican Jew turned Indian Hindu, who is in trouble with the police. Sara's dalliance with the Orient as a counterculture thus ends abruptly.

What needs to be explored in a further study are the complex cultural discourses that circulate in these twentieth-century "Orientalist" texts. The impulses toward imperial appropriation, the resistance of the Orient to this appropriation, and the failure of U.S. countercultural movements to provide viable alternatives to a superpower capitalist economy are all played out in these narratives of personal and national definition. Through the preponderance of satire and the insistent emphasis on the failure of present-day USAmericans to master the Orient, these texts engage in the dynamic tension between the powers of U.S. multinational capitalism and postcolonial resistance.

Notes

Preface

1. In his remarks to the National Press Club, Perot stated: "And what did they get in return [for the Indonesian connection]? A man named Huang—it's spelled H-u-a-n-g but pronounced 'Wong'—was given a position in the Clinton administration overseeing trade policy" (Ross Perot, National Press Club, October 24, 1996, CNN Website).

2. Another recent addition to the list of participants in Clinton's "Asian money" scandal is Taiwan-based mystic and billionaire Suma Ching Hai. See Howard Chua-Eoan's "The Buddhist Martha," *Time*, January 20, 1997, 47.

3. William Safire, "Dirty Money Actually a Green Peril," *Gainesville Sun*, December 23, 1996, 6A. As more of these funds are being investigated, the media is beginning to pay increasing attention to the stated goals of the "National Asian Pacific American Campaign Plan" to attempt to secure a political clout that had eluded Asian Americans for a century. See "Strategy Sought Asian Funds," *Gainesville Sun*, December 28, 1996, 1A.

4. I use the terms *USAmerican* and *USAmerica* in this book rather than *American* and *America* because they highlight the imperialism inherent in the slippage between the terms. Moreover, the term *USAmerican* is consonant with the current practice of historians trying to use culturally neutral and historically empirical terms, such as *the 1914–18 war* instead of *World War I* or *The Great War*.

5. Edward Said, *Orientalism* (New York: Random House, 1987), 2–3.

6. Reina Lewis, *Gendering Orientalism: Race, Femininity, and Representation* (New York: Routledge, 1996), 3. Lewis's conceptualization of the multiple positionalities within Orientalist discourse parallels my own thinking on this subject. Unfortunately, Lewis's book came out when my book was virtually complete—too late for me to have used it productively in my own arguments.

7. Lisa Lowe also argues for the specificity of particular Orientalist situa-

tions and for the heterogeneity of Orientalist discourse; see her *Critical Terrains: French and British Orientalisms* (Ithaca: Cornell University Press, 1991), ix–x, 5. Throughout this study I refer only to Algeria (and not Tunis or Tripoli) because most U.S. slaves were taken in Algiers.

8. In particular, I am most influenced by Judith Butler's *Gender Trouble: Feminism and the Subversion of Identity* (New York: Routledge, 1990) and *Bodies That Matter: On the Discursive Limits of "Sex"* (New York: Routledge, 1993).

9. Lawrence E. Buell, "American Literary Emergence as a Postcolonial Phenomenon," *American Literary History* 4, no. 3 (fall 1992): 411.

10. I am thinking in particular about Gayatri Chakrovarty Spivak's *In Other Worlds: Essays in Cultural Politics* (New York: Methuen, 1987), Rey Chow's *Woman and Chinese Modernity: the Politics of Reading Between West and East* (Minneapolis: University of Minnesota Press, 1991), Trinh T. Minh-ha's *Woman/Native/Other: Writing postcoloniality and feminism* (Bloomington: Indiana University Press, 1989) and *When the Moon Waxes Red: Representation, Gender and Cultural Politics* (New York: Routledge, 1991), and bell hooks's *Feminist Theory: From Margin to Center* (Boston: South End Press, 1984) and *Yearning: Race, Gender, and Cultural Politics.* (Boston: South End Press, 1990).

Introduction

1. My use of the term *cultural imaginary* is intended to evoke Jacques Lacan's use of the term *imaginary*. In Lacan's writings, the imaginary refers to "the world, the register, the dimension of images, conscious or unconscious, perceived or imagined" (Alan Sheridan, "Translator's Note," in Lacan's *The Four Fundamental Concepts of Psychoanalysis*, by Jacques Lacan, ed. Jacques-Alain Miller, trans. Alan Sheridan [New York: Norton, 1977], 279). As Kaja Silverman explains, the imaginary register, most classically exemplified by the mirror stage, is dominated by the poles of identification and duality and coexists with the symbolic; see Silverman, *The Subject of Semiotics* (New York: Oxford University Press, 1983), 157. Because the imaginary refers to the world of images and evokes questions of identity, it is a useful term with which to suggest both the pervasiveness of images of the Orient and issues of self-definition that are intimately connected with it.

2. Timothy Dwight, "America: Or a Poem on the Settlement of the British Colonies," in *The Major Poems of Timothy Dwight* (1752–1917); reprint, Gainesville, Fla.: Scholars' Facsimiles and Reprints, 1969), 11–12.

3. John Fiske, *American Political Ideas: Viewed from the Standpoint of Universal History*, with an introduction by Spencer Clark (Boston: Houghton Mifflin, 1911), 118.

4. Fiske, *American Political Ideas*, 119.

5. Fiske, *American Political Ideas*, 131.

6. Fiske, *American Political Ideas*, 143.

7. *Empire* and *Orient* are both complex and historically changing terms. My use of them throughout this study refers to the imaginative resonance these terms have for different writers rather than to an empirical meaning.

8. In my analysis of the imperial body formulated in relation to various Orients, I have found Judith Butler's idea of the male body contoured through its exclusions particularly useful because it complicates the gendered dichotomies of man-mind/woman-body. Butler writes: "Plato's scenography of intelligibility depends upon the exclusion of women, slaves, children. . . . This domain of the less than rational human bounds the figure of human reason, producing that 'man.' . . . This is a figure of disembodiment, but one which is nevertheless a figure of a body, a bodying forth of a masculinized rationality, the figure of a male body which is not a body, a figure in crisis. . . . This figuration of masculine reason as disembodied body is one whose imaginary morphology is crafted through the exclusion of other possible bodies" (Butler, *Bodies That Matter: On the Discursive Limits of "Sex"* [New York: Routledge, 1993], 48–49).

9. Edward Said, *Orientalism* (New York: Random House, 1978), 1.

10. Said, *Orientalism*, 3.

11. Said, *Orientalism*, 188, 206.

12. Said, *Orientalism*, 219.

13. Numerous postcolonial critics have questioned Said's model of power and an invariant Oriental tradition. B. J. Moore-Gilbert critiques Said's view that Orientalism "varied little between the regions upon which it operated" (Moore-Gilbert, *Kipling and Orientalism* [New York: St. Martin's, 1986], 1). Javed Majeed argues that nineteenth-century thinkers and poets had a sophisticated understanding of the creation of an ideological Orient beyond what Said allows. His own attention to the conflicting strands in the works of specific writers questions Said's "monolithic and ahistorical conception of orientalism"; see Majeed, *Ungoverned Imaginings: James Mill's "The History of British India" and Orientalism* (Oxford: Clarendon, 1992), 4–5. Nigel Leask takes Said to task for ignoring the anxieties and instabilities of empire, a topic his own work foregrounds; see Leask, *British Romantic Writers and the East: Anxieties of Empire* (Cambridge: Cambridge University Press, 1992), 2. Sara Mills, in a study of women's travel writing, suggests that women travel writers could not adopt the imperial voice with the ease of their male counterparts and that their descriptions focused more on particular individuals than on a race; see Mills, *Discourses of Difference: An Analysis of Women's Travel Writing and Colonialism* (New York: Routledge, 1991), 3. See also the works of Reina Lewis and Lisa Lowe cited in pref. nn. 6 and 7.

The most significant critiques of Orientalism are offered by James Clifford and Aijaz Ahmed. Clifford finds problematic Said's simultaneous use of radical antihumanists, such as Foucault, and his humanistic idea that Orientalism has distorted oriental experience. He also takes Said to task for not developing any theory of culture other than hegemonic and disciplinary. See Clifford, *The Predicament of Culture* (Cambridge: Harvard University Press, 1988), 258, 263–64. Ahmad also criticizes Said for trying to reconcile familiar values of humanist liberalism, such as tolerance and cultural pluralism, with Foucault's discourse theory. More importantly, he faults Said for positing a singular discourse, traversing precapitalist and capitalist periods, and for his preoccupation with canonical writers. See Ahmad, *In Theory: Classes, Nations, Literatures*

(London: Verso, 1992), 166–68. See also Catherine Gimelli Martin, "Orientalism and the Ethnographer: Said, Herodotus, and the Discourse of Alterity," *Criticism* 32, no. 4 (1990): 511–29.

14. Judith Butler, *Bodies That Matter*, 48–49; Homi K. Bhabha, "The Other Question," *Screen* 24 vi (1983): 18, 22.

15. For an analysis of the homoerotic nature of Western writings about the Near East, see Joseph A. Boone, "Vacation Cruises; or, The Homoerotics of Orientalism," *PMLA* 110 (1995): 89–107.

16. Bhabha's formulations (cited in n. 14 in this introduction) can sometimes lend themselves to an ahistorical application of hybridity. If we take hybridity as both the sign of colonial power and the means for subverting it, the discussion of colonialism becomes, to a large extent, irrelevant. Bhabha's excessive reliance on a Lacanian psychoanalytical model of the self as a metaphor for colonial relations can also lend itself to an ahistoricity at odds with any study related to a historical phenomenon like colonialism, no matter how variously we define this phenomenon.

17. Ella Shohat, "Notes on the 'Post-Colonial,'" *Social Text* 31/32 (1992): 109. Shohat's essay is a brilliant analysis of the problems of universally deploying the term *postcolonial* and of the institutional legitimation of PO-CO just as postcolonialists are all celebrating syncretism and hybridity. Jenny Sharpe also writes about the dangers of an ahistorical articulation of resistance within colonial discourse; see Sharpe, "Figures of Colonial Resistance," *Modern Fiction Studies* 35 (1989): 137–55.

18. Michel Foucault, *The Archaeology of Knowledge and the Discourse on Language*, trans. Sheridan Smith (New York: Pantheon, 1972; originally published in French in 1969), 32.

19. Foucault, *The Archaeology of Knowledge*, 37.

20. Michel Foucault, *Discipline and Punish: The Birth of the Prison*, trans. Alan Sheridan (New York: Random House, 1979; originally published in French in 1975), 23.

21. Rux Martin, "Truth, Power, Self: An Interview with Michel Foucault," in *Technologies of the Self: A Seminar with Michel Foucault*, ed. Luther H. Martin et al. (Amherst: University of Massachusetts Press, 1988), 10–11.

22. Michel Foucault, *The History of Sexuality*, trans. Robert Hurley, vol. 1 (New York: Vintage, 1980; originally published in French in 1976), 95.

23. Edward Said has also criticized the seeming collapse of distinction between power and resistance that Foucault's works seem to promote. Said cites Poulantzas's critique of Foucault to point to the lack of attention to struggles. He takes Foucault to task for not taking seriously his own ideas about resistances to power. "If power oppresses and controls and manipulates," Said writes, "then everything that resists it is not morally equal to power, is not neutrally and simply a weapon against that power. Resistance cannot equally be an adversarial alternative to power and a dependent function of it, except in some metaphysical, ultimately trivial sense" (Said, *The World, The Text, and the Critic* [Cambridge: Harvard University Press, 1983], 246). Said distinguishes between what he sees as the radical Foucault of the sixties and the Foucault of the eighties, who had turned from the historical to the local; see Said, *Culture and Impe-*

rialism (New York: Knopf, 1993), 26. I myself do not see the later Foucault as having given up the idea of history or the importance of power structures. In a sense, the notion of the circulation of power makes power structures even more ubiquitous.

24. Jonathan Arac and Harriet Ritvo, introduction to *Macropolitics of Nineteenth-Century Literature: Nationalism, Exoticism, Imperialism*, ed. Jonathan Arac and Harriet Ritvo (Philadelphia: University of Pennsylvania Press, 1991), 1.

25. Timothy Brennan, "The National Longing for Form," in *Nation and Narration*, ed. Homi K. Bhabha (New York: Routledge, 1990), 59.

26. Benedict Anderson, *Imagined Communities* (1983; reprint, New York: Verso, 1991); George L. Mosse, *Nationalism and Sexuality: Middle-Class Morality and Sexual Norms in Modern Europe* (Madison: University of Wisconsin Press, 1985). In *Culture and Imperialism* (83), Edward Said examines the significance of J. A. Hobson's formulation of imperialism as the expansion of nationality.

27. Toni Morrison, *Playing in the Dark: Whiteness and the Literary Imagination* (Cambridge: Harvard University Press, 1992), 44–45.

28. Although Morrison's argument is strong, it needs to be expanded to include the presence of Native Americans as well as various non-Western others that figure so prominently in the cultural imaginary. How, for example, can the Africanist presence alone explain either William Bradford's concept of culture and morality in *Of Plymouth Plantation* or the peculiarities of the literature of the yellow peril? The former depends on the Native American presence, the latter on the Chinese presence. Despite its purely Africanist focus, however, Morrison's basic idea of suppressed racial others constituting ideologies of nationhood is powerful.

29. Anderson, *Imagined Communities*, 5.

30. Mosse, *Nationalism and Sexuality*, 2.

31. Mosse, *Nationalism and Sexuality*, 40.

32. Mosse, *Nationalism and Sexuality*, 13, 23. See also Andrew Parker et al., eds., *Nationalism and Sexualities* (New York: Routledge, 1992), 6–7.

33. Rey Chow, "Violence in the Other Country: China as Crisis, Spectacle, and Woman," in *Third World Women and the Politics of Feminism*, ed. Chandra Talpade Mohanty, Ann Russo, and Lourdes Torres (Bloomington: Indiana University Press, 1991), 82.

34. Chow, "Violence in the Other Country," 86.

35. See Annette Kolodny, *The Lay of the Land: Metaphor as Experience and History in American Life and Letters* (Chapel Hill: University of North Carolina Press, 1975).

36. Philip Freneau, "American Liberty, a Poem," in *The Poems of Philip Freneau, Poet of the American Revolution*, ed. Fred Lewis Pattee (New York: Russell and Russell, 1963), vol. 1, 143. The poem was originally published in 1775.

37. The poem "Hail Columbia" was composed by Joseph Hopkinson; the music set to it is generally attributed to Philip Phile. See John Bartlett, *Familiar Quotations*, 14th ed. (Boston: Little, Brown, 1968), 508. Joel Barlow published his epic "The Vision of Columbus" in 1787 and "The Columbiad" in 1825.

38. National icons often take different sex-gender constructions depending on the qualities attributed to them. Case Wheeler, in a collection of poems

written on the occasion of U.S. independence, contrasts the proud and fierce, predatory, yet cowardly, (male) eagle, a symbol of the British, with the peaceful, yet brave, (female) crane, an apt symbol for the United States; see Wheeler, *Poems on Several Occurrences in the Present Grand Struggle for American Liberty* (Chatham, N.J.: Shepard Kollock, 1779), 3–5. Similarly, Benjamin Franklin, in his protest against the adoption of the bald eagle as a national emblem, writes, "For my own part, I wish the bald eagle had not been chosen as the representative of our country; *he* is a bird of bad moral character; *he* does not get his living honestly" (Franklin, letter to Mrs. Sarah Bache, January 26, 1784, in *The Complete Works of Benjamin Franklin,* vol. 8, ed. John Bigelow [New York: Putnam's, 1888], 444; emphasis mine). However, in Hawthorne's *Scarlet Letter,* the eagle is gendered as female and mother; see Stephanie A. Smith, *Conceived by Liberty: Maternal Figures and Nineteenth-Century American Literature* (Ithaca: Cornell University Press, 1995), 9–10.

39. Benson John Lossing, *Harper's Encyclopedia of United States History* (New York: Harper, 1902; reprint, Detroit: Gale Research Co., 1974), vol. 5: "Liberty-Cap".

40. Rana Kabbani examines in detail the European construction of the Orient as woman and sees Victorian travel writing about the Orient as part of a patriarchal discourse; see Kabbani, *Europe's Myths of the Orient* (Bloomington: Indiana University Press, 1986), 7.

41. Arthur Christy, *The Orient in American Transcendentalism* (New York: Columbia University Press, 1932), 65. Frederic Ives Carpenter's *Emerson and Asia* (1930; reprint, New York: Haskell House, 1968) similarly notes the importance of oriental literatures for Emerson but deals only with the transmission of ideas, such as mysticism and beauty. Carpenter is also at pains to point out that Emerson was not "really" indebted to oriental literatures and that his own philosophy was formed in ignorance of these literatures (2). V. K. Chari's *Whitman in the Light of Vedantic Mysticism* (Lincoln: University of Nebraska Press, 1964) is an attempt to see connections between the Vedantic concept of the self and Whitman's seemingly dual celebrations of body and soul.

42. Yu's study covers writers from Emerson to the Beat generation. Yu suggests that U.S. writers were unique in their "total absence of literary exoticism and cultural dilettantism" in their response to the Orient, because they saw the Orient in relation to Columbus's voyage; see Yu, *The Great Circle: American Writers and the Orient* (Detroit: Wayne State University Press, 1983), 22. Yu's book unfortunately perpetuates its own hegemonic Orientalism, because of Yu's eagerness to praise writers for simply showing an interest in the Orient. Talking about Henry Adams's responses to Japan, Yu writes: "Reason could not help him penetrate Japan. But he did try, even though he failed; herein lay the significance of Adams' pilgrimage to the Orient" (87). Yu's analysis itself participates in the imperialist construction of the West as a rational male attempting to "penetrate" an irrational East/woman. Similarly, Yu describes Percival Lowell's books as "a fascinating chronicle of the author's progress toward *the Asiatic mystery*" (87; emphasis mine).

43. Luther S. Luedtke, *Nathaniel Hawthorne and the Romance of the Orient* (Bloomington: Indiana University Press, 1989).

44. Fuad Sha'ban, *Islam and Arabs in Early American Thought: The Roots of Orientalism in America* (Durham, N.C.: Acorn, 1991), viii. Sha'ban's study is the only one to politicize USAmerican millennial and missionary interests in the Near Eastern Orient. It is limited, however, by his decision to foreground only the religious discourses of the period. The findings of Egyptology, the imperial narratives Egyptology generated, and the racial discourses of the period, for instance, do not figure into Sha'ban's study.

45. Perry Miller formulated the idea of Puritan origins as defining the development of U.S. culture. According to Miller, Puritanism "was not only the most coherent and most powerful single factor in the early history of America, it was a vital expression of a crucial period in European development" (Miller, *The New England Mind: The Seventeenth Century* [New York: Macmillan, 1939], viii). Miller acknowledges that the narrative of Puritan origins suppresses the history of slavery, but he writes nevertheless, "I recognize, and herein pay my tribute to, the priority of Virginia; but what I wanted was a coherence with which I could coherently begin" (Miller, *Errand into the Wilderness* [New York: Harper, 1956], viii). Amy Kaplan offers an interesting analysis of Miller's attempts to suppress the Africanist presence in his book. She suggests that Miller "represents a coherent America by constructing Africa as an imperial unconscious of national identity" (Kaplan, "Left Alone with America," in *Cultures of United States Imperialism*, ed. Amy Kaplan and Donald E. Pease [Durham, N.C.: Duke University Press, 1993], 5).

46. Leo Marx's *Machine in the Garden: Technology and the Pastoral Ideal in America* (New York: Oxford University Press, 1964) and R. W. B. Lewis's *The American Adam: Innocence, Tragedy, and Tradition in the Nineteenth Century* (Chicago: University of Chicago Press, 1955) are, in different ways, derived from this model.

47. Richard Slotkin, *Regeneration through Violence: The Mythology of the American Frontier, 1600–1860* (Middletown, Conn.: Wesleyan University Press, 1973), 5.

48. Ronald Takaki, *Iron Cages: Race and Culture in Nineteenth-Century American Culture* (New York: Knopf, 1979), xvii.

49. Richard Drinnon, *Facing West: The Metaphysics of Indian-Hating and Empire-Building* (Minneapolis: University of Minnesota Press, 1980).

50. William Appleman Williams, *The Tragedy of American Diplomacy* (New York: Dell, 1959); R. W. Van Alstyne, *The Rising American Empire* (Chicago: Quadrangle, 1960). Van Alstyne devotes a considerable part of his book to imperialism in the eighteenth century. The advantage of looking at the "American Empire," Van Alstyne points out is that "the United States can be studied as a member of the competitive system of national states, with a behavior pattern characteristic of an ambitious and dynamic national state . . . reversing the customary practice of treating national history from the standpoint of the nation preoccupied with its own internal affairs and only incidentally looking beyond its borders" (9). In *Empire as a Way of Life* (New York: Oxford University Press, 1980), Williams also devotes more attention to the late seventeenth and early eighteenth centuries. He pays particularly close attention to the contradictory rhetoric of liberty and empire in the writings of Thomas Jefferson

(59–65). Thomas R. Hietala focuses specifically on the expansionism of the United States from 1841 to 1849, a period when the country doubled its domain, and he criticizes the trend of diplomatic history to study only the period after 1890; see Hietala, *Manifest Design: Anxious Aggrandizement in Late Jacksonian America* (Ithaca: Cornell University Press, 1985), 260–61. See also V. G. Kiernan, *America: The New Imperialism: From White Settlement to World Hegemony* (London: Zed, 1978).

51. The most thorough analysis of Anglo-Saxon racial doctrines pervading the United States in the mid–nineteenth century is Reginald Horsman's *Race and Manifest Destiny: The Origins of Racial Anglo-Saxonism* (Cambridge: Harvard University Press, 1981).

52. Philip S. Foner, ed., *The Complete Writings of Thomas Paine* (New York, 1945), 1:17.

53. Van Alstyne, *The Rising American Empire*, 1. Van Alstyne takes the title of his book verbatim from Washington's phrase.

54. Cited in Wai-chee Dimock, *Empire for Liberty: Melville And The Poetics of Individualism* (Princeton: Princeton University Press, 1989), 9.

55. Thomas Jefferson, "To the Citizens of Washington," March 4, 1809, in *The Complete Jefferson* ed. Saul K. Padover (New York: Tudor, 1943), 552.

56. Cited in Samuel Flagg Bemis, *John Quincy Adams and the Foundations of American Foreign Policy* (New York: Knopf, 1949), 182.

57. Some critics have asserted that all U.S. literature is postcolonial. The relationship between postcoloniality and U.S. literature was first formulated in Bill Ashcroft, Gareth Griffiths, and Helen Tiffin's academic best-seller *The Empire Writes Back: Theory and Practice in Post-Colonial Literatures* (New York: Routledge, 1989), where the authors write: "The first post-colonial society to develop a 'national' literature was the USA. . . . In many ways the American experience and its attempts to produce a new kind of literature can be seen as the model for all later post-colonial writing" (16). The danger in such a formulation is that *The Empire Writes Back* provided a way of appropriating a very current and politically correct theory to reinscribe mainstream scholarship as formulated by theorists of national character in the line of Perry Miller. What had been called the "Puritan origins," the "city on a hill" mission, and the "jeremiad," all terms that also described "the American experience" from a strictly limited regional and gender perspective, could now be called postcolonial.

Lawrence E. Buell's suggestive use of postcoloniality as a prism for viewing nineteenth-century U.S. literature is similarly problematic. Questioning theories of Puritan or otherwise indigenous origins of U.S. literature, Buell proposes that the major texts of U.S. literature that declare literary independence are in fact texts implicated in a troubling colonized relationship to British literature. To support his thesis that canonical U.S. literature is a literature of the colonized, Buell draws together a series of parallels: Chinua Achebe's and Herman Melville's concerns with audience; Walt Whitman's and James Ngugi's concerns with language; and Whitman's and Henry David Thoreau's use of cultural hybridization, as well as Salmon Rushdie's and G. V. Desani's. Of course, Buell is well aware of the problematic politics of his comparisons and begins his essay by acknowledging the "possible hypocrisy of an exercise in imagining America of the expansionist years as a postcolonial rather than proto-imperial power" (Buell, "American Literary Emergence as a Postcolonial Phenomenon," *American Literary History* 4, no. 3 [fall 1992]: 411). However, although he promises to return to the issue at the end of the essay, he does so very briefly by suggesting that despite its imperialism, "American culture can be said to remain at least vestigially postcolonial as long as Americans are impressed by the sound of an educated British accent" (434).

The postcolonial status of U.S. literature is undeniable to the extent that one cannot simply ignore the anxieties of British influence under which seventeenth-, eighteenth-, and even nineteenth-century American writers labored and sought to create a literature appropriate to a new nation. What is left out of the aforementioned thesis, however, is that for internally colonized peoples like the African Americans and Native Americans, questions of British influence were peripheral, if not inconsequential. Even within canonical U.S. literature, in which concerns about the new USAmerican nationhood are important, to equate these concerns with the idea that postcolonial oppression from the former colonizing power formed the basic identity of (now) canonical U.S. literature—as do Ashcroft, Griffiths, and Tiffin—is problematic because it presumes no other position for this literature than that of the colonized. It is important, therefore, to pay attention to what Ella Shohat calls "the politics of location" instead of subsuming power differences with an easy stroke of the "post"; see Shohat, "Notes on the 'Postcolonial,'" 99, 102.

58. David S. Shields, *Oracles of Empire: Poetry, Politics, and Commerce in British America, 1690–1750* (Chicago: University of Chicago Press, 1990), 20.

59. Wai-Chee Dimock, *Empire for Liberty: Melville and the Poetics of Individualism* (Princeton: Princeton University Press, 1989), 8. Eric Cheyfitz, in *The Poetics of Imperialism* (New York: Oxford University Press, 1991), analyzes Burroughs's Tarzan texts in the light of U.S. foreign policy (3–21).

Chapter 1

1. For a good survey of the literary reception of the Near East in the early nineteenth century, see Dorothee Metlitsky Finkelstein's *Melville's Orienda* (New Haven: Yale University Press, 1961), 13–24. Luther S. Luedtke deals extensively with the commercial links between Salem and the Near and Far East; see his *Nathaniel Hawthorne and the Romance of the Orient* (Bloomington: Indiana University Press, 1989).

2. Thomas Goddard Wright, *Literary Culture in Early New England, 1620–1730* (1920; reprint, New York: Russell and Russell, 1966), 25. Some of the books donated to the Yale Library in 1714 included Sir Walter Raleigh's *History of the World* (1614) and Paul Ricaut's *History of the Present State of the Ottoman Empire*, (London: John Starkey and Henry Brome, 1675). See Wright, op. cit., 185–86.

3. Wright, *Literary Culture in Early New England*, 273–74, 280.

4. Cited in Wright, *Literary Culture in Early New England*, 178.

5. Wright, *Literary Culture in Early New England*, 148.

6. Mukhtar Ali Isaani *The Oriental Tale in America through 1865: A Study in American Fiction* (Ph.D. diss., Princeton, 1962).

7. John A. Wilson, *Signs and Wonders Upon Pharoah: A History of American Egyptology* (Chicago: University of Chicago Press, 1964), 36

8. John T. Irwin, *American Hieroglyphics: The Symbol of the Egyptian Hiero-glyphics in the American Renaissance* (New Haven: Yale University Press, 1980), 3–5.

9. For Schwab, the publication of the *Zend Avesta* by Abraham Hyacinthe Anquetil-Duperron in 1771 marks the beginning of an intellectual revolution; see Schwab, *The Oriental Renaissance: Europe's Rediscovery of India and the East, 1680–1880*, trans. Gene Patterson-Black and Victor Reinking (New York: Columbia University Press, 1984), 7.

10. Kenneth Walter Cameron, "Young Emerson's Orientalism at Har-vard," in *Indian Superstition*, by Ralph Waldo Emerson, ed. Kenneth Walter Cameron (Hanover, N.H.: Friends of the Dartmouth Library, 1954), 13.

11. Alan D. Hodder, "Emerson, Rammohan Roy, and the Unitarians," in *Studies in the American Renaissance*, ed. Joel Myerson (Charlottesville: University Press of Virginia, 1988), 135.

12. There is some confusion about the date of publication of this tale. John Bigelow, in his edition of Franklin's works, lists the tale as written in 1779; see Bigelow, ed., *The Complete Works of Benjamin Franklin*, vol. 6 (New York: Put-nam's, 1888), 261–66. Frank L. Mott and Chester E. Jorgenson, in their *Benjamin Framklin: Representative Selections* with Introduction, bibliography, and notes (New York: Hill and Wang, 1936), list it as "date unknown" (New York), 519, 544.

13. Frank Luther Mott, *Golden Multitudes* (New York: Macmillan, 1947), 305, cited in Luedtke, *Nathaniel Hawthorne and the Romance of the Orient*, 64, 61. Luedtke's book is thus far the best study of U.S. writing in the context of the Orient.

14. Benjamin Silliman, *Letters of Shahcoolen*, with an introduction by Ben Harris McClary (1802; reprint, Gainesville, Fla.: Scholars' Facsimiles and Reprints, 1962), 7.

15. The articles in question are "Arabian Literature: First Paper," *Southern Literary Messenger*, June 1840, 457–60; "Arabian Literature: Paper Second," *Southern Literary Messenger*, July 1840, 563–66; "Arabian Literature: Paper Third," *Southern Literary Messenger*, November 1840, 760–63.

16. Luedtke, *Nathaniel Hawthorne and the Romance of the Orient*, xv–xvi.

17. Attempts to initiate trade with the Near East started soon after the Rev-olutionary War, once the strictures of the Acts of Trade, which forbade direct trade with the Levant, were no longer applicable. U.S. ships visited Constan-tinople in 1786, Smyrna in 1797, and Alexandria in 1800. See James A. Field Jr., *America and the Mediterranean World, 1776–1882* (Princeton: Princeton Univer-sity Press, 1969), 113.

18. Other Turkish exports included fruit, nuts, silver, raw wool, and hides. Imports from the United States were varied, but the main item was New Eng-land rum. See David H. Finnie, *Pioneers East: The Early American Experience in the Middle East* (Cambridge: Harvard University Press, 1967), 30–31.

19. Finnie, *Pioneers East*, 32.

20. By 1832 Eckford had built the *Mahmud*, which at 3,934 tons was the largest battleship in the world. See Finnie, *Pioneers East*, 70–71.

21. Philip Freneau, "On the First American Ship That Explored the Route to India" in *The Poems of Philip Freneau, Poet of the American Revolution*, vol. 2, ed. Fred Lewis Pattee (New York: Russell and Russell, 1963), 261.

22. Quoted in Ernest Lee Tuveson, *Redeemer Nation: The Idea of America's Millenial Role* (Chicago: University of Chicago Press, 1968), 101.

23. Quoted in Loren Baritz, *City on a Hill: A History of Ideas and Myths in America* (New York: Wiley, 1964), 107.

24. Reginald Horsman, *Race and Manifest Destiny: The Origins of Racial Anglo-Saxonism* (Cambridge: Harvard University Press, 1981), 90–91.

25. Ships took iron, hemp, and duck from Sweden and Madeira, rum and sugar from the West Indies, and fish, flour, iron, and tobacco from New York, Philadelphia, and Virginia. They returned with tea, coffee, muslins, and silks. See William B. Weeden, *Economic and Social History of New England, 1620–1789*, vol. 1 (1890; reprint, New York: Hillary House, 1963), 820–22.

26. Customary profits on muslins and calicoes from Calcutta, for instance, were a hundred percent. It is little wonder that the younger Derby stayed in India for three years. Derby recorded 125 voyages in 1785–89, of which 45 were to India or China. See Weeden, *Economic and Social History of New England*, 825.

27. R. W. Van Alstyne, *The United States and East Asia* (London: Thames and Hudson, 1973), 19.

28. John Sweetman, *The Oriental Obsession* (New York: Cambridge University Press, 1988), 212.

29. Luedtke, *Nathaniel Hawthorne and the Romance of the Orient*, 26–27.

30. Finnie, *Pioneers East*, 165.

31. Finnie, *Pioneers East*, 155.

32. *New York Daily News*, April 18, 1856, 1.

33. *American Oriental Society* 1 (1843–49): 64–67. This list is far from complete. It does not include, for instance, Rev. Isaac Taylor's *Scenes in Asia* (cited in n. 35 in this chapter).

34. I do not mean to suggest that travel writing is somehow innocent of ideology. As many critics, including Mary Louise Pratt, have pointed out, travel writing is perhaps the most pointed illustration of the imperial gaze. I am simply pointing out that missionary writers do not foreground the conversion agenda but rather cleverly embed it within the structure of the conventional travel narrative.

35. Rev. Isaac Taylor, *Scenes in Asia, for the Amusement and Instruction of Little Tarry-at-Home-Travellers* (Hartford, Conn.: Silas Andrus, 1826), iii.

36. Bayard Taylor's works are discussed more fully in chap. 3.

37. Finnie, *Pioneers East*, 5.

38. George William Curtis, *The Howadji in Syria* (New York: Hurst and Co., 1852), 9.

39. Curtis, *The Howadji in Syria*, 17.

40. Curtis, *The Howadji in Syria*, 18.

41. Carl Bode, *Anatomy of American Popular Culture, 1840–1861* (Berkeley:

University of California Press, 1959), 105. Bode's book includes a picture of Bayard Taylor in full Arab dress. Bode deals only with Taylor's *The Lands of the Saracen,* which he calls escapist (231), a feature not common to all of Taylor's writings. Although some parts of *The Lands of the Saracen* might be in the tradition of escapist orientalist writing, his *A Visit to India, China, and Japan* closely reports current political activities and social mannerisms in a fashion hardly characteristic of escapist writing.

42. Bayard Taylor writes, for instance: "in few of the English works on India which I have read, has justice been done to the character of the native population. The Parsees, especially, form a community distinguished for its intelligence, enterprise and public spirit" (Taylor, *A Visit to India, China, and Japan in the Year 1853* [1855; reprint, New York: Putnam's, 1862], 39–40).

43. Bayard Taylor, *A Visit to India, China, and Japan,* 372.

44. Horsman, *Race and Manifest Destiny,* 47.

45. Cited in Horsman, *Race and Manifest Destiny,* 119.

46. For similarities between phrenological depictions of superior Anglo-Saxon races and the bodies Whitman celebrated in his poems, see Harold Aspiz, *Walt Whitman and the Body Beautiful* (Urbana: University of Illinois Press, 1980), 139–40, 189.

47. Samuel George Morton, *Crania Americana; or a Comparative View of the Skulls of Various Aboriginal Nations* (Philadelphia: J. Dobson, 1839), 5.

48. Morton, *Crania Americana,* 6.

49. Morton, *Crania Americana,* 7.

50. Morton, *Crania Americana,* 29.

51. Morton, *Crania Americana,* 31.

52. Morton, *Crania Americana,* 31.

53. In 1837, Morton wrote to George R. Gliddon, the U.S. consul in Cairo: "it is very important that I should get a few heads of Egyptian mummies from Thebes, &c. . . . and if twenty-five or thirty skulls, or even half that number can be obtained, . . . I am ready to defray every expense" (cited in Josiah C. Nott and George R. Gliddon, *Types of Mankind; or Ethnological Researches Based upon the Ancient Monuments, Paintings, Sculptures, and Crania of Races and upon Their Natural, Geographical, Philological, and Biblical History* (Philadelphia: Lippincott, Grambo, and Co., 1854), xxxv.

54. Cited in Nott and Gliddon, *Types of Mankind,* xxxvii.

55. Samuel George Morton, "Observations on Egyptian Ethnography, Derived from Anatomy, History, and the Monuments," *Transactions of the American Philosophical Society* 9 (1846): 157–58.

56. Nott and Gliddon, *Types of Mankind,* 84.

57. Frederick Douglass, "The Claims of the Negro Ethnologically Considered" (address delivered at Western Reserve College, July 12, 1854), published in *The Life and Writings of Frederick Douglass,* ed. Philip S. Foner, vol. 2, *Pre-Civil War Decade, 1850–1860* (New York: International Publishers, 1950), 296–301.

58. S. S. N., "Anglo-Saxons and Anglo-Africans," *Weekly Anglo-African,* August 13, 1859, 4.

59. Pauline Hopkins, "Famous Women of the Negro Race," part 7, "Educators," *Colored American Magazine* 5 (June 1902): 130.

60. Josiah C. Nott, *Two Lectures; on the Connection between the Biblical and Physical History of Man* (1849; reprint, New York: Negro Universities Press, 1969), 17.

61. Jacob Norton, *Faith on the Son of God Necessary to Everlasting Life: A Sermon Delivered before the Massachusetts Missionary Society at Their Eleventh Annual Meeting, in Boston, May 29, 1810* (Boston: Lincoln and Edmands, 1810), 25.

62. Charles L. Chaney, *The Birth of Missions in America* (South Pasadena, Calif.: William Carey Library, 1976), 187.

63. Squadron letters, Smith to Secretary of the Navy, April 19, 1845, and September 11, 1845, cited in Field, *America and the Mediterranean World*, 210.

64. Rev. C. H. Wheeler, *Ten Years on the Euphrates; or Primitive Missionary Policy Illustrated* (Boston: American Tract Society, 1868), 75.

65. "Report of the American Board of Commissioners for Foreign Missions Read at the Second Annual Meeting, 1811," in *First Ten Annual Reports of the American Board of Commissioners for Foreign Missions* (Boston: Crocker and Brewster, 1834), 23.

66. *First Ten Annual Reports*, 29.

67. *First Ten Annual Reports*, 23.

68. *First Ten Annual Reports*, 177.

69. *First Ten Annual Reports*, 211.

70. Rev. Isaac Taylor, *Scenes in Asia*, 81.

71. Rufus Anderson, *History of the Missions of the American Board of Commissioners for Foreign Missions to the Oriental Churches*, vol. 1 (Boston: Congregational Publishing Society, 1872), 2.

72. Wheeler, *Ten Years on the Euphrates*, 43.

73. John Pickering, "Address," *Journal of the American Oriental Society* 1, no. 1 (1849): 2.

74. Pickering, "Address," 2.

75. Pickering, "Address," 2.

76. Pickering, "Address," 5.

77. Pickering, "Address," 5.

Chapter 2

1. Samuel Eliot Morison, *The Oxford History of the American People* (New York: Oxford University Press, 1965), 363.

2. These details are taken from H. G. Barnby's account in *The Prisoners of Algiers: An Account of the Forgotten American-Algerian War* (New York: Oxford Press, 1966), 1, 86, 303.

3. James A. Field, Jr. *America and the Mediterranean World, 1776–1882* (Princeton: Princeton University Press, 1969), 51–53.

4. *Naval Documents Related to the United States Wars with the Barbary Powers* (Washington, D.C.: U.S. Government Printing Office, 1939), 1:22, cited in Lotfi Ben Rejeb, "'To The Shores of Tripoli': The Impact of Barbary on Early American Nationalism" (Ph.D. diss., Indiana University, 1982), 80.

5. David A. Carson, "Jefferson, Congress, and the Question of Leadership

in the Tripolitan War," *Virginia Magazine of History and Biography* 94, no. 4 (October 1986): 408.

6. Cited in Lotfi Ben Rejeb, "To the Shores of Tripoli," 82. Rejeb sees the Barbary wars as vital in the ideological construction of a powerful American nationalism at the turn of the century. Rejeb writes: "The issue was not only economic and political but also highly ideological: the United States meant to reflect the image of a national character—an odd mixture of aggressive manliness and self-righteous idealism, of power and romanticism—at once inside and beyond her frontiers. The brand of nationalism produced the prototypical idea and behavior which later ushered in the 'big stick' policy and became a pattern of American involvement abroad" (83).

7. Cited in Lotfi Ben Rejeb, "To the Shores of Tripoli," 82–83.

8. Robert J. Allison, *The Crescent Obscured: The United States and the Muslim World, 1776–1815* (New York: Oxford University Press, 1995), xvi. Allison's study is important in emphasizing the significance of the Muslim world as an adversary in cultural and political ideas of nationhood. Although Allison brings into his analysis such literary works as Royall Tyler's *The Algerine Captive* (1797) and Susanna Rowson's *Slaves in Algiers* (1794), his treatment of them is cursory.

9. Western thought had long distinguished between the power of the (Western) monarch and that of the (Eastern) despot. Beginning with Aristotle's contrast between the power of the monarch, which served the people, and that of the despot, which simply served the tyrant himself, the distinctions persisted. In France, the word *despotism* entered the dictionary in the eighteenth century and referred to arbitrary, as opposed to reasonable, power. Such arbitrary power was seen to be exemplified by Turkey, Japan, Persia, and all of the countries of Asia. See Olivier Richon, "Representation, the Despot, and the Harem: Some Questions around an Academic Orientalist Painting by Lecomte-Du-Nouy (1885)," in *Europe and Its Others*, ed. Frances Barker et al. (Colchester: University of Essex Press, 1985), 8–9.

10. Thomas Jefferson, *The Autobiography*, in *The Writings of Thomas Jefferson*, ed. A. A. Lipscomb and A. E. Bergh (Washington, D.C. Issued by Thomas Jefferson Memorial Association of the United States, 1903–1904), reprinted in *The Norton Anthology of American Literature*, 3rd ed. vol. 1, Eds. Nina Baym et al (New York: Norton, 1989), 642.

11. Lewis P. Simpson, "Jefferson and the Writings of the South," in Empire for Liberty, 131–33.

12. Benjamin Franklin, "On the Slave Trade," in *The Complete Works of Benjamin Franklin*, vol. 10, ed. John Bigelow (New York: Putnam's, 1888). The piece appeared in the *Federal Gazette* on March 25, 1790.

13. Mukhtar Ali Isaani, "The Oriental Tale in America through 1865" (Ph.D. diss., Princeton University, 1962), 74.

14. Royall Tyler, *The Algerine Captive* ed. Don L. Cook (1797; reprint, New Haven, CT: College and University Press, 1970), 224 (hereafter cited parenthetically in text).

15. See Tyler, *The Algerine Captive*, 34–35. Tyler got the details for this particular episode from Jeremy Belknap's *History of New Hampshire* vol 1 (Philadel-

phia: Printed for the author by Robert Aitken, 1784). John Engell sees *The Algerine Captive* as a satire on the country's pretensions to freedom. Engell suggests that Tyler "studied American character without the blinders of national pride, without self-congratulation or inflated rhetoric" (Engell, "Narrative Irony and National Character in Royall Tyler's *The Algerine Captive*," *Studies in American Fiction* 17, no. 1 [1989]: 19).

16. Marwin M. Obeidat writes that in *The Algerine Captive*, captivity is not a central theme: "*The Algerine Captive* is also a travel narrative, and Underhill is the first American innocent abroad, who wants to provide the American reader with fabulous information about the 'Barbary Pirates' affair, the Muslim East, the Barbary Prophet, and Algerian life in general among other things having to do with Islam" (Obeidat, "Royal Tyler's *The Algerine Captive* and the Barbary Orient: An Example of America's Literary Awareness of the Muslim Near East" *American Journal of Islamic Social Sciences* 5, no. 2 [1988]: 258).

17. John Engell calls attention to the contiguity of these dates; see Engell, "Narrative Irony and National Character," 29.

18. George L. Mosse, *Nationalism and Sexuality: Middle-Class Morality and Sexual Norms in Modern Europe* (Madison: University of Wisconsin Press, 1985), 23.

19. William Bradford's attack on Thomas Morton focuses as much on his atheism as on his lack of concern with social forms. Bradford lists Morton's excesses in drinking, dancing, consorting socially with Native American men and women, and reveling around the Maypole. See Bradford, *Of Plymouth Plantation*, ed. Harvey Wish (New York: Capricorn, 1962), 141.

20. Edward Said, *Orientalism* (New York: Random House, 1987), 188.

21. Lotfi Ben Rejeb deals at length with the differences between slavery as privateering in the North African states and slavery as practiced in the plantations of the United States. Rejeb points out that slaves in North Africa were commercial commodities that could profitably be exchanged for ransom. Many North African slaves owned livestock, and some even had servants. See Rejeb, "To the Shores of Tripoli," 9–10.

22. Cathy Davidson, *Revolution and the Word: The Rise of the Novel in America* (New York: Oxford University Press, 1986), 206. Davidson analyzes *The Algerine Captive* as a picaresque novel whose function was to provide a critique of "what was rotten in the American polis" but that "stopped short of outlining a project of political change" (210).

23. In the nineteenth century, Oriental luxury as a trope for plantation splendor and benign slavery began to be well circulated. In *Uncle Tom's Cabin*, for instance, Harriet Beecher Stowe describes St. Clare's plantation as follows: "Wide galleries ran all around the four sides, whose Moorish arches, slender pillars, and arabesque ornaments, carried the mind back, as in a dream, to the reign of oriental romance in Spain." See Harriet Beecher Stowe, *Uncle Tom's Cabin* (1852; reprint, New York: Penguin, 1981), 179.

24. See Laura Mulvey, "Visual Pleasure in Narrative Cinema," *Screen* 16, no. 3 (1975): 9. Mulvey's explanation of pleasure is still compelling despite her assumption of a male viewer. In the colonial situation, the pleasure of the look is useful in understanding the Western gaze on the Orient.

25. David Everett, *Slaves in Barbary*, in *Columbian Orator* ed. Caleb Bingham (Boston, Printed for Caleb Bingham), 1817, 118.

26. Field, *America and the Mediterranean World*, 52–53.

27. Robert Treat Paine, "Ode, Written and Sung for General Eaton Fire Society, January 14, 1810," in *Works, in Verse and Prose, of the Late Robert Treat Paine, jun., Esq.* (Printed and Published by J. Belcher, Boston, 1812), 285, cited in Allison, *The Crescent Obscured*, 201.

28. Jonathan Smith, *The Siege of Algiers* (Philadelphia: J. Maxwell, 1823), 4.

29. James Ellison, *The American Captive* (Boston: Joshua Belcher, 1812), hereafter cited parenthetically in text.

30. Joseph Stevens Jones, *The Usurper; or Americans in Tripoli*, in *"Metamora" and Other Plays*, ed. Eugene Richard Page (1841; Princeton: Princeton University Press, 1903), 174; the 1903 edition will hereafter be cited parenthetically in text.

31. *The Siege of Algiers* sets the U.S. mission against the larger context of Christendom and Islam. A character named Mahomet, for instance, solemnly swears to ward off the powers of Christendom. Another, called the "Christian Monitor," plays the voice of conscience for all the Westerners participating in the system of tribute. The Consular House is called the "United Christian Brotherhood in the West" (Jonathan Smith, *The Siege of Algiers*, 19). Citizen Yankoo exemplifies liberty and freedom, the Dey incredible cruelty and lust.

32. Ellison's characterization of Juba, a black cook, also seems designed to question complacency about U.S. slavery. Juba always addresses Jack as "massa" and yet, when asked about slavery, exclaims: "O massa, no, no; we brack gentlemen be all *free!*" (Ellison, *The American Captive*, 38).

33. Reginald Horsman supports this thesis throughout his book *Race and Manifest Destiny: The Origins of American Racial Anglo-Saxonism* (Cambridge: Harvard University Press, 1981). About racialism in the 1830s, he writes, "The most influential American scientific writing defending innate racial differences was not to appear until after 1839, but public assertions of the existence of superior and inferior races increased rapidly in the 1830s" (120).

34. Sarah Haight, *Letters from the Old World*, vol. 1 (New York: Harper, 1840), 112.

35. I have not dealt here with Rowson's novel *The Test of Honour, A Novel*, 2 vols. (London: Printed for John Abraham, 1789), which has a subplot of Algerian captivity. The novel was written before Rowson's move to the United States and does not enter into discourses on U.S. nationalism. *Slaves in Algiers* is a reworking of the Algerian subplot in the earlier novel.

36. The boisterous theater audiences of Rowson's times also delighted in patriotic themes. Patricia L. Parker writes, "They interrupted a musical number with demands to hear 'Yankee Doodle,' and threw gin bottles and orange peels if they did not get it" (Parker, *Susanna Rowson* [Boston: Twayne, 1986], 70).

37. Susanna Rowson, *Slaves in Algiers* (Philadelphia: Wrigley and Berriman, 1794), 9 (hereafter cited parenthetically in text).

38. Wendy Martin, "Profile: Susanna Rowson, Early American Novelist," *Women's Studies* 2 (1974): 2.

39. Dorothy Weil, *In Defense of Women: Susanna Rowson (1762–1824)* (University Park: Pennsylvania State University Press, 1976), 37.

40. Cathy Davidson, "Flirting with Destiny: Ambivalence and Form in the Early American Novel," *Studies in American Fiction* 10 (1982): 18. Similar arguments about sentimental novels embodying masks of femininity and ideal womanhood have been made by Ann Douglas Wood in "The Scribbling Women' and Fanny Fern: Why Women Wrote," *American Quarterly* 23 (1971): 3–24. Writing about Victorian domestic novels, Nancy Armstrong has argued that domestic narratives seized power by authorizing what was female and contested the "reigning notion of kinship relations that attached most power and privilege to certain family lines" (Armstrong, *Desire and Domestic Fiction: A Political History of the Novel* [New York: Oxford University Press, 1987], 5).

41. Cathy Davidson points out how Rowson's portrayal of Meriel's abuse at the hands of her husband, Clement, in *Trials of the Human Heart* (Philadelphia: Printed for author by Wriglay & Berriman 1795) is subversive in that it does not correspond to the "pervasive sentimental ideal of tranquil, connubial domesticity" (Davidson, "Flirting with Destiny," 21).

42. Martin, "Profile: Susanna Rowson," 3.

43. James Tilton, "An Oration, Pronounced on the 5th July, 1790," *Universal Asylum and Columbian Magazine* 5 (December 1790): 372.

44. Benjamin Silliman, *Letters of Shahcoolen,* with an introduction by Ben Harris McClary (1802; reprint, Gainesville, Fla: Scholars' Facsimiles and Reprints, 1962), 22, 23.

45. Mary Wollstonecraft, *A Vindication of the Rights of Women,* ed. Charles W. Hagelman (1792; reprint, New York: Norton, 1967), 206.

46. Weil, "In Defense of Women," 40.

47. Patricia L. Parker sees this speech only as an exemplification of Rowson's criticism of the subordination of women; see Parker, *Susanna Rowson,* 71.

48. Joseph Buckminster, "A Sermon Preached before the Members of the Boston Female Asylum, September 1810," cited in Nancy F. Cott, *The Bonds of Womanhood: 'Woman's Sphere' in New England, 1780–1835* (New Haven, Conn.: Yale University Press, 1977), 148.

49. See Cott, *The Bonds of Womanhood,* 153.

50. Malek Alloula has brilliantly shown how harems fulfilled fantasies for male voyeurs and how the passivity of the women in them was assumed. By analyzing French postcards of Algeria in the early twentieth century, Alloula shows how the eroticized bodies of Algerian women were part of photographers' own voyeurism and how the imaginary possession of the women was a surrogate for the conquest of the Algerians. See Alloula, *The Colonial Harem,* trans. Myrna Godzich and Wlad Godzich (Minneapolis: University of Minnesota Press, 1986), xi.

51. Jonathan Smith, *The Siege of Algiers,* 65.

52. Sara Mills, in *Discourses of Difference: An Analysis of Women's Travel Writings and Colonialism* (New York: Routledge, 1991), argues, for instance, that British women writers formulated a counterhegemonic discourse that questioned the orientalist presumptions of male writers.

53. Although *Salmagundi* appeared as the combined work of Washington

Irving, William Irving, and James Kirk Paulding, I generally refer to Washington Irving as the main author of the work. William Irving is known to have contributed most of the sentimental poetry scattered in the volume. Evert A. Duyckinck, the editor of the 1860 edition of *Salmagundi* (New York: Putnam's), noted that the writing anticipated Washington Irving's *Sketch Book* and the humor of his *A History of New York, by Diedrich Knickerbocker*. In his introduction to the 1860 edition, Duyckinck states, "The book in fact, is every way in place in company with the series of Mr Irving's writings. It was not all of his composition to be sure . . . ; but, without separating his part from the rest, and making every allowance for inexperience of style, we may readily enough detect throughout its pages the genius of Washington Irving" (vi).

54. The Mustapha letters in *Salmagundi* are numbered III, V, VII, IX, XI, XIV, XVI, XVIII, and XIX. See the 1860 edition of *Salmagundi*, cited in the preceding note.

55. On the Oriental Renaissance in Europe, see the work of Raymond Schwab cited in chap. 1 n. 9.

56. Cited in Stanley T. Williams, *The Life of Washington Irving* (New York: Oxford University Press, 1935), 2:221.

57. Warren S. Walker, "Two- and Three-Tailed Turks in *Salmagundi*," *American Literature* 53 (1981): 477–78. Walker presents interesting evidence to illustrate the historical bases of the Mustapha letters. Mustapha's letter in which he bemoans the lack of adequate clothing and the inability of his captors to provide easily for his needs, for instance, is not entirely fictitious. Walker points out that the Turkish prisoners had in fact "appeared several times at theatres during benefit performances given in part to finance new wardrobes for them, their only clothes at the time of their capture having grown tattered" (477).

58. See p. 113 of the 1860 edition of *Salmagundi* (cited in chap 2 n. 52); the 1860 edition will hereafter be cited parenthetically in text.

59. Peter Markoe, *The Algerine Spy in Pennsylvania* (Philadelphia: Prichard and Hall, 1787), 18 (hereafter cited parenthetically in text).

60. Silliman, *Letters of Shahcoolen*, 22–23.

61. Silliman, *Letters of Shahcoolen*, 41–42.

62. Barnby, *The Prisoners of Algiers*, 303–4.

63. See Lotfi Ben Rejeb, "To the Shores of Tripoli," viii.

Chapter 3

1. Josiah C. Nott and George R. Gliddon, *Types of Mankind; or Ethnological Researches Based upon the Ancient Monuments, Paintings, Sculptures, and Crania of Races and upon Their Natural, Geographical, Philological, and Biblical History* (Philadelphia: Lippincott, Grambo, and Co., 1854), 87.

2. Nott and Gliddon, *Types of Mankind*, 52.

3. James A. Field Jr., *America and the Mediterranean World, 1776–1882* (Princeton: Princeton University Press, 1969), 181.

4. David H. Finnie, *Pioneers East: The Early American Experience in the Middle East* (Cambridge: Harvard University Press, 1967), 155.

5. Mark Twain, *The Innocents Abroad* (1869; reprint, New York: Signet, 1966), 477.

6. John Sweetman, *The Oriental Obsession* (New York: Cambridge University Press, 1988), 219.

7. Finnie, *Pioneers East*, 5.

8. Ahmed M. Metwalli, "Americans Abroad: The Popular Art of Travel Writing in the Nineteenth Century," in *America: Exploration and Travel*, ed. Steven E. Kagle (Bowling Green, Ohio: Bowling Green State University Press, 1979).

9. Ann Douglass, *The Feminization of American Culture* (New York: Knopf, 1977), 14–17, 48–49.

10. Douglass, *The Feminization of American Culture*, 8.

11. Rev. Ross C. Houghton, *An Account of the Religious, Intellectual, and Social Condition of Women in Japan, China, India, Egypt, Syria, and Turkey* (Cincinnati: Hitchcock and Walden, 1877), 5.

12. A. L. Tibawi, *American Interest in Syria, 1800–1901: A Study of Educational, Literary, and Religious Work* (Oxford: Clarendon, 1966), 29, 303.

13. "The United States: A Commissioned Missionary Nation," *American Theological Review* 1 (January 1859): 154.

14. By 1848 there were thirteen women's missionary societies in New England alone. See Helen Barrett Montgomery, *Western Women in Eastern Lands* (New York: Garland, 1987), 19.

15. Rev. Dr. Anderson, *Journal of the American Oriental Society* 1, no. 4 (1848): xl.

16. The most prominent examples of domestic novels would be Susan Warner's *Wide, Wide World* (London: J. Nisbett 1851) and Maria Susanna Cummins' *The Lamplighter* (Boston: J. P. Jewett 1854).

17. "Orientalism," *Knickerbocker* 41 (June 1853): 479–80.

18. Henry J. Brent, "The Mysterious Pyramid," *Knickerbocker* 35 (April 1850): 304.

19. Brent, "The Mysterious Pyramid," 304.

20. Brent, "The Mysterious Pyramid," 306.

21. Maturin Murray Ballou, *The Turkish Slave: Mahometan and His Harem* (Boston: E. Gleason, 1850), 11 (hereafter cited parenthetically in text).

22. Many critics have argued the importance of African literature and culture to U.S. literature. See, for instance, Eric Sundquist, *To Wake the Nations: Race in the Making of American Literature* (Cambridge: Harvard University Press, Belknap Press, 1994), 2–3.

23. Anna Jameson, *Lives of Celebrated Female Sovereigns and Illustrious Women* (Philadelphia: Porter and Coates, 1870), 28. Some of the other women included in Jameson's collection are Joan of Arc, Anne Boleyn, Empress Josephine, and Lady Jane Grey.

24. William Gibbon, *The History of the Decline and Fall of the Roman Empire* (New York: Harper, 1851), 1:350.

25. William Ware, *Letters of Lucius M. Piso From Palmyra to His Friend Marcus Curtis at Rome*, 2 vols. (New York: C. S. Francis, 1837), 1:97 (hereafter cited parenthetically in text).

26. Cited in Field, *America and the Mediterranean World*, 89.

27. John DeForest, *Oriental Acquaintance; or Letters from Syria* (New York: Dix, Edwards, 1856), 3.

28. DeForest, *Oriental Acquaintance*, 4.

29. DeForest, *Oriental Acquaintance*, 5.

30. John DeForest, *Irene the Missionary* (Boston: Roberts Brothers, 1879), 40–41 (hereafter cited parenthetically in text).

31. Anna Julia Cooper, *A Voice From the South, by a Black Woman of the South* (Xenia, Ohio: Aldine, 1892), 51, cited in Hazel Carby, *Reconstructing Womanhood: The Emergence of the Afro-American Woman Novelist* (New York: Oxford University Press, 1987), 101.

32. Robert Rydell, *All the World's A Fair: Visions of Empire at American International Expositions, 1876–1916* (Chicago: University of Chicago Press, 1984), 6, 10.

33. Barbara Welter, *Dimity Convictions: The American Woman in the Nineteenth Century* (Athens: Ohio University Press, 1976), 21.

34. Caroline Ticknor, *Hawthorne and His Publisher* (Port Washington, N.Y.: Kennikat, 1969; orig. pub. 1913), 140.

35. Nina Baym, *Woman's Fiction: A Guide to Novels by and about Women in America, 1820–1870* (Ithaca: Cornell University Press, 1978), 11–12.

36. Maria Susanna Cummins, *El Fureidis* (Boston: Ticknor and Fields, 1860), 1 (hereafter cited parenthetically in text).

37. Leila Ahmed, "Western Ethnocentrism and Perceptions of the Harem," *Feminist Studies* 8 (fall 1982): 524. Male writers wrote about the horrors of lesbianism in harems they had never visited. George Sandys reported, for instance, that "it is not lawful for anyone to bring ought in unto them [harems] with which they may commit the deeds of beastly uncleanliness." Some writers considered the blight of lesbianism to be spread through Muslim women in general. Robert Withers wrote: "much unnatural and filthy lust is said to be committed daily in remote closets of the darksome baths: yea women with women; a thing incredible." Both Sandys and Withers are cited in Ahmed, op. cit., 524–25.

38. Elizabeth Stuart Phelps, *The Story of Avis*, ed. Carol Farley Kessler (New Brunswick, N.J.: Rutgers University Press, 1985), 142.

39. Phelps, *The Story of Avis*, 205.

40. Phelps, *The Story of Avis*, 83.

41. Billie Melman has shown how nineteenth-century British women also desexualized the harem and mapped onto it the middle-class home; see Melman, *Women's Orients: English Women and the Middle East, 1718–1918; Sexuality, Religion, and Work* (Ann Arbor: University of Michigan Press, 1992), 101.

42. Carby, *Reconstructing Womanhood*, 39.

43. The following description of a woman being beaten to death by her husband clearly violates all probability: "One of my Moslem neighbors once beat one of his wives to death. I heard her screams day after day, and finally,

one night, when all was still, I heard a dreadful shriek, and blow after blow falling upon her back and head. I could hear the brute cursing her as he beat her. The police would not interfere and I could not enter the house" (Rev. Henry Harris Jessup, *The Women of the Arabs* [New York: Dodd and Mead, 1873], 9). As a neighbor, Jessup might well have heard screams, but he could not possibly have heard where the blows were falling. His addition of imaginary details to an event that is obviously horrendous suggests not simply concern on the part of the writer but also a vicarious, misogynistic thrill.

44. David F. Dorr, *A Colored Man round the World* (Ohio: Dorr, 1858), 11.

45. Dorr, *A Colored Man round the World*, 12.

46. Dorr, *A Colored Man round the World*, 192.

47. The only African American fictional works published prior to Dorr's travel narrative were William Wells Brown's *Clotel, or the President's Daughter* (London, 1853) and Frank Webb's *The Garies and Their Friends* (New York: AMS Press, 1971; orig pub 1857). Webb's novel was legitimated by an introduction by Harriet Beecher Stowe. Harriet Wilson's *Our Nig* (Boston: G. C. Rand and Avery, 1859) was a failure and sold only one hundred copies at the time of its publication. The only works sure to find a large reading audience were slave narratives published under the auspices of the abolitionists.

48. Dorr, *A Colored Man round the World*, 128.

49. Dorr, *A Colored Man round the World*, 128.

50. Similarly, Dorr also joined in the popularly expressed USAmerican outrage at the dominance of signifiers of Islam in the Holy Land. Dorr notes that during his travels in Jerusalem, he was offended when he saw how "the mosque of the Turk looked down upon our glorious sepulchre, as it were with contempt" (Dorr, *A Colored Man round the World*, 184).

51. Frederick Douglass, "The Claims of the Negro Ethnologically Considered" (address delivered at Western Reserve College, July 12, 1854), published in *The Life and Writings of Frederick Douglass,* ed. Philip S. Foner, vol. 2, *Pre-Civil War Decade, 1850–1860* (New York: International Publishers, 1950), 289–90.

52. Douglass, "The Claims of the Negro," 291.

53. Douglass, "The Claims of the Negro," 301.

54. Dorr, *A Colored Man round the World*, 123.

55. Dorr, *A Colored Man round the World*, 126–27.

Chapter 4

1. John T. Irwin, *American Hieroglyphics: The Symbol of the Egyptian Hieroglyphics in the American Renaissance* (New Haven: Yale University Press, 1980), 45.

2. Irwin, *American Hieroglyphics*, 43. Irwin sees Champollion as a model for the character of Dupin, "that intuitive decipherer of clues, with his fondness for enigmas, conundrums, and hieroglyphics" (44).

3. Moffitt L. Cecil, "Poe's Arabesque," *Comparative Literature* 18 (1966): 58.

4. Sidney Kaplan, introduction to *The Narrative of Arthur Gordon Pym of Nantucket,* by Edgar Allan Poe (New York: Hill and Wang, 1960), xxv.

5. Kenneth Silverman, *Edgar A. Poe: Mournful and Never-Ending Remembrance* (New York: Harper Collins, 1991), 207.

6. Questions about Poe's political leanings and about the politics of his works are highly debatable. While most critics acknowledge Poe's pro-slavery stance, there is considerable difference of opinion about whether this stance affects his literary works. An editorial article on the defense of slavery for which Poe is acknowledged as author was published in the *Southern Literary Messenger* vol 2, 5 (April 1836), 336–39 in 1836 and has long been thought by critics to have been written by Poe himself; see Kenneth Alan Hovey, "Critical Provincialism: Poe's Poetic Principle in Antebellum Context," *American Quarterly* 39 (1987): 347. James A. Harrison included the piece in his *The Complete Works of Edgar Allan Poe*, vol. 8 (New York: The University Society, 1902), 265–75. Robert D. Jacobs writes that "except for occasional thrusts against Jacksonian democracy, his [Poe's] writings showed little concern for political affairs. Reviewing Poe in the context of Southern literature, one may correctly say that he wrote on topics common to Southern poets, but with a tone and a range of symbolic reference all his own" (Jacobs, "Edgar Allan Poe," in *The History of Southern Literature*, ed. Louis D. Rubin Jr. [Baton Rouge: Louisiana State University Press, 1985], 135).

7. The American movement into the Pacific was heralded by many as a precursor to even greater influence in Asia. In the California constitutional convention of 1849, H. W. Halleck saw an expansionist destiny for the state: "The people of California will penetrate the hitherto inaccessible portions of Asia, carrying with them . . . the refining and purifying influence of civilization and Christianity" (cited in Reginald Horsman, *Race and Manifest Destiny: The Origins of Racial Anglo-Saxonism* [Cambridge: Harvard University Press, 1981], 287). Secretary of Navy John P. Kennedy put the matter more bluntly when he declared that no country had the right to refuse ports to Americans (see Horsman, op. cit., 289).

8. Marie Bonaparte read *Pym* as an enactment of a symbolic journey back to the womb; see Bonaparte, *The Life and Works of Edgar Allan Poe: A Psycho-Analytic Interpretation*, trans. John Rodker (London: Hogarth, 1949). Her reading has been repeated in various forms by psychoanalytic critics. Dennis Pahl, for instance, sees the different places Pym visits as "external manifestations of Pym's psychic journey toward himself" (Pahl, *Architects of the Abyss* [Columbia: University of Missouri Press, 1989], 54). Symbolic critics are similarly ahistorical. Edward H. Davidson argues, for instance, that the whiteness at the end of Pym's journey signifies "the blankness of eternal mystery [that] engulfs him the moment he faces the white light of revelation" (Davidson, *Poe: A Critical Study* [Cambridge: Harvard University Press, 1966], 177). Toni Morrison's powerful racialized interpretation of the black and white images in Poe's works reveals how politicized Poe's writings were. Morrison sees Poe as one of the most important writers to deal with the presence of American Africanism. She interprets the image of whiteness at the end of *Pym* as both an antidote for and a meditation on the Africanist presence. See Morrison, *Playing in the Dark: Whiteness and the Literary Imagination* (Cambridge: Harvard University Press, 1992), 32–33.

9. Edgar Allan Poe, *The Narrative of Arthur Gordon Pym of Nantucket* (1838; reprint, New York: Hill and Wang, 1960), 169. Wilson Harris points this slip out in *The Womb of Space: The Cross Cultural Imagination* (Westport, Conn.: Greenwood, 1983), 23.

10. See Burton R. Pollin, *Discoveries in Poe* (New York: Oxford University Press, 1970), 25–26.

11. Bedlo describes the scene in familiar Oriental terms but includes a political dimension that is unusual for most Eastern tales: "The houses were wildly picturesque. On every hand was a wilderness of balconies, of verandas, of minarets, of shrines, and fantastically carved oriels. Bazaars abounded; and in these were displayed rich wares in infinite variety and profusion. . . . A small party of men, clad in garments half Indian half European, and officered by gentlemen in a uniform partly British, were engaged, at great odds, with the swarming rabble of the alley. I joined the weaker party, arming myself with the weapons of a fallen officer, and fighting I knew not whom with the nervous ferocity of despair" (Edgar Allan Poe, "A Tale of The Ragged Mountains," in *The Short Fiction of Edgar Allan Poe: An Annotated Edition*, ed. Stuart Levine and Susan Levine [Urbana: University of Illinois Press, 1976], 179).

12. Poe, "A Tale of The Ragged Mountains," 129.

13. Poe, "A Tale of the Ragged Mountains," 131.

14. Poe, "A Tale of the Ragged Mountains," 132.

15. Poe's uncompleted novella "The Journal of Julius Rodman," serialized over six issues in *Burton's Gentleman's Magazine* (Jan–June 1840), presents itself as a true account of the first expedition of white men to cross the Rocky Mountains. R. A. Stewart in his "Notes" on "The Journal of Julius Rodman" writes: "This tale appeared anonymously in *Burton's* but the internal evidence is fully sufficient to set at rest all question as to the authorship." *Complete Works of Edgar Allan Poe* vol. 4, Ed. James A. Harrison (New York: AMS Press, 1965), 277. Harrison includes the novella in this volume, 9–101.

16. Maturin Murray Ballou, *The Turkish Slave: Mahometan and His Harem* (Boston: E. Gleason, 1850), 16.

17. Maria Susanna Cummins, *El Fureidis* (Boston: Ticknor and Fields, 1860), 287.

18. Edgar Allan Poe, "Ligeia," in *The Short Fiction of Edgar Allan Poe*, 79 (hereafter cited parenthetically in text).

19. Daniel Hoffman suggests that Ligeia is "described, admired, adored, nay worshipped, not so much for what she looks like, or for who she is, but for what she *knows*" (Hoffman, "The Marriage Group," in *Edgar Allan Poe: Modern Critical Views*, ed. Harold Bloom [New York: Chelsea House, 1985], 90). But if we examine "Ligeia" in the light of Western interest in Egyptology, we see that Ligeia's oriental looks and her unsurpassable knowledge go hand in hand.

20. Jay B. Hubbell, *South and Southwest: Literary Essays and Reminiscences* (Durham, N.C.: Duke University Press, 1965), 104.

21. Cynthia Jordan, *Second Stories: The Politics of Language, Form, and Gender in Early American Fictions* (Chapel Hill: University of North Carolina Press, 1989), 134–35.

22. Walt Whitman, *Leaves of Grass,* ed. Sculley Bradley and Harold W. Blodgett (New York: Norton, 1973), 245.

23. Whitman, *Leaves of Grass,* 111.

24. Ralph Waldo Emerson, "An Address: Delivered before the Senior Class in Divinity College, Cambridge, Sunday Evening, July 15, 1838," in *Complete Works of Ralph Waldo Emerson,* vol. 1, ed. Edward W. Emerson (1903; reprint, New York: AMS Press, 1968), 126.

25. Jerry A. Herndon sees "Ligeia," published two years after Emerson's "Nature," as a "satirical portrait of Emersonian Transcendentalism" (Herndon, "Poe's 'Ligeia': Debts to Irving and Emerson," in *Poe and His Times,* ed. Benjamin Franklin Fisher [Baltimore: Edgar Allan Poe Society, 1990], 119).

26. Few cultural critics have noted that New England was increasingly involved in trade with the Far East. Luther S. Luedtke, however, presents a fascinating reading of Hawthorne's work in the light of the extensive contact with the East; see Luedtke, *Nathaniel Hawthorne and the Romance of the Orient* (Bloomington: Indiana University Press, 1989).

27. Bill Ashcroft, Gareth Griffiths, and Helen Tiffin, *The Empire Writes Back: Theory and Practice in Post-Colonial Literatures* (New York: Routledge, 1989), 159.

28. I am grateful to Susan Mickleberry for pointing out this connection.

29. Ruth P. Thomas, "Montesquieu's Harem and Diderot's Convent: The Woman as Prisoner," *French Review* 52, no. 1 (October 1978): 37, 38.

30. Hazel Carby points out the reluctance of scholars to condemn the rape of black women and to rewrite rape as complicity. Carby suggests that this kind of patriarchal rewriting is responsible for the "institutionalized rape of black women" not being seen as a powerful symbol of black oppression. See Carby, *Reconstructing Womanhood: The Emergence of the Afro-American Woman Novelist* (New York: Oxford University Press, 1987), 22, 39.

31. Anne Goodwyn Jones, *Tomorrow Is Another Day: The Woman Writer in the South, 1859–1936* (Baton Rouge: Louisiana State University Press, 1981), xii, 4, 9.

32. Edgar Allan Poe, *The Complete Works of Edgar Allan Poe,* ed. James A. Harrison, 17 vols. (New York: Crowell, 1929), 8:14, cited in Ernest Marchand, "Poe as a Social Critic," *American Literature* 6 (1934): 36.

33. Clark Griffith, "Poe's 'Ligeia' and the English Romantics," in *Edgar Allan Poe: Modern Critical Views,* ed. Harold Bloom (New York: Chelsea House, 1985), 76.

34. Lasley J. Dameron sees similarities between Dupin, the disinherited aristocrat, and Poe: "both have aristocratic origins, superior intellects, and alienated personalities" (Dameron, "Poe's Auguste Dupin" in Eds., Lasley J. Dameron and James W. Matthews *No Fairer Land: Studies in Southern Literature before 1900* (Troy, New York: Whitston, 1986), 160.

35. John McCardell, *The Idea of a Southern Nation: Southern Nationalists and Southern Nationalism, 1830–1860* (New York: Norton, 1979), 4. McCardell points out that the tariff crisis led to a systematic "defense of the South's peculiar institution of slavery. Proslavery quickly became the position around which all Southerners, no matter how much they might disagree with one another on

other questions, could unite. . . . Calls arose and spread for a distinctive Southern literature. Religious nationalism became more intense" (7).

36. Rana Kabbani, *Europe's Myths of the Orient* (Bloomington: Indiana University Press, 1981), 68; Kabbani quotes Andrea Rose's *Pre-Raphaelite Portraits*
(London, 1981), 9.

37. Morrison, *Playing in the Dark*, 31–33.

38. Joseph G. Kronick sees the political implications of these writings but
finally views them as secondary to Poe's interest in language: "Although this
may be a coded allegory of antebellum America, it is but another of Poe's puz-
zles created for the express purpose of being deciphered" (Kronick, "Edgar
Allan Poe: The Error of Reading and the Reading of Error," in *Southern Literature and Literary Theory*, ed. Jefferson Humphries [Athens: University of Georgia Press, 1990], 217). Kronick sees the Poe resurrected by John T. Irwin as a
writer who, like his contemporaries Whitman, Melville, and Emerson, tried to
"discover the origin of man by deciphering the origin of language" (207).

39. Harriet Elizabeth (Prescott) Spofford, "Desert Sands," in *"The Amber
Gods" and Other Stories* (1863; reprint, Freeport, N.Y.: Books for Libraries Press,
1969), 191, 190 (hereafter cited parenthetically in text). For an analysis of Spofford's critique of the dichotomies of the angel and the voluptuous woman see
Robin Riley Fast's "Killing the Angel in Spofford's 'Desert Sands' and 'The
South Breaker'" *Legacy* 11, i (1994), 37–39, 45. Fast also observes that the sug-
gestion of sympathy between Eos and Vespasia subverts "not only patriarchal
assumptions about gender but also European-American beliefs about race"
(45).

40. Susan Gubar, "'The Blank Page' and the Issues of Female Creativity,"
in *Writing and Sexual Difference*, ed. Elizabeth Abel (Chicago: University of
Chicago Press, 1982), 77.

41. Herman Melville, "Bartleby, the Scrivener: A Story of Wall-Street" in
The Writings of Herman Melville: The Piazza Tales, ed. Harrison Hayford et al.
(Evanston, Ill., and Chicago: Northwestern University Press and Newberry
Library, 1987), 9:28.

42. Melville, "Bartleby," 27.

43. Melville, "Bartleby," 44.

44. Herman Melville, "I and My Chimney," in *The Writings of Herman
Melville*, 9:355.

45. Melville, "I and My Chimney," 358.

46. Herman Melville, journal entry, December 17, 1856, in *The Writings of
Herman Melville*, 15:67.

47. Herman Melville, journal entry, January 23, 1857, in *The Writings of
Herman Melville*, 15:81; see also 70, 92, 94.

48. Herman Melville, journal entry, December 13, 1856, in *The Writings of
Herman Melville*, 15:61.

49. Herman Melville, journal entry, January 3, 1857, in *The Writings of Herman Melville*, 15:75.

50. Herman Melville, journal entry, January 26, 1857, in *The Writings of
Herman Melville*, 15:86.

51. Nina Baym, "The Erotic Motif in Melville's *Clarel*," *Texas Studies in Language and Literature* 16, no. 2 (summer 1974): 316.

52. Warren Rosenberg, "'Deeper Than Sappho': Melville Poetry and the Erotic," *Modern Language Studies* 14, no. 1 (1984): 74.

53. Finkelstein's book *Melville's Orienda* (New Haven: Yale University Press, 1961) is still the most complete work on Melville and the Orient. Finkelstein situates Melville's representations of the Near East through his readings of popular Near Eastern literatures in translation and of travel writers, such as Bayard Taylor. Finkelstein writes that for Melville, the Near East signified both the oppressiveness of history and the power of decipherment (11). He writes: "The Hero as Explorer is the Melvillean hero par excellence. It is his image that is reflected in Melville's preoccupation with the explorers, prophets, and conquerors of the ancient Near East—the inevitable focus of a vision in which the totality of being is apprehended at its 'original' historical source" (120). The central idea of *Clarel*, writes Finkelstein, is "the experience of 'sacred geography' both in its physical and metaphysical aspects . . . which resolve themselves in the hero's progress from religious disillusionment to a triumphant affirmation of the force of the human spirit that transcends the limitations of creed" (91). Franklin Walker's *Irreverent Pilgrims: Melville, Browne, and Mark Twain in the Holy Land* (Seattle: University of Washington Press, 1974) is a descriptive account of Melville's journey and summarizes Melville's observations. Jalaluddien Khuda Bakhsh's "Melville and Islam" (Ph.D. diss., Florida State University, 1988) concentrates mainly on Melville's journal and Clarel and points out how impressed Melville was with Islam (84, 131).

54. Walter E. Bezanson, "The Characters," in his edition of *Clarel* (cited in the following note), 530.

55. Herman Melville, *Clarel: A Poem and Pilgrimage in the Holy Lands*, ed. Walter E. Bezanson (New York: Hendricks House, 1960), part I, ii, lines 84–87, p. 10 (hereafter cited parenthetically in text).

56. Fuad Sha'ban, *Islam and Arabs in Early American Thought: The Roots of Orientalism in America* (Durham, N.C.: Acorn, 1991), 151. Different leaders posited different versions of the Second Kingdom. William Miller, whose followers grew into the thousands, announced that 1843 would be the year of the Second Coming of Christ. To many of these groups, Jews were the foundations of this Second Coming (Sha'ban, op. cit., 151). Many evangelists also left the United States to establish settlements in Palestine in expectation of the Second Coming, which was to occur there (Sha'ban, op. cit., 158). Melville had probably familiarized himself with travelers accounts of these settlements.

57. See Nina Baym's "The Erotic Motif in Melville's *Clarel*," 316.

58. Bezanson, in his edition of *Clarel* (cited in n. 55 in this chapter), xxiv, xciii.

59. Hershel Parker is one of the few critics who has paid some attention to what Vine is saying. He views the interaction between Vine and Clarel as comic, because they seem to be oblivious to each other's thoughts and talk past each other. See Parker, "The Character of Vine in Melville's Clarel," *Essays in Arts and Sciences* 15 (June 1986): 104–5.

60. In *Nile Notes of a Howadji* (New York: Harper, 1851), George William

Curtis wrote: "For what more are these orientals than sumptuous savages? As the Indian dwells in the primeval forests . . . so lives the Oriental, the pet of natural luxury, in a golden air, at the foundations of History . . ." (12).

61. In the section titled "Under the Minaret," Clarel's attention is caught by the sight of Arabs in prayer. Melville momentarily suspends the actions of Celio and Clarel as he sketches the prayer scene.

> But ere they might accost or meet,
> From minaret in grounds hard by
> Of Omar, the muezzin's cry—
> . . . .
> . . . Along the walls
> And that deep gulf over which these tower—
> Far down toward Rogel, hark it calls!
> Can Siloa hear it, yet her wave
> So listless lap the hollow cave?
> Is Zion deaf? But, promptly still,
> Each turban at the summons shrill,
> Which should have called ere perfect light,
> Bowed—hands on chest, or arms upright.

(I.xv.21–23, 27–35)

Chapter 5

1. Kenneth Walter Cameron, appendix B to *Indian Superstition*, by Ralph Waldo Emerson, ed. Kenneth Walter Cameron (Hanover, N.H.: Friends of the Dartmouth Library, 1954), 67–68.

2. Richard Henry Stoddard's Eastern poems are mainly poems about pining lovers, lovely women waiting to be rescued, unlimited sensuality, and indolence. They are divided into sections, such as "Persian Songs," "Chinese Songs," "Tartar Songs," etc. See Stoddard, *The Book of the East and Other Poems* (Boston: James R. Osgood, 1871).

3. Raymond Schwab, *The Oriental Renaissance: Europe's Rediscovery of India and the East, 1680–1880*, trans. Gene Patterson-Black and Victor Reinking (New York: Columbia University Press, 1984), 4, 7.

4. Schwab, *The Oriental Renaissance*, 11.

5. Schwab, *The Oriental Renaissance*, 26.

6. Schwab's language tends to obliterate the facts of colonization. Schwab writes, "Some rather surprising events had occurred coincidentally within a short span: a spiritualist revival, the outburst of historical studies, the English conquest of Bengal, and the French expedition to Egypt. In such ways the soul of Europe was carried toward an unknown future" (15). The irony of the "soul" being carried forward through "conquest" simply escapes Schwab's otherwise perceptive study.

7. R. W. Van Alstyne, *The United States and East Asia* (London: Thames and Hudson, 1973), 21, 44.

8. Cited in W. La Feber, *The New Empire: An Interpretation of American Expansion, 1860–1898* (Ithaca, N.Y.: 1963), 24–32.

9. Van Alstyne, *The United States and East Asia,* 18–19.

10. Kenneth Walter Cameron, "Notes on Massachusetts Orientalism," in *Indian Superstition,* by Ralph Waldo Emerson, ed. Kenneth Walter Cameron (Hanover, N.H.: Friends of the Dartmouth Library, 1954), 64.

11. Cited in Henry Nash Smith, *Virgin Land* (Cambridge: Harvard University Press, 1950), 22–23.

12. V. I. Lenin, *Imperialism: The Highest Stage of Capitalism* (New York: International Publishers, 1939), 62–64.

13. William B. Weeden, *Economic and Social History of New England, 1620–1789,* vol. 1 (1890; reprint, New York: Hillary House, 1963), 820.

14. Rev. Dr. Anderson, informal statement of the relation of the *American Oriental Society* to U.S. missionaries in the East, *Journal of the American Oriental Society* 1, no. 4 (1845): xliv.

15. Bayard Taylor, *A Visit to India, China, and Japan* (1855; reprint, New York: Putnam's, 1862), 45.

16. Schwab, *The Oriental Renaissance,* 25.

17. William Rounseville Alger, *The Poetry of the East* (Boston: Whittemore, Niles, and Hall, 1856), 8.

18. I will deal later with missionary writing, which almost always saw British colonization as the salvation of the pitiable masses of Indians.

19. Rev. Isaac Taylor, *Scenes in Asia, for the Amusement and Instruction of Little Tarry-at-Home-Travellers* (Hartford, Conn.: Silas Andrus, 1826), 81, 73–74.

20. Bayard Taylor's *A Visit to India, China, and Japan,* originally published by Putnam's in 1853, had gone through sixteen editions by 1862.

21. Bayard Taylor, *A Visit to India, China, and Japan,* 273.

22. Bayard Taylor, *Central Asia: Travels in Cashmere, Little Tibet, and Central Asia* (New York: Scribner, Armstrong, 1874), 11.

23. Bayard Taylor, *A Visit to India, China, and Japan,* 273.

24. Edward E. Salisbury, "Memoir on the History of Buddhism read before the Society May 24, 1844" *Journal of the American Oriental Society* vol lii (1844): 81–82.

25. Ralph Waldo Emerson, *The Journals and Miscellaneous Notebooks of Ralph Waldo Emerson, 1847–1848,* vol. 10, ed. Merton M. Sealts Jr. (Cambridge: Harvard University Press, Belknap Press, 1973), 360.

26. I have made this argument about multiculturalism in Malini Johar Schueller, "Multiculturalism as a Strategy of Reading," *Prose Studies* 17, no. 1 (April 1994): 1–20.

27. Both works are cited in Lucius Outlaw, "Toward a Critical Theory of 'Race,'" in *Anatomy of Racism,* ed. David Theo Goldberg (Minneapolis: University of Minnesota Press, 1990), 63.

28. Reginald Horsman, *Race and Manifest Destiny: The Origins of Racial Anglo-Saxonism* (Cambridge: Harvard University Press, 1981), 47.

29. Horsman, *Race and Manifest Destiny,* 62.

30. Charles Caldwell, *Thoughts on the Original Unity of the Human Race*

(New York, 1830), 134–35, 136, cited in Horsman, *Race and Manifest Destiny*, 119–20.

31. Horsman, *Race and Manifest Destiny*, 134–35.

32. Linda Frost, "'Living Curiosities' and the 'Wonder of America': Freaks, Savages, and the Construction of National Identity in the Civil War Union" (paper presented at the American Studies Association Conference, Boston, Mass., November 1993), 5. For a detailed examination of freak shows in mid-century, see Robert Bogdan, *Freak Show: Presenting Human Oddities for Amusement and Profit* (Chicago: University of Chicago Press, 1988).

33. I am referring here to Macaulay's Minute of 1835 on Indian education. Macaulay wrote, "It is, I believe, no exaggeration to say that all the historical information which has been collected in the Sanskrit language is less valuable than what may be found in the paltry abridgments used at preparatory schools in England" (cited in Edward Said, *The World, The Text, and the Critic* [Cambridge: Harvard University Press, 1983], 12).

34. Lucretia M. Davidson, "Amir Khan," in *Amir Khan and Other Poems* ed. Samuel F. B. Morse, A. M. (New York: G. and C. and H. Carvill, 1829) 10.

35. H. W. Longfellow, "The Kalif of Baldacca," *Atlantic* 13 (June 1864): 664.

36. James Russell Lowell, "Dara," *Graham's*, July 1850.

37. James Russell Lowell, "An Oriental Apologue," *National Anti-Slavery Standard*, April 12, 1849, stanza lines 5–6.

38. Lowell, "An Oriental Apologue," stanza Xiii, lines 1–4.

39. Bayard Taylor, "Smyrna," in *Poems of the Orient* (Boston: Ticknor and Fields, 1854), 123.

40. Bayard Taylor, "An Oriental Idyl," in *Poems of the Orient*, 80.

41. Bayard Taylor, "An Oriental Idyl," 81.

Chapter 6

1. Frederick Ives Carpenter, *Emerson and Asia* (1930; reprint, New York: Haskell House, 1968), 103. Beongcheon Yu writes that "the Oriental influence on Emerson was primarily Indian—Indian religion and philosophy . . ." (Yu, *The Great Circle: American Writers and the Orient* [Detroit: Wayne State University Press, 1983], 28).

2. Kenneth Walter Cameron, "Young Emerson's Orientalism at Harvard," in *Indian Superstition*, by Ralph Waldo Emerson, ed. Kenneth Walter Cameron (Hanover, N.H.: Friends of the Dartmouth Library, 1954), 17–19. Buchanan had students write essays with such titles as "On the Best Means of Civilizing the Subjects of the British Empire in India, and of Diffusing the Light of the Christian Religion throughout the Eastern World."

3. Cameron, "Young Emerson's Orientalism at Harvard," 19.

4. Cited in Alan D. Hodder "Emerson, Rammohan Roy, and the Unitarians," in *Studies in the American Renaissance*, ed. Joel Myerson (Charlottesville: University of Virginia Press, 1988), 134.

5. Cited in Hodder, "Emerson, Rammohan Roy, and the Unitarians," 146.

6. Emerson uses the British term *juggernaut* to refer to an annual proces-

sion of deities honoring Jagganath (lord of the world); during the procession, the very devout sometimes throw themselves in front of the carriage wheel so as to be blessed.

7. Throughout this discussion, I cite Cameron's edition of "Indian Superstition," cited in n. 2 in this chapter.

8. Rey Chow, "Violence in the Other Country: China as Crisis, Spectacle, and Woman," in *Third World Women and the Politics of Feminism,* ed. Chandra Talpade Mohanty, Ann Russo, and Lourdes Torres (Bloomington: Indiana University Press, 1991), 86.

9. Cameron, "Young Emerson's Orientalism at Harvard," 37. Cameron suggests that these lines might have been part of an earlier version of the poem. Authenticated earlier versions of the poem have not yet been found.

10. Recent critical works have attempted to historicize Emerson's ideas and examine them in the context of his age. Mary Kupiec Cayton, for instance, foregrounds the urban, capitalist culture of Boston and looks at Emerson as a product of his time and place. She sees Emerson's philosophy of self-reliance as a response to the urbanization of New England and the development of a commercial culture. See Cayton, *Emerson's Emergence: Self and Society in the Transformation of New England, 1800–1845* (Chapel Hill: University of North Carolina Press, 1989), 221–22. In a similar vein, Richard A. Grusin offers a more radical historical revisionism of common transcendental oppositions, such as heart and head, intuition and institution. Instead of simply showing how the oppositions resist yet also serve institutional interests, Grusin reexamines the oppositions "in the discursive context from which they emerged" (Grusin, *Transcendental Hermeneutics: Institutional Authority and the Higher Criticism of the Bible* [Durham, N.C.: Duke University Press, 1991], 3).

11. Ralph Waldo Emerson, "Self-Reliance," in *The Complete Works of Ralph Waldo Emerson,* ed. Edward W. Emerson, 12 vols. (1903–1904); (reprint, New York: AMS Press, 1968), 2:61.

12. Emerson, "Self-Reliance," 44.

13. David Leverenz, in *Manhood and the American Renaissance* (Ithaca: Cornell University Press, 1989), has argued that the major writers of the American Renaissance were at odds with their culture because they repudiated the masculine values of competition and aggression that were valorized in mid-nineteenth-century America.

14. Ralph Waldo Emerson, "Nature," in *Complete Works,* 1:3, 59.

15. Ralph Waldo Emerson, *The Journals and Miscellaneous Notebooks of Ralph Waldo Emerson, 1822–1826,* ed. William H. Gilman et al. (Cambridge: Harvard University Press, Belknap Press, 1961), 218.

16. Cited in Carpenter, *Emerson and Asia,* 30.

17. Hélène Cixous, "Sorties," in *New French Feminisms,* ed. Elaine Marks and Isabelle de Courtivron (New York: Schocken, 1980), 90–91.

18. I am thinking here about the many critiques of patriarchal othering of women, such as Derrida's critique of woman as untruth in *Spurs: Nietzsche's Styles,* trans. Barbara Harlow (Chicago: University of Chicago Press, 1978), and Irigaray's critique of woman caught within the specular, patriarchal logic of

Freudian psychoanalysis in *Speculum of the Other Woman,* trans. Gillian C. Gill (Ithaca: Cornell University Press, 1974).

19. For recent distinctions between sex and gender drawn by such theorists as Gayle Rubin and Eve Sedgwick, see Henry Abelove, Michele Aina Barale, and David M. Halperin, ed., *The Lesbian and Gay Studies Reader* (New York: Routledge, 1993).

20. Michel Foucault, *The History of Sexuality,* trans. Robert Hurley, vol. 1 (New York: Vintage, 1980; originally published in French in 1976), 101.

21. George L. Mosse, *Nationalism and Sexuality: Middle-Class Morality and Sexual Norms in Modern Europe* (Madison: University of Wisconsin Press, 1985), 31.

22. Ralph Waldo Emerson, *The Journals and Miscellaneous Notebooks of Ralph Waldo Emerson,* vol. 10, ed. Merton M. Seatts (Cambridge: Harvard University Press, Belknap Press, 1973), 90.

23. Ralph Waldo Emerson, *The Journals and Miscellaneous Notebooks of Ralph Waldo Emerson,* vol. 14, ed. Susan Smith et al. (Cambridge: Harvard University Press, Belknap Press, 1978), 166.

24. Emerson, *Complete Works,* 2:10.

25. Ralph Waldo Emerson, *Representative Men,* in *Complete Works,* 4:234, 252.

26. Ralph Waldo Emerson, "Plato," in *Complete Works,* 4:47.

27. Emerson, "Plato," 52.

28. Ralph Waldo Emerson, "The Superlative," in *Complete Works,* 10:179.

29. Emerson, "Plato," 53–54.

30. Emerson, "Plato," 53.

31. Marianna Torgovnick's *Gone Primitive: Savage Intellects, Modern Lives* (Chicago: University of Chicago Press, 1990) is an excellent examination of primitivism (as a Western construct) as an omnivorous category, one that can encompass the primitive as both revered and reviled.

32. For an analysis of Emerson's simultaneous hatred of slavery and derision of abolitionists, see Leonard Neufeldt, "Emerson and the Civil War," in *Critical Essays on Ralph Waldo Emerson,* ed. Robert E. Burkholder and Joel Myerson (Boston: G. K. Hall, 1983), 413–24.

33. Ralph Waldo Emerson, "Address: Emancipation in the British West Indies," in *Complete Works,* vol. 12, 101.

34. Ralph Waldo Emerson, "The Fugitive Slave Law: Address to Citizens of Concord, 3 May, 1851," in *Complete Works,* vol. 12, 211.

35. Len Gougeon, *Virtue's Hero: Emerson, Antislavery, and Reform* (Athens: University of Georgia Press, 1990), 66.

36. In a thorough examination of *English Traits,* Philip Nicollof writes: "While there was much in this American inheritance from the English which Emerson deplored (the materialism, for example), he never questioned the supreme value of . . . English traits. . . . It was first Emerson's bias, then his philosophical conviction, that the American was derived from the one best race and the one best national history" (Nicoloff, *Emerson on Race and History: An Examination of English Traits* [New York: Columbia University Press, 1961], 11).

37. Ralph Waldo Emerson, *English Traits,* ed. Howard Mumford Jones (Cambridge: Harvard University Press, Belknap Press, 1966), 29.

38. Emerson, *English Traits,* 30.

39. Philip L. Nicoloff suggests that Emerson was fascinated with scientific theories of hybrid vigor that were commonly accepted in the American North before the great midcentury immigration; see Nicoloff, *Emerson on Race and History,* 128.

40. Emerson, *English Traits,* 32, 42–43.

41. Emerson, *English Traits,* 201.

42. Richard Bridgman sees *English Traits* as an ambivalent document about Emerson's attitude toward the Britain as the empire of the past and the United States as that of the future. Bridgman writes, "He [Emerson] respected much in England yet thought he perceived its limitations. He wanted to believe that America would succeed England in moral leadership, but he was all too aware of his nation's immaturity" (Bridgman, "From Greenough to 'Nowhere': Emerson's *English Traits,*" *New England Quarterly* 59, no. 4 (December 1986): 469.

43. Emerson, *English Traits,* 201.

44. Emerson, "Plato," in *Complete Works,* 4: 49.

45. About Emerson's oriental writings, James Russell Lowell wrote: "Where is his system? What is the use of it all? What the deuse have we to do with Brahma?" (Lowell, "The Conduct of Life," in *Critical Essays on Ralph Waldo Emerson,* ed. Robert E. Burkholder and Joel Myerson [Boston: G. K. Hall, 1983], 175).

46. Ralph Waldo Emerson, "Brahma," in *Complete Works,* 9:195.

47. Emerson writes, "Nature is the tyrannous circumstance, the thick skull, the sheathed snake, the ponderous, rock-like jaw; necessitated activity; violent direction" (Emerson, "Fate," in *Complete Works,* 6:15).

48. Emerson, "Fate," 5.

49. Emerson, "Fate," 20.

50. Emerson, "Fate," 32.

51. Emerson, "Fate," 18.

52. Emerson, "Fate," 16.

53. Emerson, "Fate," 16–17.

54. Emerson, "Fate," 9.

55. Emerson, "Fate," 23.

56. It was very late in his life when Emerson began to represent the Eastern countries in less than abstract terms. In a speech given at a banquet in honor of the Chinese embassy, Emerson praised China for its contributions to astronomical science, block printing, vaccination, and so on. Interestingly, Emerson also makes a clear distinction in the speech between "republic" and "empire." He opens the speech by commenting on the "remarkable occasion of meeting the embassy sent from the oldest Empire in the world to the youngest Republic" (Emerson, "Speech: At the Banquet in Honor of the Chinese Embassy," in *Complete Works,* 11:471. Yet this essay is preceded by an epigraph about the nature of the East in abstract terms.

Chapter 7

1. Cited in Gay Wilson Allen, foreword to *Whitman in the Light of Vedantic Mysticism*, by V. K. Chari (Lincoln: University of Nebraska Press, 1964), vii..

2. Cited in Beongcheon Yu, *The Great Circle: American Writers and the Orient* (Detroit: Wayne State University Press, 1983), 55.

3. Whitman wrote this explanation in a November 16, 1857, piece in the *Brooklyn Times*. Cited in Yu, *The Great Circle*, 235–36.

4. Cited in Yu, *The Great Circle*, 55.

5. Allen, foreward to *Whitman in the Light of Vedantic Mysticism*, viii.

6. V. K. Chari, *Whitman in the Light of Vedantic Mysticism*, xii, 17.

7. Walt Whitman, *Notebooks and Unpublished Prose Manuscripts*, 6 vols., ed. Edward F. Grier (New York: New York University Press, 1984), vol. 5 1974–75.

8. Whitman, *Notebooks and Unpublished Prose Manuscripts*, vol. 5, 1982.

9. Whitman, *Notebooks and Unpublished Prose Manuscripts*, vol. 5, 1983.

10. Whitman, *Notebooks and Unpublished Prose Manuscripts*, vol. 5, 1975.

11. Walt Whitman, "To Foreign Lands," in *Leaves of Grass*, ed. Sculley Bradley and Harold W. Blodgett (New York: Norton, 1973), 3. Further references to this edition of *Leaves of Grass* are hereafter cited parenthetically in text, with the abbreviation *LG*.

12. Walt Whitman, *Walt Whitman's Workshop: A Collection of Unpublished Manuscripts* ed. Joseph Clifton Furness (Cambridge: Harvard University Press, 1928), 163.

13. Whitman, *Walt Whitman's Workshop*, 164.

14. Whitman, *Walt Whitman's Workshop*, 164.

15. Cited in Harold Aspiz, *Walt Whitman and the Body Beautiful* (Urbana: University of Illinois Press, 1980), 11. Aspiz sees the Columbus myth as significant only in connection with Whitman's poor health after his paralytic stroke in 1873 and his consequent personal identification with the battered figure of Columbus; see Aspiz, op. cit., 10–11.

16. See William H. Shurr, "Irving and Whitman: Re-Historicizing the Figure of Columbus in Nineteenth-Century America," *American Transcendental Quarterly* 6, no. 4 (1992): 237–38.

17. William H. Shurr sees Irving's biography of Columbus as an early document of abolitionist literature; see Shurr, "Irving and Whitman," 241–42.

18. Washington Irving, *The Life and Voyages of Christopher Columbus*, vol. 11 ed. John Harmon McElroy of *The Complete Works of Washington Irving*, general editor, Richard Dilworth Rust (Boston: Twayne, 1981), 564.

19. Irving, *Life and Voyages of Christopher Columbus*, 567.

20. Betsy Erkkila, *Whitman the Political Poet* (New York: Oxford University Press, 1989), 123, 125. Erkkila's book is extremely useful in seeing Whitman's ideas about race and slavery in the context of the discourses of the time. Erkkila also deals at length with Whitman's job as editor of the *Brooklyn Daily Eagle* and the pressures on him to take a pro-slavery stance. Whitman's refusal to budge on the issue of extending slavery led to his losing his job; see Erkkila, op. cit., 49–51. Yet little more than a decade later, Whitman's map of democratic Amer-

ica would include "negroes at work in good health" and "the planter's son returning after a long absence, joyfully welcom'd and kiss'd by the aged mulatto nurse" (Whitman, "Our Old Feuillage," lines 35, 37, *LG* 173).

21. Harold Aspiz shows how popular phrenological and physiognomical depictions of superior Anglo-Saxon races found their way into the bodies and faces Whitman celebrated in his poems; see Aspiz, *Walt Whitman and the Body Beautiful*, 139–40, 189.

22. Walt Whitman, "The Eighteenth Presidency," in *Walt Whitman's Workshop*, 112.

23. Whitman, "The Eighteenth Presidency," 113.

24. For a discussion of the fascination with Hottentot women see Sander L. Gilman, "Black Bodies, White Bodies: Toward an Iconography of Female Sexuality in Late Nineteenth-Century Art, Medicine, and Literature," in *"Race," Writing, and Difference,* ed. Henry Louis Gates (Chicago: University of Chicago Press, 1986), 232–33.

25. Jacques Lacan, *Ecrits: A Selection,* trans. Alan Sheridan (New York: Norton, 1977), 18.

26. Nancy Chodorow, *The Reproduction of Mothering* (Berkeley: University of California Press, 1978), 59.

27. Chodorow, *The Reproduction of Mothering,* 61.

28. Julia Kristeva, "Stabat Mater," in *The Kristeva Reader,* ed. Toril Moi (New York: Columbia, 1986), 161.

29. Annette Kolodny, *The Lay of the Land: Metaphor as Experience and History in American Life and Letters* (Chapel Hill: University of North Carolina Press, 1975), 6. The realities of settlement and the conquest over the Native Americans, however, led to the imaging of the land as a female body requiring control. By the nineteenth century, Kolodny suggests, the literary imagination had to choose between filial responses and "the more active responses of impregnation, alteration, and possession" (71).

30. Although postcolonial theory has repeatedly shown how the female body figured as nation is used as a justification for colonization, not all such personifications need be associated with colonizing. There are, for instance, big differences between images of the veiled woman, the temptress, woman as nature, woman as avenger, and so on.

31. See Byrne R. S. Fone, *Masculine Landscapes: Walt Whitman and the Homoerotic Text* (Carbondale: Southern Illinois University Press, 1992), 92–93. Fone looks closely at Whitman's early writings, prior to 1855, to examine the maternal aspect in Whitman's poems.

32. Harold Aspiz points out that Whitman, like some reformists of his time, saw sexual appetite and procreative ability as important aspects of women's well-being. In Whitman's work, writes Aspiz, "Woman's sexuality symbolized the evolutionary yearning to complete the human race and to supply it with physically sound and spiritually sensitive children" (Aspiz, *Walt Whitman and the Body Beautiful,* 235–36). I would go further and suggest that Whitman not only translated sexuality into procreativity but, by sexualizing the maternal body, broke through gender restrictions that traditionally separated the maternal and the erotic.

33. Annette Kolodny, *The Lay of the Land*, 6.

34. Walt Whitman, manuscript entry written between 1857 and 1860, in *Notebooks and Unpublished Prose Manuscripts*, vol. 5, 1920.

35. Walt Whitman, *The Collected Writings of Walt Whitman*, General Eds. Gay Wilson Pollen and Sculley Bradley vol. 1, *Specimen Days*, ed. Floyd Stovall (New York: New York University Press, 1963), 175–76.

36. Martin K. Doudna, for instance, sees the poem as Whitman's feeling that the West was spiritually incomplete. Repeating Whitman's overt rhetoric, Doudna writes, "Where the West has turned to the exploitation of natural resources, the East in Whitman's view, has remained closer to the ultimate source of truth, Nature itself" (Doudna, "'The Essential Ultimate Me': Whitman's Achievement in 'Passage to India,'" *Walt Whitman Quarterly Review* 2 [winter 1985]: 6; see also 1–9). Similarly, Harsharan Singh Ahluwalia reads the poem as a contrast between "two kinds of achievements, material and spiritual, only one of which has been completed by the New World" (Ahluwalia, "A Reading of Whitman's 'A Passage to India,'" *Walt Whitman Quarterly Review* 1 [June 1983]: 10). James E. Miller also concurs with the theme of spiritual fusion and sees the poem as a call for "an achievement of the soul to match the marvelous achievement of the hands" (Miller, *Walt Whitman* [Boston: Twayne, 1990], 85). Betsy Erkkila, in her otherwise astute study of Whitman's politics, sees the poem as moving to a dialectical union of opposites: "past and present, East and West, religion and science, spirit and matter, fiction and fact" (Erkkila, *Whitman the Political Poet*, 267). Beongcheon Yu also sees the poem as a metaphysical one, a journey back to the cradle of mystic wisdom; see Yu, *The Great Circle*, 70–71.

37. T. J. Jackson Lears, *No Place of Grace: Antimodernism and the Transformation of American Culture, 1880–1920* (New York: Pantheon, 1981), 218.

38. In 1757, at the Battle of Plassey, the East India Company had overthrown Siraj-ud-Daulah, the nabob of Bengal. In 1765 the company forced the Mogul emperor to recognize its rights to collect the revenue of Bengal. See John A. Garraty and Peter Gay, ed., *The Columbia History of The World* (New York: Harper, 1972), 634.

39. Walt Whitman, manuscript entry written between 1857 and 1859, in *Notebooks and Unpublished Prose Manuscripts*, 1978. Whitman mistakenly substitutes *Mongol* for *Mogul* in the entry.

40. "India and China," *New York Daily News*, April 18, 1856. Other news items on the same day included news from Britain, Greece, Russia, France, Spain, Sweden, and Greece.

41. Michel Foucault, *Discipline and Punish: The Birth of the Prison*, trans. Alan Sheridan (France 1975; reprint, New York: Random House, 1979), 27.

Afterword

The epigraph is from William Gibson, *Neuromancer* (New York: Ace, 1984), 6, 89.

1. Marcus Cunliffe, *The Age of Expansion, 1848–1917* (Springfield, Mass.:

Merriam, 1974), 200. I wish to thank Janet Walker for bringing some of these ideas to my attention.

2. John Luther Long, *Madame Butterfly, Purple Eyes, etc.* (1898; reprint, New York: Garrett, 1968), 13.

3. Mosco Carner, *Puccini* (New York: Holmer and Meier, 1977), 363–64, 380. Marxist productions of Puccini's *Madame Butterfly* in fact presented the opera as a lesson against colonial imperialism; see Carner, op. cit., 381.

4. Hwang's interpretation of the ritual suicide at the end of *Madame Butterfly* can be seen in the exchange between Gallimard and Song. To Gallimard, the French diplomat, who finds the ending beautiful and "a pure sacrifice," Song says: "Consider it this way: what would you say if a blonde homecoming queen fell in love with a short Japanese businessman? He treats her cruelly, then goes home for three years, during which time she prays to his picture and turns down marriage from a young Kennedy. Then, when she learns he has remarried, she kills herself. Now, I believe you would consider this girl to be a deranged idiot, correct? But because it's an Oriental who kills herself for a Westerner—ah!—you find it beautiful" (Hwang, *M. Butterfly* [New York: Plume, 1989], 17).

5. Eugene O'Neill, *Marco Millions*, in *The Plays of Eugene O'Neill*, vol. 2 (New York: Random House, 1964), 418. I wish to thank Aeron Haynie for pointing out this reversal. Kublai Kaan forms his judgment of Marco much earlier in the play. He confides in one of his courtiers, Chu-Yin: "Marco's spiritual hump begins to disgust me. He has not even a mortal soul, he has only an acquisitive instinct" (O'Neill, op. cit., 387).

6. John P. Marquand, *Thank You, Mr. Moto* (Boston: Little, Brown, 1936), 6–7.

7. Marquand, *Thank You, Mr. Moto*, 71.

8. John Hersey, *A Single Pebble* (New York: Knopf, 1956), 138.

9. Perhaps Beat works are able to give a redemptive status to the Orient because, unlike other orientalist works in the postwar period, Beat texts are not set in the Orient.

10. Jack Kerouac, *The Dharma Bums* (1958; reprint, New York: Penguin, 1976), 31.

11. Jay McInerney, *Ransom* (New York: Vintage, 1985), 73.

12. As is well known, Allen Ginsberg and Jack Kerouac were intellectually inspired by Hinduism and Zen Buddhism. In this afterword, however, I limit myself to texts specifically set in the Orient.

Index

Frost, Linda, 235
Fuller, Thomas, 24
El Fureidis, 12, 14, 97–104

Garrison, William Lloyd, 121
Gibbon, William, 86, 225
Gibson, William, 199, 204
Gilman, Sander L., 240
Ginsberg, Allen, 203
Gliddon, George S., 13, 36–38, 75, 77, 153, 224
Goldsmith, Oliver, 68
Gougeon, Len, 237
Griffith, Clark, 121, 230
Grusin, Richard A., 236
Gubar, Susan, 125, 231

Haight, Sarah, 60, 222
Hakluyt, Richard, 24
harems
    and illicit sexuality, 118
    popularity of, 83
    as social space, 103
Harte, Bret, 142
Herndon, Jerry A., 230
Hersey, John, 202–3, 242
heteronormativity, 99
heterosexuality threatened, 100, 119, 122, 165
Hietala, Thomas R., 214
Hodder, Alan D., 216
Hoffman, Daniel, 229
homoeroticism, 6, 126, 171
    and race, 135–38
homosexism, 115
hooks, bell, 208
Hopkins, Pauline, 38, 218
Horsman, Reginald, 152–53, 214, 217, 222, 228, 234, 235
Houghton, Ross, Rev., 78, 225
Hovey, Kenneth Alan, 228
Huang, John, vii
Hubbell, Jay B., 115, 229
Hwang, David Henry, 200, 242

imperial imaginary, 2
imperialism, U.S., 9, 200

and Asia, 144
critiqued, 134–35, 200–201
and gender, 147
and maternal Orient, 184–98
and missionary work, 39, 40
and the Orient, 123
and spirituality, 171–74, 184–98
India as spiritual, 157–58, 165, 171–74, 184–98
Irene the Missionary, 3, 14, 91–97
Irigaray, Luce, 236
Irving, Washington, 3, 49, 179, 239
    Salmagundi (Mustapha letters), 68–73
Irwin, John T., 110, 216, 227
Isaani, Mukhtar Ali, 216, 220

Jacobs, Robert D., 228
Jameson, Anna, 85, 225
Jefferson, Thomas, 19, 27, 28, 47–48, 112, 144, 220
Jessup, Henry Harris, Rev., 83, 104, 227
Jones, Anne Goodwyn, 119, 230
Jones, Joseph Stevens, 49
    Usurper, The, 60–61
Jones, William, 25
Jordan, Cynthia, 115, 229

Kabbani, Rana, 212, 231
Kaplan, Amy, 17, 213
Kaplan, Sidney, 110, 227
Kerouac, Jack, 203, 242
Kristeva, Julia, 183–84, 188, 240
Kronick, Joseph G., 231
Kolodny, Annette, 184, 188, 240, 241

Lacan, Jacques, 208
Lears, T. J. Jackson, 241
Leask, Nigel, 209
Lenin, V. I., 234
Leverenz, David, 236
Lewis, R. W. B., 213
Lewis, Reina, x, 207
Long, John Luther, 199–200, 242
Longfellow, Henry Wadsworth, 142
Lowe, Lisa, 207